THE THEOLOGICAL METHODOLOGY
OF HANS KÜNG

American Academy of Religion
Academy Series

Editors
Carl Raschke
William Gravely

Number 39

THE THEOLOGICAL METHODOLOGY
OF HANS KÜNG

by
Catherine Mowry LaCugna

Catherine Mowry LaCugna

The Theological Methodology of Hans Küng

Scholars Press

Published by
Scholars Press
101 Salem Street
P.O. Box 2268
Chico, CA 95927

The Theological Methodology
of Hans Küng

by
Catherine Mowry LaCugna

Ph.D., 1979   Fordham University

New York, New York

Library of Congress Cataloging in Publication Data

LaCugna, Catherine Mowry, 1952–
    The theological methodology of Hans Küng.

    (American Academy of Religion academy series ;
no. 39) (ISSN 0277-1071)
    Originally presented as the author's thesis (Ph.D.—
Fordham University, 1979)
    Bibliography: p.
    1. Theology—Methodology—History of doctrines—
20th century. 2. Küng, Hans, 1928–   . I. Title. II.
Series.
BR118.L23   1981   230'.2'0924   81-16654
ISBN 0-89130-546-7   AACR2

Manufactured in the U.S.A.

TABLE OF CONTENTS

TABLE OF CONTENTS--<u>Continued</u>

ABBREVIATIONS

The following abbreviations are used in the text and frequently in footnotes. The full reference is given in the bibliography.

A	"Anmerkungen zu Walter Kasper, 'Christologie von unten?'"
CIT	"Toward a New Consensus in Catholic (and Ecumenical) Theology"
CRR	Council, Reform and Reunion
EC	"'Early Catholicism' in the New Testament as a Problem in Contro-versial Theology
EG	Does God Exist? An Answer For Today
F	Fehlbar? Eine Bilanz
FT	Freedom Today
Inf	Infallible? An Inquiry
J	Justification. The Doctrine of Karl Barth and a Catholic Reflec-tion
KD	The Küng Dialogue
MIT	The Church Maintained in Truth
MG	Menschwerdung Gottes. Eine Einführung in Hegels theologisches Denken als Prolegomena zu einer künftigen Christologie
OBC	On Being a Christian
SC	Structures of the Church
TC	The Church
Th&Ch	The Theologian and the Church
T	Truthfulness: The Future of the Church
W&W	Hans Küng. His Work and His Way
*	An asterisk following a reference indicates the author's own trans-lation of a text

FOREWORD

In the spring of 1979, a few months after this dissertation was completed, Hans Küng published another Theological Meditation, The Church Maintained in Truth, and a Preface to A. B. Hasler's book, How the Pope Became Infallible, both of which reiterated his views concerning papal infallibility. Küng wrote in a letter to Bishop George Moser, "No new infallibility debate should be provoked by my preface and by the theological meditation that accompanies it. Yet it is important to me, now as before, that the infallibility issue should be explored exegetically, historically and systematically with objectivity and scholarly honesty." (KD 164) Moser replied on April 5, 1979,

> I am entirely unable to understand how you can possibly think that your present utterances should not provoke a new infallibility debate. In my opinion, your conduct cannot be understood as anything but as a provocation. I, therefore, assume that unpleasant consequences are inevitable and that great difficulties will ensue.
> Although I do not at the moment know where we should go from here, especially in view of the fact that, as a theology teacher, you are still involved in the formation of the theologians of our diocese, I am still as prepared as ever to talk and to seek a tenable reconciliation. (KD 165)

Eight months later, on Dec. 15, 1979 (published Dec. 18), the Vatican issued a Declaration against Küng and withdrew his canonical mission. The document reads in part, "Professor Hans Küng, in his writings, has departed from the integral truth of Catholic faith, and therefore he can no longer be considered a Catholic theologian nor function as such in a teaching role." (KD 201)

In the days immediately following the Vatican action, conversations took place among Bishop Moser, other diocesan officials, Prof. Küng, and some of Küng's colleagues; additional statements were issued by both parties, including the German Bishops' "last word" (read in all Churches in W. Germany) and Pope John Paul II's statement of May 15, 1980 in support of

the German Bishops' Conference. In the interim there was some confusion
over whether Küng's civil tenured appointment was subject to Vatican action,
and the fairness of the proceedings was disputed. At one point Küng's
colleagues on the Catholic Theological Faculty at Tübingen withdrew their
support. The 'compromise' eventually reached entailed the removal of Küng
as a teacher of seminarians, but he still retains his post as Director of
the Ecumenical Institute at the University of Tübingen.

These developments in "the Küng case" make the following study all the
more apposite. Who could have foreseen that after nine years of an
infallibility debate, including a close call in 1973 at which time his
teaching license was not revoked, the Vatican would now take such shocking
action. The obvious question is why Küng has elicited this latest condemnation. Although the German Bishops had repeatedly voiced grave objections
about Küng's Christology, it was again the infallibility question which
provoked the Vatican Sacred Congregation to disclaim Küng as a legitimate
teacher of Catholic theology. Was Küng simply naive when he presaged in the
Preface to Hasler's book, "Until now excommunication, suspension, and the
withdrawal of the authorization to teach have not happened in the new
infallibility debate and are also unlikely to happen in the future"?

Those who are interested in the equity of the process may consult
documentation contained in the volume edited by W. Jens, Um nichts als die
Wahrheit (Nothing But the Truth) (Piper, 1978); the United States Catholic
Conference has published its own version, The Küng Dialogue (1980). But
beyond procedural matters there are systematic theological and methodological questions: what does Küng say about infallibility (and other topics),
and what is the theological method which leads him to these conclusions?
The latter question is the topic of the following study. In the course of
the infallibility debate the divergence among theological methods became

xi

quite clear; the events of 1979 and thereafter show beyond any doubt that
the fundamental objection of the hierarchy pertains to method, to what it
considers to be Küng's less-than-catholic view of Tradition. This renders
our study all the more open-ended, all the more appropriate.

INTRODUCTION

"Who is Hans Küng?" begin the editors of a recent book on the life and work of the Swiss Catholic theologian. To many he is known, they write, but only a few know him; many cliches surround him, but only a few know what he really thinks and wishes. Still, Hans Küng is an undeniably controversial figure: for one person, he is too critical, for another, not critical enough; for one, too Catholic, for another, no longer Catholic; for one, too submissive, for another, too outspoken. Who is he, this theologian and scholar, pastor and writer, preacher and professor, priest and polemicist, Catholic and ecumenist? (W&W 8)

Indeed, many answers are possible. The official Roman Catholic Church's reaction has been unambiguous. Dossier No. 399/57/i began to be compiled by the Vatican Holy Office (later called the Sacred Congregation For the Doctrine of the Faith) in 1957, with Küng's first publication, Rechtfertigung. Die Lehre Karl Barths und eine katholische Besinnung (E.T., Justification. The Doctrine of Karl Barth and a Catholic Reflection), which was the dissertation he wrote under Professor Louis Bouyer in Paris. Despite the dossier, Küng was asked by Pope John XXIII to be a peritus at Vatican II. Every subsequent major publication has elicited some sort of disapprobation, sometimes expressed in meetings or colloquia held between Küng and hierarchical officials, in other cases, through formal proceedings initiated by the Holy Office, but always and consistently through correspondence between Küng and the hierarchy.

The books which have drawn the most protest from ecclesiastical authorities have been Structures of the Church; The Church; Truthfulness: The Future of the Church; Infallible? An Inquiry; On Being A Christian; and The Church Maintained in Truth. In particular, in 1967 the Sacred Congregation began official proceedings and forbade The Church to be translated or discussed until a colloquium had taken place in Rome. In the meantime Küng

wrote Infallible? An Inquiry which unleased a world-wide debate, and

prompted condemnations by the Sacred Congregation and various Bishops'

Conferences in different nations. In 1973 the Vatican issued Mysterium

Ecclesiae; no author was named but it obviously was directed against Küng.

Then in 1975 formal proceedings against The Church and Infallible? were

ended. From 1975-1977 the German Bishops' Conference issued three separate

Declarations against On Being A Christian. Finally, on December 18, 1979,

Küng's canonical mission was revoked by the Vatican.

In the present study it is our intention to draft a portrait from the

angle of Küng's theological methodology. We are guided in this by two con-

victions. First of all, much of the controversy and disagreement encircling

Küng seems to have resulted from insufficient consideration of the theologi-

cal methodology which lies behind his theological formulations. In this

sense, the present study is intended as a counterbalance to prevailing

assessments of Küng's theology. But this is not to imply that if Küng's

methodology is elaborated, many will not hold fast to their dissent. His

theology, especially his Christology, certainly warrants further critical

evaluation, although an understanding of his methodology will surely aid the

enterprise since many of the salient areas of disagreement are methodologi-

cal at base.

Second, the analysis of Küng from the standpoint of methodology makes

it possible to be both constructive and critical. Readers who hope to find

in this dissertation a one-sided, uncritical "defense" of Küng against his

reviewers will be disappointed; even the most sympathetic reader of Küng

could hardly conclude that he himself bears no responsibility whatever for

the serious rifts generated by "the Küng case." At the same time, those who

look for an out-and-out refutation or denunciation of him (in the style of a

very recent book[1]) will also be disappointed, for anyone familiar with the
infallibility debate knows how utterly fruitless such a stance has proven to
be. It is not that we claim to be able to sketch a so-called "objective"
portrait, and Chapter I will explain some of the reasons this is impossible.
But writers beginning from either an entirely positive or entirely negative
perspective do not do justice to Küng. They superimpose a transparency
through which they read his works, a transparency which ultimately obscures
their vision. We have by no means overlooked the fact that critical evaluation of Küng's methodology is called for; questions that arise along the
course of the study are disengaged for handling in Chapter V. The constructive side of this study comprises the first three chapters, which attempt to
spell out what Küng's theological methodology is.

Generally speaking, what is Küng's theological method and why has it
raised such acute problems in contemporary theology? The nearly twenty
years of theological writings which followed Küng's historical-critical
studies represent his attempt to work out the various implications of
historical-critical methods in the systematic areas of ecclesiology and
Christology. But in his endeavor to bridge the gap between exegesis and
dogmatic theology by means of historical criticism, Küng has come into a
seemingly inevitable collision with different ecclesiastical authorities,
notably over the matter of Tradition and its normative authority. Yet, even
if it were agreed that in the infallibility controversy the Vatican
Congregation failed to understand the distinctive priorities of Küngian
methodology, it would be naive to suppose that, had Rome better understood,
its same objections would not remain. As we shall see, the German Bishops'
Conference better perceived the methodological issues informing the theological dispute, hence their dissent extends to Küng's methodology as well
as to his theology.

There are many difficulties to surmount in a study such as this. First of all, Hans Küng is not only a living theologian, he is relatively young. Judging from his productivity so far (he has averaged one major book a year, in addition to numerous articles, shorter books, lecture tours, and other scholarly activities), we may expect many other publications to appear. This plainly confers a provisional character to the study, for it cannot in any way ensure that Küng will not in the future change his interests, style, or even his methodology.

A second matter to be reckoned with derives from the varied kinds of publications he has authored. Küng tells us he originally aspired to be a pastor, and in fact, his seven years' training in Rome (1948-1955) were geared for pastoral work. During those years Humani Generis and the definition on Mary's Ascension were issued, both of which, surprisingly, he accepted without reservation. But largely for pastoral reasons a gradual dissatisfaction emerged in Küng's mind, concerning the crisis in Church leadership under Pius XII, developments in theology, and the excessive discipline with which he came into conflict as a college chaplain. Although Küng was a pastor for only a brief time (1957-1959 in Luzern), and from 1960-1980 Professor of Dogmatic and Ecumenical Theology at the University of Tübingen, the pastoral sense has never departed from him. Consequently, among his total works one finds not only several pieces written in pastoral fashion (for example, That the World May Believe; Why Priests? and many others), but his theological positions are very much shaped by pastoral considerations. In terms of our study this will be explained under the rubric, "hermeneutical principles."

Despite the very provisional nature of this study, it is still possible to move forward in a positive formulation of Küng's theological methodology. Chapter I is divided into two parts. The first defines the terms of the study and describes methodology to consist of two 'moments': the starting point (philosophical and theological assumptions), and the sources proper to theology which are ordered in light of the starting point (Scripture and Tradition). The second half of this chapter elaborates Küng's methodological starting point and explores the interplay between faith and history as the two dominant noetic strands in Küngian methodology. The Chapter ends with a description of the general Küngian theological hermeneutic.

Chapters II and III take up the second 'moment' in theological methodology, namely, the ordering of sources in light of the starting point. Chapter II is devoted to an examination of the influence of the ecumenical hermeneutic--with all that entails--on what Küng defines as the norma normans non normata: Scripture. In particular we shall see his historical-critical studies as the turning-point in his understanding of the Word of God, of biblical inspiration and inerrancy, and the matter of the Canon.

Chapter III takes up the second theological source: Tradition, which Küng defines as norma normata. As in the previous chapter, we shall look at Tradition from the standpoint of his methodology. This means ascertaining the effect of the ecumenical hermeneutic on Tradition, which will be seen to explain the secondary status Küng assigns to Tradition. Of special importance is the fact that the faith-perspective seems to play a rather mitigated role with respect to the normativity of Tradition, whereas with respect to Scripture, it is important that Scripture is seen by faith as the Word of God.

Having described the essential form of Küng's theological method, Chapter IV will illustrate it with a test-case: papal infallibility. The methodology which is utilized by Küng will be extracted mainly from the pages of his Inquiry, but as well from additional supporting materials. Moreover, those areas in his methodology which generated numerous

controversies are discussed in order to demonstrate both the character and
potential shortcomings of Küngian methodology.

In the final chapter critical questions are asked of Küng concerning
two chief areas. The first concerns the relationship between theoretical
and applied methodology, and tries to come to terms with the degree of disparity between what Küng professes to be, and what functions as, his
ultimate criterion in theology. The second concerns the relationship
between catholicity and Tradition. Primarily because of the infallibility
controversy, doubts were raised about Küng's catholicity, and in this part
of the final chapter we shall identify the central problem and venture an
answer.

There can be no substitute for reading Küng himself; a study of his
methodology cannot give a feel for his style, his wit and passion, his out-
spokenness and courage, his anger and hurt, his obvious commitment to Christ
and the Church, his immense erudition and also his humility. Yet, it may be
hoped, the positive contribution of this study--however limited its angle of
vision--will be to complement other portraits presently available.

CHAPTER ONE

THEOLOGICAL METHODOLOGY

The organization and structure of this study is intended to reflect certain convictions we hold about theological methodology in general, and it is the task of Part I of this chapter to make clear what these convictions are. But here it may be noted by way of introduction that the dissertation proceeds according to the logical order of (Küng's) methodology. That is to say, it is usually the case that a theology is written first, and reflection (by the theologian or others) on the operative theological methodology comes later, if indeed it comes at all. But a theologian always works within a given framework which in the most general terms consists of both metaphysical convictions and the data to be analyzed. Most broadly conceived, then, a study of methodology would seek to identify and understand the 'framework' within which the theologian operates. And so, in terms of logical progression (because method antecedes theological results), in this study, formal consideration is given first to Küng's epistemology and ontology.

This kind of study could have taken other forms. For example, it is conceivable that one might attempt to present every Küngian text for individual analysis, something along the lines of individual pericopes in contemporary biblical exegesis. The assumption would be that (theological) texts are ultimately transparent, and will yield insights into their meaning and intent, provided the researcher follows hermeneutical principles which forestall eisegesis. But such an approach must first state its own hermeneutical principles and its understanding of "objectivity," else it would fail to grapple with a very difficult hermeneutical problem. That is to say, how could one know what one is looking for in a text (in terms of

7

the theologian's methodology) unless one does not already have in mind some
idea of the constituents of methodology? Concretely, how could one say, for
example, "In this passage, Küng's interpretation of the resurrection hinges
on his historical-critical understanding of causality," unless one did not
already assume--as a partial description of methodology--that a writer's
interpretation can be explained in terms of his or her metaphysical convictions. It seems crucial, then, that before stating what a particular
theologian's method is, one must first state what methodology is. This is
the task of Part I of Chapter I. Part II enunciates Hans Küng's methodological starting point in terms of its epistemological, ontological and
hermeneutical aspects.

Part I: A Definition of Methodology
The Problem of Objectivity

The so-called problem of objectivity begins this section because the
position we take with respect to it determines the definition of methodology
with which we choose to work, and this in its turn determines the procedure
of the study.

Had Hans Küng written any bona fide metaphysical tracts on theological
method at some point in his career, a study of his own theological methodology rightly could commence by investigating the philosophical system
informing the theological elaboration. Having seen the justification for
the metaphysics, we then could proceed to the theological works in order to
see the application (modifications, augmentations) of those philosophical
principles to various theological data. The underlying conviction in this
procedure would be that the conclusions reached by any author, theological
or not, are largely the result of hermeneutical principles; that is to say,

the particular way he or she looks at reality (epistemology) in its turn influences (and perhaps fully determines) what he or she sees (ontology).

Hans Küng has not provided us with any such metaphysical works,[1] but the same assumption--that Küng's theological interpretation results from his hermeneutic (which is itself the consequence of those metaphysical assumptions he finds convincing)--is not an altogether unwarranted one. It is, after all, part of our twentieth-century heritage to think that what we see is influenced (often in undetectable ways) by our general historical and cultural location. Indeed, it has been cogently argued and is generally accepted nowadays, that thinking can never be entirely bias-free, value-free, or belief-free. Thus we cannot imagine there to be some sort of pure Weltanschauung, itself untouched by the Welt in which the anschauung is located.

Most scientists today have finally eschewed the lofty ideal--once even elevated to an epistemological criterion--of (absolute) objectivity. As a matter of fact, based on the modern modification of Kantian metaphysics which is commonly called 'relativity', scientific theoreticians have expanded Kant's critical question (whether the human mind can know noumena behind the phenomena) to ask whether the human mind can be sure if it can know even phenomena.[2] This shift of Kant's question is strikingly illustrated in mathematics, wherein one is able to write several geometries, each independent, each cogent, each comprehensive, but each entirely different. Metaphysical doubt, then, has extended even to the supposed certainty that correct ways of thinking (different methods or routes) necessarily guarantee application to the world apart from the mind.[3] Philosophical and hence scientific method finally stands accused by its own methical skepticism about the ability of the human mind to know anything with (absolute) certainty.[4]

However one wishes to view the matter of objectivity, certainty and knowledge, what is defensible is that the content of knowledge is shaped--perhaps more than we always realize but perhaps less than sheer relativists would have it--ineluctably by the <u>manner</u> in which we know. Or, the interpretation of an event, meaning or value, is inestimably affected by the mode of interpreting. This conviction guides this thesis on two major counts. First, the rather elusive characteristic called "pure objectivity" neither can be nor will be naively claimed to attach to this study of Hans Küng, as if one is ever unaffected by one's own presuppositions. But neither is pure "relativity" ascribed to it, as if lasting and true statements could not be made about Küng's methodology due to a prior epistemological problem. One cannot remain in a methodological limbo wherein steps cannot be taken for fear that the ground will not be there to support one's feet. Consequently, the attempt has been made to remain cognizant of all the philosophical difficulties and simultaneously to move forward in a positive formulation of Küng's method.

Second, we will be working at Küng with the assumption that it is possible to identify certain metaphysical assumptions which circumscribe his thinking, and which are decisive for his theological hermeneutic and therefore for his conclusions. The procedure by which we will identify Küng's theological "horizon" needs now to be formulated.

A Definition of Methodology

It was suggested in the foregoing that a strictly "objective" analysis is an impossibility due to the structures of the mind which are said to be themselves historically contingent. But the question of "objective truth" remains to be answered, that is, whether there exists such truth and whether it can be known as such. Thus the crucial matter is to ascertain whether one's working assumptions ('truth claims') about reality have their basis in

reality. Our methodological investigation does not have as its purpose the
formulation of an epistemological position by which one can determine the
relationship between the knower and the known; rather it has the more
modest, yet still very difficult task of investigating what the methodology
of a particular theologian is, and whether the method does justice to the
subject matter being investigated. This first requires a definition of
methodology.

It has been argued that epistemology and ontology belong indisputably
to one's interpretation of reality. This implies that epistemology and
ontology belong to methodology, too, inasmuch as methodology may be defined
as the means of arriving at an interpretation. The method is not identical
either with its point of origin (starting point) nor with its terminus (the
conclusions), nor with the link which connects them. However, the peculiar
character of the starting point greatly prevails upon the kind of route
chosen to arrive at the end point, and the route itself greatly prevails
upon the kind of end point reached.[5] The term 'method' is often thought to
refer to both the starting point and the actual route taken, though the two
are distinguishable 'moments'. In this dissertation, 'method' or
'methodology' will be used to indicate and include both.

The Starting Point

The point of origin for any method may include some or all of such
diverse elements as cultural, chronological, geographical location, intellectual ability and subjective mood states of a particular investigator,
explicit or implicit metaphysical convictions, et. al. But every point of
origin always implies a particular way of knowing.[6] This has bearing on the
rest of methodology in two ways, or on two levels.

First, within the starting point there takes place a 'dialectic' of
sorts. We have been saying that how one sees (epistemology) influences what

one sees (ontology). While this is true, it would be mistaken to conceive these as two static, well-defined, independent 'moments' within the starting point. As a matter of fact, the interchange between the two is rather more fluent, such that _what_ one has come to see often modifies _how_ one previously saw, which in its turn modifies what one will see from thereon, and so on. Despite the numerous problems with the term, what best describes this transmutation is the term _dialectic_. Although this is not intended in an Hegelian (or Barthian) sense, it does signify that there are two 'moments' which continuously mold each other, and can be said to "combine" into a general interpretive standard. This synthesis is what is meant by the term _hermeneutic_. All this takes place within the starting point.

Second, the hermeneutic reached (which retains the character of a way of knowing) significantly affects the conduit chosen to link together starting point and end point (results). As the interchange between starting point and conduit proceeds, each contributing to and modifying the other, another synthesis is reached: the end point, the actual conclusions, the real results of the investigation. Because in a 'dialectical' movement all previous moments are preserved (though sublated), the starting point is the crucial element that should be isolated, if possible.

Theological method is no different in principle. It is no secret that in history and especially today there are numerous (sometimes even anti-thetical) interpretations of the very same event of God in Jesus. What accounts for the variety are two items: different epistemological or onto-logical assumptions which comprise the starting point, and dissimilar routes determined by the starting point. The resultant endpoint (results) may be unique, but it is not itself a cause for the variety of interpretations. Only the plurality of 'methods' accounts for the plurality of conclusions.

If we were to catalogue the major disciplines in terms of their
broadest characteristics, two fundamental types of methods emerge.[7]
Scientific method, which views its data (matter as such) in terms of
proximate or penultimate causes (the 'what' rather than the 'whence' of
things), presupposes that the nature of reality is fully explainable in
terms of its facticity, its cause-and-effect nexus, its patterns of
probability, and, further, that other (non-empirical) ways of knowing are
inferior, however ideologically successful they may be. Non-scientific
method, which has as its object the meanings and values which people assign
to various aspects of human life (including human institutions and
structures), and which regards these in terms of both internal and ultimate
causes, presupposes that a world-view is incomplete if it does not
acknowledge the levels of meaning behind mere existence, if it does not
admit the different view of reality constituted by things seen in relation
to us. Non-scientific method may be bifurcated into interpretive method
(literature; philosophy) and social-scientific method (sociology;
psychology; economics; politics; anthropology; history;[8] and others).
History seems to straddle scientific and interpretive methods inasmuch as it
seeks to employ the tools and assumptions of scientific method, and hopes
thereby to be enabled to adjudge internal and ultimate causes for human
meanings and values.

In terms of this schema, theology obviously has most in common with
interpretive method. Recent literary study and modern historiography both
have contributed a great deal to theology in such methodological areas as
literary criticism, textual criticism, and redaction criticism. And
theology's debt to and alliance with philosophical reasoning is also well-
known and frequently acknowledged. With respect to social-scientific
method, theology of late has utilized more and more the various findings and

methods of these disciplines in its attempt to re-state the Christian message. One can think, for example, of the current theological sensitivity to the sundry psychological factors which work in the religious (or irreligious) person, or of the current theologico-economic analysis of third-world countries, or of sociological theory being consulted when reorganizing diocesan structures. But theological method is not strictly social-scientific, because certain methodological principles of the latter are beholden to a view of religion which is untenable for Christian theology.

Least of all has theology something in common with scientific method, not because theology is anti-science, or because theology disdains scientific progress, but because in terms of methodological starting points, the positivistic scientific view restricts itself to an explanation of reality in the limited natural terms of causes and effects. This starting point obviously rules out in principle other kinds of explanations, including God himself being the cause of an event.[9] From the theological viewpoint, the possibility that God could 'break' or 'suspend' the empirically observable causal chain if He would so choose cannot at any rate be ruled out a priori. It would be at least problematic for theology uncritically to take over scientific criteria as its own, without inquiring whether such criteria might not militate against something which theology ought to strive to uphold. Theological method need not be antagonistic towards scientific method and results, nor need it doubt its own integrity as a rigorous and cogent discipline; theology need only recognize how different are its "warrants"[10] from those of science.

The issue of theology's relationship to scientific method begins to bring into focus those elements which are unique to theological method. Put negatively, the "study of God," for example, is not unique to theology, since philosophy, without ceasing to be philosophy (by becoming theology), also studies God or ideas about God. Nor is the study of Scripture unique to theology, for Scripture is a literary document studied by philologists and literary critics who do not cease to be such. Nor is the study of religious history unique to theology, for church historians freely, and without ceasing to be historians, examine historically locatable claims made about God through the ages. Nor is the study of revelation in other religions unique to theology, for phenomenologists and sociologists of religion, without ceasing to be such, also survey other religions. But when any one of these areas of study is consciously and purposefully viewed from within the perspective of Christian _faith_, with the intent of articulating that faith for its adherents, then the element has been added that specifies the investigation as _bona fide theological_. In other words, if one is talking about Christian theologians,[11] one should be able to assume that one is referring to Christian believers who engage in theology for their particular community, for, if the so-called 'theologian' is not a believer who works out of a religious tradition, then he or she is an anthropologist, or sociologist, or philosopher of religion, but not a theologian.

This position--that the theologian must be a believer--is not a popular one. Many assumptions operate in the minds of those who hold the contrary; one is that faith is a bias whereas, they incorrectly assume, not having faith is not a bias. But precisely this cannot be demonstrated. Faith is a way of knowing, just as non-faith is also a way of knowing. Within this so-called bias of faith, it is argued, there are elements that predispose the believer to see certain things that may be unwarranted--a miracle, to use a frequent example. Is it not also the case, though, that the bias of unbelief predisposes the unbeliever not to see what may really be there? We are brought back to the initial claim in this discussion, namely, that

the way one sees affects (or determines) what one sees. If one's way of
seeing is not faith-based, then one sees Scripture, for example, as merely
an historical document. But in faith one receives Scripture as the Word of
God. Those who claim that theologians need not be nor should not be
believers seem to have missed the point about the nature of both faith[12] and
of theology.

As a way of knowing, then, faith may belong to a theologian's starting
point and as such will affect both the route chosen and the interpretation
arrived at. The noetic form of Christian faith even rules out certain
routes and hence certain conclusions (which, when reached, are deemed
'heretical').[13] For example, faith in the God who reveals Himself in Jesus
Christ would discourage an undiscriminating use of the linguistic-analytic
method in which it is asserted that "God" is a non-sensical term. But it is
easier to decide the routes which faith must exclude, than to indicate all
those routes which the starting point of faith conceivably could countenance. Still, it would be false to judge the suitability of methods solely
on the basis of their results, for it is not unthinkable that a method could
be fitting despite conclusions drawn from it.

However one wishes to resolve these problems, what does remain tenable
is that faith is a way of knowing, a way no less respectable than other ways
of knowing, and as such it decisively affects what is known. In a study of
theological methodology, then, one would want to know precisely if and how
faith fits into the epistemology and ontology of that method.

The Ordering of Sources

What we have been calling the methodological starting point (metaphysics) is not the sole element that distinguishes one method from another.
If that were the case, one still could not explain how one interpretive

discipline differed from another. The reason rests in the second moment in methodology: the route which links together the starting point and the end point, or the conduit which is constituted by the sources or data peculiar to the discipline. But more than this, the way these sources are ordered, the priorities that are assigned to them, is what differentiates one method from another. Again, the ordering would depend on the starting point, which explains why one psychological method, for example, can be distinguished from another psychological method.

In theology it is no different. Fortunately, the controversial element of faith (as an element in the starting point) is not the singular factor that distinguishes the theological method from other methods. Theological method, too, consists of a conduit which embraces certain sources. Theology relies on the following: Scriptural and extra-scriptural writings; documents of church history (including dogma and doctrine; other theologians; church councils; church practices and discipline); extra-church history; the social sciences; the physical sciences; other humanities (art; music; philosophy; literature; and others); other religious traditions; the current cultural and historical consciousness (intellectus); current world events; an individual's faith; the faith of the Church. Again, several of these areas are not unique to theology, for they are studied by scholars from other fields. But what differentiates the theological craft is the priority assigned to some sources over others. It is almost self-evident that in a theologian's deliberations, Tradition normally would have priority over, say, psychology,[14] but the field becomes muddier when trying to decide the exact relationship of Scripture and Tradition, or dogma and history, or previous church practice and current demands. The manner in which the relationship among the sources may be worked out depends in part on the starting point of the investigation.

Methodology, then, as a means of arriving at an interpretation, includes both the point of origin (metaphysical assumptions) and a connecting link between the starting point and the end point; the link or route is the ordering of the sources germane to the discipline. To repeat what was pointed out earlier, the starting point significantly affects the ordering of sources which, in its turn, largely affects the conclusions reached. That is why there are a number of potential variations in methods, hence also in conclusions and results.

As explained in the Introduction to this dissertation, our task is to identify and formulate Hans Küng's theological method in the terms just described. As the first step in that direction, then, Part II of the present chapter lays out Küng's starting point in terms of the epistemological and ontological convictions which together comprise his general theological hermeneutic. Chapter II and III will examine the ways Küng orders the prominent theological sources, Scripture and Tradition.

Part II: Küng's Methodological Starting Point

The definition of methodology with which we are working in this study is one that serves to allow a formal distinction to be made between method and content, yet serves also to make one conscious of the real proximity between method and content. This connection was explained by reference to the characteristic we ascribed to methodology: dialectical. That is to say, there is no such thing as a 'pure' starting point existing somewhere (not even in the mind) which is itself devoid of all content. Similarly, there is no 'pure' epistemology untouched by the ontology which it generates, or by the hermeneutic of which it becomes part. Even though one's way of knowing is logically prior to what one knows, still, the way of knowing only comes about in reference to what is known. Thus "to know" is

both a transitive verb, "I know something," and an intransitive verb, "I
know." Another way of saying it is that ontology and epistemology mutually
condition each other, both formally and in terms of content.

Consequently, when we come to actually set out the formal principles in
the ordo cognoscendi of Küng's theological methodology, it must be borne in
mind that the epistemology does not exist in a vacuum of sorts but has in
fact much to do with ontology and everything to do with content. However,
the attempt has been made for the purpose of analysis to isolate and
formulate these 'moments' in their formal aspects.

Epistemology

There are two basic strands in Küng's epistemology--faith and history--
which, when interwoven, constitute the epistemological rudiments of Küng's
methodology.[15] In Küng's view, history and faith are the two prime noetic
elements since revelation is a matter of both faith and history.[16] Faith
and history are 'ways of knowing' which determine how a certain reality
(such as revelation) is known, and what aspect of that reality is known. In
Küng's formal methodology, faith is the pre-eminent and normative of the
two.[17] However, as we shall see shortly, for Hans Küng, present-day faith
cannot do without the historical mode of knowledge.

Although it is difficult to separate faith and history because of the
way Küng has woven them together, still, for discussion purposes each will
be discussed independently of the other, and then in terms of the other.

Faith as a Way of Knowing

Hans Küng has tried to formulate and utilize a definition of faith that
is both rational and biblical. The attempt to define it rationally results
from his intense desire to make accessible to modern people the original
message of Jesus Christ; this means adopting to some degree many of the

scientific criteria which inform today's consciousness.[18] The attempt to define faith biblically results from his adherence to the principle of Scripture as _norma normans_.

Biblical Faith

Küng came to his understanding of faith partly in the context of his study of the doctrine of justification by faith according to Karl Barth, Trent, and, of course, Scripture. Küng has also been involved for several years in ecumenical dialogue with the dialectical theology of Barth (and others) and the natural theology of Catholic theology (especially of Vatican I).

Küng's study of Barth began quite early[19] and culminated in the doctoral dissertation published as <u>Justification</u>. <u>The Doctrine of Karl Barth and a Catholic Reflection</u>. At one point in his analysis of the Scriptural definition of faith, he echoes Paul who says that it is faith, not love, which justifies. Küng stresses that the character of justifying faith is <u>trust</u>. (J 252ff.)[20]

When Küng moved on from justification to ecclesiology, the same definition of faith appropriately found its way into the context of a theology of the Holy Spirit and the Church. In <u>The Church</u> Küng writes that according to Scripture (especially Pauline texts) the Holy Spirit, through faith, effects freedom from sin, death and law. (TC 150-159) It is the Holy Spirit who "gives faith in the cross and resurrection of Christ and gives the power to live a life of faith. He is the 'spirit of faith' (II Cor. 4:13; cf. II Cor. 5:5, 7)." (TC 167) Christians believe in the God revealed in Jesus <u>through</u> the Holy Spirit. God as Holy Spirit is, according to Küng, totally and absolutely free, yet overwhelmingly <u>faithful</u>. Even when God binds Himself to (word and sacrament in) the Church, "We do not demand something of him, he demands something of us: our unconditional <u>faith</u> . . . faith in

God's free grace and faithfulness." (TC 178) Both we and the Church are
simul justus et peccator, justified by faith yet contradicting faith by sin.
Hence the object of faith cannot be either man or the Church but only God
Himself. Only God is perfectly free and faithful, thus only on His promises
can our faith rely, as unconditional trust.[21]

In the Christological context, Küng has worked with the same definition
of faith but he has described it more in terms of its essential connection
with the resurrection of Jesus. The singularly problematic character of the
resurrection (whether it be historical or not) brings out extremely clearly
the character of faith as trust. Regarding the 'empty tomb' Küng makes
clear--presumably following the New Testament--that "the empty tomb never
led anyone to faith in the risen Christ . . . . the disciples never appeal
to the evidence of the empty tomb in order to strengthen the faith of the
Church or to refute and convince opponents." (OBC 365-366) On the contrary,
Küng remarks, (Easter) faith is always oriented to the living Jesus himself;
"The one who called men to believe has become the content of faith, God has
forever identified himself with the one who identified himself with God."
(OBC 383; cf. A 178f.) Persons are called to faith on the grounds that
Jesus was really raised to life, but not on the grounds of post-resurrection
appearances or an empty tomb. As we shall see in more detail presently, not
even an empty tomb could compel faith, else faith would cease to be trust
and hence cease to be faith.[22]

Rationality of Faith

Recently Küng has argued philosophically and theologically in On Being
A Christian and Does God Exist? that the dynamic operative in one's choice
about belief in God's existence has its epistemological analog in one's
fundamental choice about 'the reality of reality'. The lengthy discussion,

in which Küng eruditely spans the history of modern philosophy and theology, need not be reiterated here, (cf. EG; OBC Part A. II. 2; MG) but the following is the shell of his argument.

While modern atheism denies the existence of God, nihilism has cast into doubt the very reality of reality (die Wirklichkeit der Wirklichkeit). Both nihilism and atheism are unproved yet irrefutable. (OBC 73) One's answer to the questionability of reality (fraglichen Wirklichkeit) is not intellectual but volitional: one chooses either to trust or mistrust (mißvertraut) reality. Basic trust (Grundvertrauen) is the affirmative answer to nihilism, it is a 'yes' to reality. Küng writes that nihilism is factually though not philosophically overcome through basic trust; it is possible to live and act in basic trust without grounding reality, but the reality which grounds basic trust still appears itself to be ungrounded. (EG 425ff.)

The fundamental question of basic certainty (Grundgewißheit) about reality appears to be, then, a matter of 'faith' not of reason. That is, one is presented with a choice, but there are no rationally compelling reasons either for or against trusting in reality. It is the same with the question of God's existence: one can neither rationally prove nor disprove God's existence, yet one must opt for one or the other. The affirmative answer to atheism, the 'yes' to God, is faith (Glauben). Still, is there any degree of 'rationality' to the affirmative choice one may make?

Küng writes that the two basic answers have been that of dialectical theology, which maintained the absolute unknowability of God apart from revelation, and of natural theology, which argued for a 'natural' knowledge of God (in creation, for example) to which could be added the supernatural knowledge of God from revelation. Küng argues against the dominant strains of each: the Catholic neo-scholasticism of Vatican I and Karl Barth's (and others') dialectical theology. (EG 509ff.; OBC 64ff.) In Küng's view, the

perimeters of an answer are quite clear: there can be no reduction of reason

to faith and _vice_ _versa_.

> As against dialectical theology firstly: belief in God must not only
> be asserted, it must be verified;
> As against natural theology now: belief in God is to be verified but
> not proved;
> The right way, then, would lie between the purely authoritative
> assertion of God in the spirit of dialectical theology and the
> purely rational proof of God in the spirit of natural theology,
> would lie between Karl Barth and Vatican I. (EG 536)

As in the case of the reality of reality, God's existence also cannot be

accepted based on a proof of pure reason (as in natural theology), nor by

virtue of a moral postulate of practical reason (Kant), nor even by virtue

of the biblical witnesses (dialectical theology); that God is can only be

accepted in a trust grounded in reality itself. (EG 570; OBC 74) If God

does exist, then the questionability of reality would be answered, for God

would be the Grund, Halt und Ziel der Wirklichkeit (ground, support and goal

of reality). Still, this does not compel basic trust or faith. But a 'no'

to God would mean a finally ungrounded basic trust in reality. "If someone

denies God, he does not know why he ultimately trusts in reality." (EG 571)

The 'yes' to God, on the other hand, would mean a finally grounded basic

trust in reality. Again, neither reality as such nor God's existence as

such is compelling. "Yet here, too, man remains free--within limits. He

can say 'No'." (EG 573; OBC 77) Basic trust and belief in God, then, are

identical in form.

Küng's argument, then, has proceeded methodologically neither from

dialectical theology nor from natural theology. No "vertical from above"

was set up to try to refute or ignore either nihilism's fundamental critique

of the reality of reality or atheism's denial of God's existence, as

dialectical theology has done through its assertions about the Bible. Nor,

as in Vatican I's natural theology was there accepted autonomous reason

which could demonstrate a foundation of faith having nothing to do with
faith itself. There was also no continuous, gradual, rational ascent from
man to God, nor was there asserted any arbitrariness on our part whereby
we replace God. Finally, there was no praeambula fidei as the rational
substructure of dogmatics based on the rational arguments of pure reason.
(OBC 84; EG 578)

In summary, then, Küng has argued for a notion of faith that pertains
to the "supra-rational" choice one must make about reality and hence about
God. In terms of faith being an epistemic mode, reality known in Glauben
(that is, God's existence) is markedly different from reality known in
Unglauben. Faith is also different from trust because faith is a gift from
God whereas trust need not necessarily be. Thus in terms of noetic content,
reality known in Glauben is different from what is known in Unglauben.
Moreover, in terms of noetic form, knowing reality in Glauben is
substantially different from knowing reality in Unglauben. Objective
reality as such does not change in either case (that is, God exists whether
He is known or not), but the reality for the knower (ontology) is different
because the epistemological mode is different.

History as a Way of Knowing

The affirmations of faith pertain to God's activity in historical
events (for example, the Exodus) and other historical structures (for
example, the Bible). Although Christians affirm God to be acting in
history, God still does so in ways that preserve the freedom of the
believer; not even God's activity in history is sufficient to compel faith.
To wit, not all those who lived around Jesus of Nazareth saw him as Son of
God; only those with faith "believed in his name." Still, every affirmation
of Christian faith concerning God, Jesus, the Church, appertains to these

realities as they occur or are known in history. In Küng's view, then, to make more understandable the "object" of faith as well as the medium of revelation, one may investigate the very same event from another standpoint: the historian's. He writes, "Christian faith speaks of Jesus, but historiography also speaks of him. Christian faith is interested in Jesus as the 'Christ' of the Christians, historiography in Jesus as a historical figure." (OBC 150)

It is because faith and history intersect at the decisive point of revelation that historical investigation is warranted. Historical thinking means proceeding "from below" (von unten), which entails examining by means of critical historical tools the affirmations of Christian faith which pertain to God's activity in history. (OBC 83) Or, as Küng put it to W. Kasper concerning Christology, "The historical-critical method of verification is advisable today for two reasons: (1) systematic Christology is supported by the scientific study of the New Testament, (2) Jesus Christ can be made understandable only with this method to modern men and women who live in an entirely different conceptuality." (A 172)*[23]

The second factor (different Verstehenshorizont) is important in understanding why Küng favors the historical way of thinking. He is a twentieth-century theologian who originally intended to be a pastor,[24] and who has tried through his theological writings to reach non-theologians as well. He insists that theologians must appreciate the biases, prejudices and predispositions that are obstacles to modern men and women. Theology and homiletics are ineffective if they fail to address twentieth-century women and men as twentieth-century individuals; theology must strive to understand the unique character of modern thinking in order to make its own apologetic effective. (Cf. OBC 83f.)

It is characteristic of current thinking to hold in great esteem scientific knowledge along with its criteria (factuality; objecivity; exactitude), and to denigrate other kinds of knowledge (for example, faith in the unseen). But many Christian professions of faith are explained in ways unacceptable to scientifically-oriented minds: miracles, resurrection, preexistence, to mention but a few. (OBC 227ff., 359ff., 445f.) Traditional theology employs the metaphysical natural-supernatural paradigm, so that God's activity in the world is explained as a supernatural occurrence and interference within the natural realm. This two-storey world leads to insuperable difficulties in contemporary thought. (W&W 139f.) Küng rejects this schema and asserts that it is better to speak as the Bible does simply of "God" and "man" rather than of "nature" and "supernature." (MG 575, 580, 594) And so, in order to make Christian truth-claims intelligible today, and to show that God need not be conceived in a-historical or suprahistorical terms, Küng has utilized the principles and methods of historical criticism. Presumably historical research can assist in the reformulation of faith so that impossible intellectual demands are not placed upon the believer. (OBC 163f.)

Modern historiography has had a history of its own, in the course of which many different versions of historical thinking have gained currency. Küng commonly speaks of the necessity of historical criticism for theology today, but relatively infrequently of the particular presuppositions and convictions of historical criticism which he finds compelling. Thus a slight degree of extrapolation is necessary to know what he means by the term. (Cf. TC 41; OBC 155ff.; MG Chap. VII)

As we mentioned above, history is the category which explains both how being is and how being may be known. History itself is the continuum on

which all things take their place, from which things draw their significance, and in terms of which their ultimate meaning is to be registered.
Historical thinking has replaced the natural-supernatural framework, for
human history consists of clusters of causes and effects which occur in time
and space. The question of whether to include 'outside' or supra-historical
causes has been anwered differently by various historical schools.[25] What
is Küng's position? In the context of a discussion of the resurrection Küng
remarks, "Everything will depend on our not imagining God's call within the
supernaturalist system as a divine intervention from above or from outside."
Yet he is evidently not really a positivist historian. He continues,

> If historical science, as a result of its philosophical presup-
> positions, considers man alone as creator of his history and a
> priori methodically excludes and is bound to exclude God, it
> obviously cannot verify God's action historically. If it could be
> historically verified, it would not be God's action at all. The
> fact that God is at work in the history of the world and of the
> individual person is not an observation demonstrated by historical
> criticism, but--and this must constantly be stressed--a matter of
> trusting faith. (OBC 377)

Elsewhere he writes, "History entirely free of presuppositions is a priori
impossible." (OBC 165)

Since all things occur in history, they may be explained in terms of
their individual location in history; the historical framework views all
meanings and values as historically conditioned, that is, ineluctably shaped
by their particular slot in history. This conditioning has to do with
conceptual horizon, language, intent, and other factors. Because things are
so conditioned by their history (historicity), there accrues to them a
relativity which is a function of their historicity. No human meaning or
value escapes historical conditioning or relativity. Indeed, Küng writes
that even divine truth is historically conditioned when it becomes
historical.[26]

Another matter is Küng's admission that historical methods are capable
of producing only probable results, not absolutely certain (positivistic)
ones. (Cf. OBC 158ff.) There are degrees of probability, and as far as
theology is concerned, modern critical thinking is able to arrive at a very
high degree of probable knowledge concerning the original form of the Church
(TC 20f.) and the "typical basic features and outlines of Jesus' preaching."
(OBC 159) Yet even probable knowledge is highly esteemed; Küng gives the
impression that historical methodology is a "better" tool than any available
to the Church in the past.[27]

Küng's major encounter with historical criticism took place under the
aegis of Ernst Käsemann at Tübingen. Küng acknowledged that this study was
extremely influential on his own theological thought, as it enabled him to
make the transition from a deductive to an inductive Christology. (W&W
152ff.) The first fruit of Küng's study was the very fine 1962 article,
"Frühkatholizismus im Neuen Testament als kontroverstheologisches Problem,"
wherein Küng wrestled with exegetical decisions regarding early Catholicism
in the pastoral epistles and Acts. The tremendous ramifications for Küngian
method by no means ended there; one could say that Küng is still working out
the implications of historical criticism for dogmatic theology. After all,
exegetical research can and should be applied to Church Tradition as well,
to the dogmatic and doctrinal decisions of councils, and to ecclesiastical
practices and policies. Chapter III of this dissertation consists of an
examination of the fruits of just such a procedure.

In addition to Küng's study of historical criticism, he wrote a lengthy
and dense book on Hegel's theological thought, entitled Menschwerdung
Gottes. Eine Einführung in Hegels theologisches Denken als Prolegomena zu
einer künftigen Christologie. It was this work, coupled with Küng's historical studies, that proved decisive for his later Christology. From Hegel

Küng appropriated the emphasis on understanding God in himself (ad intra) as historical, as having a history. The study of Hegel was originally intended to bolster Barth's 'high Christology' which Küng had advocated in his book on Justification.[28] But mid-stream Küng's convictions were altered; he ended his study of Hegel with the foundation of his own later Christology 'from below' (von unten) which proceeds from the concrete historical Jesus of Nazareth (up) to God's working in him. (OBC 448ff.; A 172; W&W 164f.) Christology 'from above' thinks about the interpretations of the New Testament witness deductively, based on the premise of a trinitarian and incarnational teaching down to the humanity of Jesus. Christology 'from below', on the other hand, thinks inductively-interpretatively from the human Jesus, up towards God. (A 172) Küng explicitly states that Christology 'from above' is not declared illegitimate by him.[29] "According to the New Testament we cannot have one without the other. There is not a Jesus of Nazareth who is not proclaimed as the Christ of God. There is not a Christ who is not identical with the man Jesus of Nazareth. Hence there cannot be either an untheological Jesusology or an unhistorical Christology."[30]

The noetic form of historical knowledge, which Küng terms "meta-dogmatic,"[31] clearly proceeds from economy to theology, from the concrete historical realities (up) to God as God exists in se. (See MG 548f.) Hence Küng says, for example, that the trinitarian question hinges on the Christological one: how God was in Jesus.[32] Küng's ecclesiology is no different in terms of epistemological principles. "Ecclesiology is essentially historical," meaning that "the 'essential nature' of the Church is not to be found in some unchanging Platonic heaven of ideas, but only in the history of the Church." (TC 13) At the same time, the Church can be affirmed in faith as having its ultimate referent in God himself.

Apart from history, then, neither God _in se_, God in Christ, nor God in the Church can be known. At the same time, Küng is clear and explicit about the limitations of historical research; history cannot yield a decision as to whether a miracle such as bodily resurrection actually occurred or not; more importantly, trusting faith does not rely entirely on such historical knowledge anyway. The conjunction with faith dictates the need for understanding each aspect of revelation in terms of history as well as theology.[33]

Faith and History

The methodological priorities assigned to faith and history are of utmost importance in theology. Küng is by no means unaware of the different vantage points of each, and of the significant difficulty involved in bringing the two into harmony with each other. But as far as he is concerned, Christian faith does not know God apart from his historical revelation, hence a theological understanding of faith cannot dispense with the method which today makes history most understandable: historical criticism.

By steering a middle course between dialectical and natural theology, and by adhering to a biblical notion which is re-interpreted in the modern term of rationality, Küng accomplishes several things of theological importance. Most important for our present purposes is to take note of the exact relationship between the two strands in Küng's epistemology. In terms of phenomenology, when faith is characterized as a free confident choice, then belief in God is equally as possible as non-belief. Neither can be brought about by scientifically, historically, philosophically or psychologically compelling reasons, for if any one of these were possible, faith would be a conviction but not confidence.[34] As opposed to natural theology, then, Küng's (biblical) definition virtually strips faith of any 'rationality' or rational content as its pre-condition or pre-ground. Nevertheless, against dialectical theology faith cannot be 'irrational' or contentless, especially since faith is a way of knowing, and ways of knowing arise only in response to something that is known. In Küng's account, the 'something' of faith cannot be a rationally compelling argument; rather, the 'content' of faith, as it were, is trust in a person, apart from whom there would be neither cause nor need for a decision of faith to be made. The Küngian epistemological shift, then, pertains to the noetic content of faith, for when a person--and not an event about the person (such as resurrection)--is made the object of faith, then the exact divergence of faith and history becomes clear. Küng's position mediates dialectical and natural theology by postulating that the sine qua non of faith is an event-- in which God addresses men and women. The added subtlety is that even this (historical) event--even though it be the content of faith--also cannot compel faith any more than can rational argumentation. One may still regard this event as an historical occurrence only, in which case the knower is restricted to the historical mode of knowledge. But from the vantage of faith, one is presented in this event with a choice for or against God, either of which is equally possible, but only one of which is correct.

Both faith and history converge in the same Jesus of Nazareth, but in one case he is known as God's viceroy, in the other he is merely an influential historical figure. Thus the faith and historical perspectives plainly are not mutually exclusive, though they differ in terms of noetic content and, we may now add, noetic form. That is to say, the sine qua non of the faith-mode is belief in God who really reveals himself to men and women. Although this revelation has been explained in the Churches in multifarious ways, what is common to all is the conviction that somehow the living God makes himself known as God, and that this involves some sort of participation by God in the created order.[35] The perspective of faith, then, has no trouble referring created entities to their origins in God, nor explaining relationships among creatures by reference to God. God may be cited as the cause for many realities, however mediated or restricted this causality may be by created contingencies such as time, space and human freedom. The historical form, on the other hand, prescinds from using divine causation as an explanation of reality.

With respect to the old but by no means finished debate over "the historical Jesus" and "the Christ of faith" (or, an ecclesiologist might add, "the historical Church" and "the Church of faith"), Hans Küng regards the alternative of either kerygma or history as a false one. Rather, he declares, in the New Testament there is both history and proclamation, history and kerygma, history and faith. (OBC 156ff.) Yet the 'historical Jesus' is not irrelevant to faith. "The kerygma of the community cannot be understood unless we begin quite concretely with the historical Jesus of Nazareth . . . ." (OBC 157) Or, ". . . only in the kerygma can history be understood, and indeed, only in history can the kerygma be known." (MG 592)* Similarly, the 'historical Church' is not irrelevant to faith. The New Testament faith is recorded in history; there is no 'pure' (viz., a-historical or un-historical) kerygma or proclamation. Consequently, historical research becomes an appropriate method of investigation for theology, inasmuch as the basis for faith is embedded in historical events with all the strata which that entails.

Yet, however helpful historical-critical research may be, it cannot produce faith, nor provide compelling reasons for faith. Faith as confident trust is not the product of any rational process or historical proof, but comes about by free decision in "God as he addresses me in this Jesus." (OBC 161; MG 592) Nor, by the same token, can historical research destroy faith. Again, faith is the gift of God, not the result of conclusions drawn solely from history. But historical criticism may be helpful to faith insofar as its methods help distinguish between historical 'fact' and interpretation of historical fact. Historical criticism, in tandem with Christian faith, can help root out both "uncritical credulity and critical skepticism." (OBC 163)

Faith in itself, then, is not accessible to, or able to be judged by, historical investigation, since knowledge of ultimate reality is contingent on accepting revelation; this is admittedly outside the provenance of historical research. (OBC 164) Yet the external consequences of faith can be historically established and verified. In Küng's view, it is amply possible for confident faith to live in harmony with history, for there is no need to fear the outcome of any research. In fact, understood correctly, one may say that faith 'needs' history, not as its cause, but only as its referent. That is, faith and history intersect at one crucial point: Jesus of Nazareth. When one responds in faith to God in Jesus, one never does so apart from the real, historical Jesus of Nazareth.

Ontology

This discussion concerns the second 'moment' within Küng's method-ological starting point, and is undertaken to show the influence of the epistemological strands on formal ontological principles, especially as they apply to three fundamental doctrines: how God is related to the world; how God was in Christ; how God is in the Church. The fundamental mode of all being (the "how") is historical, but as the previous section should have made clear, bare historicity needs the eyes of faith to discern its 'full' reality. Thus in the following pages the interplay between faith and history will again surface as the controlling strands in Küng's theological methodology.

Hans Küng remarked on two occasions that "the problem of God is more important than the problem of the Church, but the latter often stands in the

way of the former." (TC, Foreword; EG 32f.) This might seem to call for
ordering the following remarks with ecclesiology first, theo-logy last. But
Küng elsewhere astutely remarks that the how (Wie) of God's existence often
determines for many whether God exists, and certainly therefore whether
Jesus is God's Son and whether the Church in any sense continues the work of
Christ. Since this discussion pertains to the "how" of both intra-mundane
and transcendent existence, it was thought that the ordering would best
proceed by beginning with God and ending with the Church. For reasons of
intelligibility, the ultimate problem of the manner of God's existence is
presented first in terms of God's own manner of being, and then in terms of
God as he is known in his successive historical forays in Christ and in the
Church.

The Historicity of God

> . . . in the ontic perspective all God-world-occurrences are seen to
> be grounded in God's free grace instead of in speculative necessity,
> and in the noetic-ethical perspective all God-world-mystery is
> grounded in trusting faith rather than in absolute knowledge. (MG
> 517*, 553; EG 162-169, 182)

The position Küng reached concerning the "how" of God's relationship to
the world was advanced a great deal in his lengthy study of Hegel.[36] He
later remarked that his purpose therein was "to take seriously both the
modern development of the new understanding of God and the decisive element
of the biblical faith in God in a new understanding of God's historicity."[37]
Specifically he sought to investigate the possibilities of a "Christology
of the future" utilizing the insight of Hegel into the historicity of God
and the world. Hegel had identified God and the world in his speculative
dialectic of Absolute Spirit, so that the (absolute) difference between God
and world was sublated (aufgehoben) in the process of history. But, as the
above citation from Küng indicates, in his own analysis he has subordinated
Hegel's theology to the Christian biblical doctrine of God's transcendent

freedom. Against Hegel's affirmation of any speculative necessity in God, Küng affirms (with the Bible) the sheer gratuitousness of free grace. (MG 353)

From the standpoint of Christian theology, the decisive difference between Hegelian Christology and biblical Christology cannot be effaced: namely, the un-sublatable (Unaufhebbar) difference between God and the world. (MG 516f; EG 183) Still, Küng saw Hegel's as the honest attempt to go beyond traditional Greek metaphysics (and even traditional Christian Christologies) and, supported by specifically Christian motifs, to take seriously the suffering of God, the dialectic in God, and the becoming in God. (MG 553-554) It was these latter themes which made Hegelian thought all the more attractive for a theologian attempting to speak cogently and appealingly to modern men and women.

When Hegelian philosophy and Christian theology are set vis-à-vis each other, Küng writes, the central point which again emerges is Hegel's identification of God and world. When Christian theology criticizes Hegel on this point (Hegel's "differentiated unity"), theology is, in effect, allowing itself also to be criticized since apparently it presupposes a "differentiated identity." (MG 523)[38] Küng's intention, then, is to critique Hegel's speculative Christology from the biblical point of view, and then to critique classical Christian Christology from the Hegelian and from the biblical point of view. In so doing, Küng believed, one would arrive at a Christology both biblically based and philosophically tenable. (MG 556f.)

Classical Greek philosophy portrayed God as the unchangeable, unmovable, unaffected, immutable, timeless, infinite being. The use of Greek metaphysics in early Christian preaching and teaching tended to emphasize less the historical nature of God's action in Christ and more the metaphysical character of the Incarnation. As Küng puts it, early Christian theology viewed reconciliation and redemption more as the conquering of Platonic dualism between God and man, than as the freeing from sin, guilt and law. Juxtaposing biblical and metaphysical categories, he remarks that it would be as if the opposition between God and man as such was overcome and not that between God and sinful man; as if the entrance of God into humanity happened through incarnation and not much more through death and resurrection; as if redemption could be expressed in pure categories of being (nature, person, hypostasis) and not above all in concrete historical terms such as those used in the New Testament and in the first professions of faith. (MG 532-533) Because early Christian theology was saddled with the philosophical problems of being and becoming, the one and the many, its theological formulations viewed God's eternity more as Platonic timelessness than as a powerful living simultaneity to all time; his omnipresence was seen more as an objective dimension in the universe than as an omnipotent lordship over space; his goodness was seen more as a natural emanation of good than as a free, loving gracious gift of the historically active God; Küng draws other parallels, which contrast the Greek and the biblical expressions. (MG 534; OBC 304ff.)

In particular, Küng singles out the immutability (Unveränderlichkeit) of God which, he writes, contradicts the witness of Scripture, for the Bible speaks of the living God who created the world out of nothing, who knew and loved its most insignificant, who preserved, conducted and ruled its history. When the early Church, in its admittedly difficult apologetic task, heard the Bible, it listened, according to Küng, with Hellenistic ears. (OBC 129ff.)

The Greek notion of the unchangeability of God stands behind classical Christology.

The thought of a creator—God, who as the living God takes hold of
the world (and of matter!) directly and without mediation in Being
and Becoming, who makes possible the world and its history, and who
guides, knows and loves it . . . stands in sharp contrast to the
Greek view of the fixed transcendence of a changeless God. (MG 531)*

But the problem is to explain how, as Scripture puts it, "the Word became

flesh" or "God was in Christ." If one stresses the unity of God and man,

then against monophysitism one needs to show that "the word truly becomes

flesh." If one accents the duality, then against Nestorianism one needs to

show that "the Word itself became flesh." (MG 537)*

By means of a three-fold parallel reflection (on suffering in God, the

dialectic in God, the becoming in God) Küng plays off classical metaphysics

and the biblical message to arrive at the historicity of God. (Cf. OBC

304-309)

The 'impassibility' of God

In Greek metaphysics suffering is synonomous with deficiency. But God

is not deficiency, he is plenitude. To maintain that God suffers is

therefore impossible for Greek metaphysics.

But philosophy, Küng adds, can only speak of God 'in abstracto'. What

is the Christian theologian to say about suffering in God, since according

to Scripture God took on flesh? Not that there is any a priori necessity

for God's suffering: "God need not suffer. And yet he does so in his Son.

That is God's mystery from God's free grace, known by men and women only

through revelation and in faith." (MG 540)* God himself suffers in his Son;

in human flesh. Yet God's suffering is not a lack but plenitude: the

fullness of love. (Jn 3:16) That is why the Cross is the Christian image of

God.[39]

Other Attributes of God

What has been said of the suffering of God can be applied to the other
classical attributes of God. In Greek thought, God is the Simple, the
Infinite, the Immutable, the Incommensurable, the Onmipresent, the Eternal,
the Spirit, the Highest Good, the Omnipotent. God is absolute perfection
and needs no one, neither us nor our world: "God is God. He needs
nothing." (MG 543*; Exkurs IV)

But again, according to Scripture, God became man, God was in Christ,
God identified himself with this man. The perfect appears imperfect, the
simple many, the infinite finite, the immutable mutable, and the acutest
paradox of all: the Highest Good has become cursed (Gal 3:13) and the
Holiest has been made to be sin. (II Cor 5:21) (MG 544)

God's identification with this man is, then, not in "abstract" being
but "in flesh." Human salvation depends on God's not absenting Himself from
our history, but involving Himself in the historical plan, in the flesh. (MG
544) God reveals himself truly in Christ; who He truly is he has shown in
what he has done. He has done it because he wished to, in perfect freedom,
not because of any dialectical or speculative necessity. God reveals
himself in his humanity and co-humanity, but not therefore in a non-
divinity; on the contrary, he reveals precisely "the profoundest divinity of
his divinity" (die tiefste Göttlichkeit seiner Gottheit). (MG 545) Moreover, God has not revealed himself simply in the doxa of a divine figure,
but in the kenosis of a human servant-form; he has revealed at the same time
a superabundance of grace. (Rom. 5:20)

Such a possibility was not even envisioned by Greek metaphysics,
because it would be viewed automatically as a lack in God. But of the God
of revelation in Jesus Christ it must be said that precisely because this
God is not only 'somehow' reality but is pure reality, not somehow absolute

but the Absolute, not only actus but actus purissimus, can he be identified
with the passion and death under Pilate. Only because this God is not the
abstract God of philosophy but the living God of the Old and New Testaments,
can he enter into such pitiful humanity. (MG 564f.)

The God who acted freely in Jesus Christ is the same God attested in
the Old Testament: his activity comes not as any necessity, but as unmerited
grace (propter nos homines et propter nostram salutem). What the living God
does in history he "must" not do but "can" do. The essence of God is an
essence which is capable of self-humiliation (Selbsterniedrigung), an
essence which has within itself the power for the exteriorization of grace.
(MG 548)

The Christian God is also a God who does not exclude but includes his
contrary. This, too, as against Greek metaphysics, does not show a weakness
in God but a real power, as a positive "possibility" which appears at the
beginning of this full reality. Concretely this means a life which includes
death, a wisdom that includes folly, domination-servitude, eternity-time,
incommensurability-commensurability, infinitude-finitude. (MG 548) In terms
of methodology, Christology proceeds from God's way to God's being,
". . . or, as the ancients said, from economy to theology. Not by his
abstract but by his concrete reality will that way be known." (MG 548f.)*
This is the living God of the Old and New Testaments; infinitely superior to
all opposites, he cancels them in his being: the superabundance of grace.

The immutability and becoming of God

According to Greek metaphysics "becoming" in God signifies deficiency
in God. Again, however, the biblical testimony says something quite
different about the God in Christ, the God who has taken on flesh. God has
identified himself with a particular man: the divine Logos became flesh,
the Son of God became man. If God is immutable perfection, he has no need

(nor possibility) of becoming. Classical Christology is therefore unable to explain exactly how God becomes man--it can neither prove nor deduce a "becoming-man" of God. (MG 551; MG Exkurs IV)

Küng's three parallel reflections have approached the center: the historicity of God.

> We have sought to make clear this historicity of God as it is immanent in the system, while trying to draw consequences from a certain classical Christology based on the Greek metaphysical idea of God, which in its final outcome must 'cancel' (aufheben) this metaphysical notion of God. (MG 552)*

That is to say, there is no God who knows and loves the world but remains in himself immutable and unchangeable. God is not to be found in a supra-historical realm, out of which he breaks miraculously into the history of world and man. Even as the Eternally Perfect, God has in his freedom the eternal "possibility" of becoming historical. "God is thus the eternal, who founds, sustains and completes history, the historical primal reason and primal meaning of the whole reality of world and man." (EG 188) God is the beginning (creator), middle (power) and end (fulfillment) of history.

> "Historicity," then (as a "transcendental concept transcending the categories), is used of both man and world on the one hand and God on the other, not equivalently (univocally), nor unequivalently (equivocally), but as similar in a still greater dissimilarity (analogously): analogy of historicity. (EG 188; cf. MG Chap. VIII.2 & Exkurs IV)

Similarly, it is proper to say that God is secular (Weltlich). God is in the world and the world is in God. God is transcendence in immanence, absoluteness in relativity. Thus "Weltlichkeit" can be used as well of man as of God, not univocally nor equivocally but analogously: the analogy of "secularity" (Analogie der Weltlichkeit).[40] As the God who is secular and historical, "He has a history and brings history about. The historical nature (Geschichtlichkeit) of God is the primal history (Urgeschicht-lichkeit) of all the forces of history with regard to man and his world."[41] Küng sees God's agency in the world, therefore, not as that of the unmoved

mover, but as the 'most real reality' working from within the developmental-
process of the world, in, with and under persons and things.

> God operates not only at particular, especially important points or
> gaps in the world process but as the creating and consummating
> primal support and thus as the world-immanent, world-transcendent
> Ruler of the world . . . fully respecting the laws of nature, of
> which he is himself the source. He is himself the all-embracing and
> all-controlling meaning and ground of the world process, who can of
> course be accepted only in faith. (EG 649)

Recalling what was said previously under epistemology, the emphasis on
the historicity of God mediates another opposition between natural and
dialectical theology: the God of the philosophers cannot be dissociated
from the God of the Bible (as in dialectical theology), nor falsely
harmonized (as in natural theology), but can be seen dialectically: "the
'God of the philosophers' is--in the best Hegelian sense of the
term--'canceled-and-preserved' (aufgehoben) positively, negatively and
supereminently in the 'God of Israel and of Jesus'." (OBC 309; EG 666)

To conceive of God in terms of God's historicity is in Küng's view
both biblically warranted and more intelligible to today's way of thinking.
It is also, he writes, only in light of the historicity of God that the
condition of the possibility of a Christology of the future can be
constructed. (MG 557)

The Historicity of God in Jesus

The historicity of God was made known to Israel in its salvation
history. The same God who revealed to Israel the name Yahweh reveals
himself as Father in Jesus Christ. The incarnation of God--the becoming
historical of God--in Jesus means: in Jesus' whole preaching, proclamation,
deeds, and fate, God's word and will have assumed a human form: Jesus has in
all his words and deeds, suffering and death, in his whole person,

proclaimed, manifested and revealed God's word and will. He is the human form of God's Word, Will and Son. (EG 685; OBC 391ff.)

Just as surely as Küng rejects not the intent but the form of the classical presentation of God as immutable and static, so he rejects also not the intent but the form of traditional Christological formulations. Indeed, the Christological programme adumbrated in the previous section is one that proceeds "from below," that is, from the historical Jesus of Nazareth (up) to God's work in him. What Küng is trying to get at from the viewpoint of history is "Jesus as he really was;" from faith, "What Jesus means to us here and now." (cf. OBC 132f.) The historical method obviously aids the first of these, hence indirectly also the second. Küng makes a very interesting remark in Menschwerdung Gottes about Christology 'from below', that it should be careful not to limit itself to "knife-sharpening" but that it arrive at the facts. This means, Küng writes, that Christology, "in all its legitimate talk about historicity, must not lose sight of the concrete history of Jesus and his preaching. It would be a pity if it no longer troubled itself with the texts of Scripture but was content with abstract general theses." (MG 598)* The interplay between history and faith is clear here, that history should serve faith in order that affirmations of faith may be all the more authentic. But there is certainly no historical proof that "God was in Jesus;" this is a matter of trusting faith. Or, as Küng later said in reply to G. Baum,

> Viewed historically this Jesus constitutes the beginnings of the church. Viewed theologically he constitutes at the same time the abiding normative origin of the church, insofar as the faith of this community confesses him to be the Christ. In this way that which historically happened 'once' enjoys a validity for faith that is 'once and for all'.[42]

Similar to the previously-discussed problem of the unity between God and the world, in Christology the central question is the meaning of divine sonship, or how "this particular man Jesus" is related to God his Father. Since the historical Jesus—who is also the Christ affirmed in faith—is made accessible in the Bible, and since the Bible may be subjected to historical analysis, a Christology formulated along historical-critical lines will be substantially different from classical Christology. In fact, the shift is away from the metaphysical framework of the two-nature dogma of Chalcedon, which attempted to solve ontologically the question of the unity of the Godhead and the humanity of Christ, towards more biblical expressions and themes. Küng writes that the original biblical perspective (that is, the one delineated to be such by historical criticism) is not ontological but functional:[43] the decisive question in the Bible is the unity of the man Jesus with God his Father (or the unity of the earthly Jesus with the raised Christ). (A 176f.)[44]

It is noteworthy that Küng's starting point 'from below', while not vitiating Christologies formulated 'from above', does not contain within itself the means by which one can make an easy transition from 'below' to 'above'. That is to say, once one has determined historically-critically what Jesus' function is, one cannot pass easily to ontological statements about his nature or pass from personal communion with the Father to communion of natures, or from the salvific-soteriological testimony of Scripture to later dogmatic ontological declarations regarding the God-Man. In other words, there is no easy transition from

> . . . a functional Christology to an essentialist, metaphysical, ontological Christology, from a mission-Christology to a being-Christology, from the original two-step Christology to a . . . two-substance or two-nature Christology. . . . (A 175)[*]

Implied in such a transposition would be a different understanding of the relationship between Tradition and Scripture; dogmatic traditions cannot, according to Küng, facilely be equated with the biblical view. (A 173)

Thus Küng criticizes the Chalcedonian formula because (1) it is not
necessarily identical with the original New Testament message about Jesus;
(2) such a formula is unintelligible to modern ways of thinking. (OBC 131,
158; MG 565f., Exkurs I; A 173f.) Each of these objections obviously
results from one or the other epistemological strands mentioned in the
previous section--the former from historiography, the latter from faith.
In place of an ontological understanding of the relationship between Christ
and the Father, Küng writes:

> But this unity must be understood as personal, relational, func-
> tional, and not restricted ontologically in the sense of a two-
> natures doctrine: certainly not as a pre-given ontological unity of
> being (which neither John's prologue nor the Philippians-hymn--both
> of which are hymns, not dogmas!--supports) and as a unity of reve-
> lation which is to be understood historically, or, . . . as unity of
> activity. (A 176f.)*

The fundamental 'core' affirmation of Chalcedon remains true for Küng; that
is, he is clearly willing to affirm that "Jesus is the Son of God,"
"Although for me, the 'classical' fixation on this one title seems warranted
by neither the New Testament nor current thinking. Even according to Kasper
there is no single title which adequately expresses who Jesus is; . . . the
decisive question in all this is how "Son of God' and "is" are to be
understood." (A 174*; Cf. OBC 287ff., 384ff.) For Küng, the biblical
meaning of divine sonship, rather than its classical dogmatic formulation,
renders the ideas of incarnation and pre-existence more understandable for
modern persons.

> In the New Testament, the death and raising to life of Jesus are
> central, not the Incarnation motif (which plays practically no role
> in the oldest gospels and in the Pauline writings). Also in the
> whole New Testament nowhere is there any mention of a becoming-human
> (Menschwerdung) or a being-born (Geborenwerden) of God himself, but
> only of a becoming-human of the Word or Son of God. (A 177)* .

What Küng sees from his dual perspective is that "The Christ of the
Christians is a quite concrete, human, historical person; the Christ of the
Christians is no other than Jesus of Nazareth. And in this sense

Christianity is essentially based on history, Christian faith is essentially

historical faith." (OBC 146) That is, historical research is able to

establish that Jesus of Nazareth was a real human being with a locatable

history. (OBC 148) The New Testament witnesses (which are committed

testimonies of faith) do provide some historical information but they are

not intended as historical biographies. (Cf. OBC 150-158; Chap. II below)

After spelling out in detail what historical research (in tandem with

faith) _is_ able to know about the historical Jesus, Küng arrives at his

theological reinterpretation of the Chalcedonian formula, true God and true

man. The lengthy text is cited here in full:

> _Truly God_: The whole point of what happened in and with Jesus
> depends on the fact that, for believers, God _himself_ as man's friend
> was present, at work, speaking, acting and definitively revealing
> himself _in this Jesus_ who came among men as God's advocate and
> deputy, representative and delegate, and was confirmed by God as the
> Crucified raised to life. All statements about divine sonship,
> pre-existence, creation mediatorship and incarnation—often clothed
> in the mythological or semi-mythological forms of the time—are
> meant in the last resort to do no more and no less than substantiate
> the _uniqueness, underivability_ and _unsurpassability_ of the _call,
> offer_ and _claim_ made known in and with Jesus, ultimately not of
> human but of divine origin and therefore absolutely reliable,
> requiring men's unconditional involvement.
> _Truly man_: Against all tendencies to deify Jesus, it must
> constantly be stressed even today that he was _wholly_ and _entirely_
> man with all the consequences of this (capacity for suffering, fear,
> loneliness, insecurity, temptations, doubts, possibility of error).
> Not merely man, but _true man_. In describing him as such we insisted
> on the truth which has to be made true, the unity of theory and
> practice, of acknowledging and following him, of faith and action.
> As true man, by his proclamation, behavior and fate, he was a _model
> of what it is to be human_, enabling each and everyone who commits
> himself to him to discover and to realize the meaning of being man
> and of his freedom to exist for his fellow men. As confirmed by
> God, he therefore represents the permanently reliable _ultimate
> standard of human existence_ (OBC 449f.)[45]

Finally, it may be pointed out that Küng's commitment to faith clearly

surfaces when he states that the real matter of decisive importance is not

whether one agrees with this or that lofty dogma about Christ, but the final

test of being a Christian is "the acceptance of _faith in Christ_ and

<u>imitation</u> of Christ." (OBC 450; A 178f.) Even in Christology, then, it becomes clear how the dual strands in epistemology bear themslves out in the ontology. From the perspective of faith, God reveals himself truly in his Son, in history. From the vantage of history, in so revealing himself God partakes in all the limitations and contingencies of human existence: God takes on flesh and hence becomes historical in Jesus of Nazareth. The two perspectives work hand-in-hand with each other, for there is no Christ of faith apart from the historical Jesus and there is no historical Jesus who is not also the Christ of God.

The Historicity of God in the Church

Since God was affirmed by Israel to be involved in its history, and since God became historical in a definitive way in Jesus Christ, it is part of Christian belief that God continues to love men, women and the world in an on-going, historical fashion. The trinitarian pattern of God's relation-ship to His creation progresses from revelation and redemption to sanctifi-cation. Hence one is involved in ecclesiology.

If the ontological reality of both God in himself and God in Jesus Christ is historical, the Church would hardly be exempt, nor, in Küng's view, would that be a desideratum. Although he worked at ecclesiology before Christology, it can be verified that the same epistemology and hence same ontological principles are operative.

Just as there is the "Jesus of history" who is none other than the "Christ of faith," so there is no Church known in faith apart from the historical Church, nor is there any historical Church which is not also the Church of faith. Clearly, the Church is not "of faith" in the same way that Jesus Christ is said to be the object of faith. Yet formally speaking, there is a similarity which permits one to speak of the "Church of faith" and the "Church of history" as long as these terms are understood properly.

For the purpose of bringing out the two perspectives of faith and history, these expressions will be employed in this discussion.

Küng's is an ecclesiology 'from below', despite the strangeness of the term. That is, just as in Christology, so too in ecclesiology, theological investigations must proceed from the concrete, historical Church (up) to God's agency in it as Holy Spirit. There is an "essence" of the Church which is "drawn from the permanently decisive origins of the Church." (TC 4) But this "essence" can be known only in constantly changing historical forms. The real Church is the Church as it exists in history; "The real essence of the real Church is expressed in historical form." (TC 5) There never was an a-historical Church-ly essence existing somewhere apart from historical embodiments. "While there are permanent factors, there are no absolutely irreformable areas." Yet, "For all its relativity, historical form should not be seen as totally irrelevant and contrasted with an essence existing somewhere 'beyond' or 'above' it." (TC 5) At the same time, it is in light of the "essence" that all historical forms must be adjudged as legitimate or not, but no historical form of the Church, not even the New Testament form, perfectly manifests the Church's essence. The essence of the Church, then, though Küng does not say it explicitly here, would be identical with what was accomplished perfectly or definitively in Christ: God's Word and Will. These can be accomplished only imperfectly in the Church.

The origin of the Church does not lie merely in an historical situation, and "still less in a transcendental 'principle', fabricated or interpreted philosophically, which supposedly set the history of the Church in motion." (TC 14) Rather, the origin is both in history yet knowable only in faith: the origin is "given," "appointed" or "laid down" by the historical action of God himself in Jesus Christ. This salvific act is decisive and thus defines the essential nature of the Church. "Those origins determine what is permanently true and constantly valid in the Church, despite all historical forms and changes and all individual contingencies." (TC 14)

The Church's origin is spelled out concretely in the New Testament. Historical criticism is able to distinguish therein several different "ecclesiologies," all attesting the same origin. The perspective of faith, on the other hand, knows only the one God in the one Christ, hence the Church's origin and purpose must also be one, not several. The theologian's task is to seek discriminatingly the deeper unity in the New Testament as a whole. Of course, historical criticism has its own criteria for this task, but these should serve, not counter, the knowledge of faith of the unity of all things in Christ. (TC 18ff.)

Historical reflection on the Church's origin means historical reflection on the Gospel from which the Church took and continues to take its origin. The purpose of ecclesiology is not to determine the original shape of the Church in order that it may be imitated today, but in order to best translate into modern terms the Church's original design. (TC 24)

Because of the essential historicity of the Church, it is plagued with an "un-nature (Unwesen) which consists of all developments in the Church which conflict with its essential nature. But the positive nature of the Church comes to light only through seeing its un-nature. All aspects of the Church are subject to the eroding effects of its un-nature: "the Church is historically affected by evil." (TC 28) And lest there be confusion concerning these predicates, Küng writes, "To attack the 'un-nature' of the Church is to attack the real church but not its real nature." (TC 29)

The Church is the "object of faith" inasmuch as it cannot be judged properly from outside, from the viewpoint of a neutral observer. In faith

Christians believe that the Church is where the Holy Spirit is at work.
Belief in the Church is more properly belief in the Holy Spirit. It is
better, writes Küng, to say "I believe the Church" in contrast to "I believe
in God." (TC 32ff.) What is believed pertains to the Originator of the
Church.

It was once popular to describe the Church as being both 'visible' and
'invisible', the latter term being used to refer to the 'essence' of the
Church. But in Küng's ecclesiology, although the essence of the Church is
hidden to all but the eyes of faith, there are not two Churches, one visible
and one invisible, nor is the visible a platonic-like reflection of the
invisible, nor is the invisible identical with its essential nature.
Because of the emphasis on the unmitigated historicity of the Church, the
one real Church is both invisible and visible; the real Church has both a
nature and an un-nature. (TC 39)

Since the Church is essentially historical, all aspects of its
existence are historically conditioned. This includes all institutional
forms, all teaching, all practices, in short, all of so-called Tradition.
(Cf. Chap. III below) But to be historically conditioned does not mean to
be without value, untrue, or even non-perduring; conditioning is simply an
ontological characteristic of being historical. It is identifiable by
historical-critical tools, but as this chapter has argued, faith is not on
that account rendered superfluous but all the more necessary. The fear, as
Küng puts it, of sinking "without trace in the changeability of everything
historical" (TC 21) is negated by confident faith in God's promises to the
Church. But in ecclesiology—perhaps more than in Christology—there is far
greater room in which one has to decide which elements are more historically
conditioned, which elements are less so. For Küng there is no aspect of
reality which escapes historical conditioning: even God (ad extra) is

historically conditioned. But what perhaps differentiates Küng here from other theologians is his prior theoretical position that historicity extends to all existence because historicity is first true of God himself.

To continue with the parallelism between Christology and ecclesiology, it may be said that just as there are permanent features about God or Jesus, though both are historically conditioned, so also in the Church there are permanent features. But these apply to the Church's essential nature (Body of Christ; Creation of the Holy Spirit) as it is worked out in history, not to this or that historical form. The Church has been given a concrete, historical, and even historically conditioned yet permanently decisive criterion for its life: the Bible.[46] Just as in Christology, it is Scripture which yields the data both for a scientific ecclesiology as well as for the affirmations of faith. Hence Scripture must be investigated historically-critically but interpreted through the perspective of faith. (Cf. OBC 478ff.; Chap. II below) It is according to Scripture that one is able to identify those historical forms which are justified by its origin, and those which are not.[47] But even historical forms which are congruent with the essential nature of the Church are still historically conditioned and hence in principle not irreformable.[48]

Within the purview of ecclesiology we come to one of the most important areas of Küng's theology and methodology: ecumenism.[49] It seems to be the case that the perspective of faith and history are somewhat at odds in ecclesiology, since they arrive at two different and perhaps contradictory realities: the existential, historical reality does not accord with the theological reality. That is to say, from the standpoint of faith, the Church is already one in the one Christ. The unity of the Church is a spiritual entity which depends ultimately on the unity of God which is efficacious through Jesus Christ in the Holy Spirit. There is one and the same God, one and the same Jesus Christ, one and the same Holy Spirit, one and the same Lord's Supper, one and the same Baptism, one and the same confession of faith. "The Church is one and therefore should be one." (TC 273) This is a perspective of faith which knows the unity of the Church to be already real in Christ.

But from the standpoint of history the Church is not one; for it is divided in doctrine and practice. In Küng's mind, a believer looking at this can only be scandalized. Standing in the way of re-union are various historical developments which were not necessarily authorized by the Church's origin (in his view, the Marian and papal dogmas). Where historical criticism enters in--as an aid to faith--is in investigating and clarifying heterogeneous historical accretions (both in Church practices and dogmas) which need not remain. Historical research is also able to distinguish among different strata in the Bible and so approach that which is attested as the origin of the Church.[50]

Ecumenicity does not exclude a plurality of historical forms or expressions. Plurality and disunity are not identical. There is one faith, though there are different (historical) professions of faith, about the one Christ, though different (historical) doctrines, derived from the one Scripture, though containing different (historical) testimonies, accepted by the one Church, though it exists in different historical forms. What becomes questionable for Küng is whether the multiplicity of historical forms are authentic witnesses to Jesus Christ or are unbiblical, unauthorized doctrinal or practical developments in Tradition.

The Küngian Hermeneutic

Hermeneutics is generally defined as the study or science of methods of interpretation; theological hermeneutics usually pertain to principles of

interpretation of Scripture, though modern interpretation is now extended to
various elements of ecclesiastical Tradition as well. In the description of
methodology given above, it was further stipulated that a hermeneutic is
comprised by epistemological and ontological principles. Specifically, the
two previous sections of this chapter showed that Küng's formal principles
of interpretation are both historical and theological. In terms of the
relationship between faith and history, the theoretical subordination of
history to faith renders Küng's methodology a theological method. Yet, the
historical mode of knowledge substantially conditions the faith mode, for
faith in Küng's scheme is inconceivable apart from history.

Because of the nearly equal weighting of faith and history in Küng's
starting point, one would expect his general hermeneutic to be propor-
tionate. And so, when the formal principles discussed thus far are drawn
together and formulated in more analytic terms, it becomes possible for us
to isolate and formulate two basic hermeneutical principles which comprise
the overall hermeneutic and are thus operative and decisive throughout
Küng's theological methodology.

The first is apologetic in nature. Küng has seen quite clearly that
the historical-critical framework achieves a great deal in terms of
appealing to contemporary ways of thinking. The re-presentation of biblical
themes in ways understandable to moderns is plainly of great value to the
Church's mission of proclamation. Through historical analysis Küng has
endeavored to preserve the central truths of faith affirmed throughout
Christian history, while reworking the limited language and ideas in which
the truths have been expressed. He has performed an equivalent task by
presenting many of the Church's practices (ritual; legal; disciplinary) in
light of their historical locus and relative forms. From the standpoint of

apologetics, then, Küng's use of modern historiography is an appropriate and fruitful means of retranslating the Gospel for today.

But the apologetic task is not the dogmatic task. While Küng's apologetic principle is making Christian ways of thinking intelligible to modernity, it seems that he performs also a dogmatic task. That is to say, specific doctrines or dogmas may be recast in terms which are not only modern but patently ecumenical. And if the measure of good theology from the apologetic viewpoint is its ability to re-translate the original Gospel into the contemporary idiom, the measure of good theology from the dogmatic viewpoint is its ecumenicity (also in re-translating the original Gospel).

Seen in this light, it is not incidental that Küng's methodology is historical-critical, for it is precisely this approach which enables both tasks to be executed: it enables Küng's theology to be pastorally effective, and it gives him passage to ecumenical theology. That is to say, for apologetic theology, historiography makes possible the unmasking of old ways of thinking (for example, the two-storey universe; miracles; pre-existence; et. al.) which need no longer stand in the way of modern theology's arduous task of re-interpretation. As far as dogmatic theology is concerned, one immediate result of historical criticism is the emphasis on the unrivalled normativity of the Bible, which means the ground common to all Christian communions is reaffirmed and even raised to the level of a methodological criterion. A second result of historical criticism is that Tradition recedes into the background of theological work (Cf. Chap. III below) which means that a much subordinated place is assigned to those his-torical and doctrinal developments which divide Christendom (especially papacy and Mariology).

Apologetic and dogmatic theology are basically different tasks, even though both attempt to render clear and intelligible some aspect of

Christian faith. Dogmatic theology makes its case only within the Christian community and may presuppose that its recipients are believers. Apologetic theology, on the other hand, may make its presentation either _intra_ or _extra_ the Christian community, and so does not presume likewise about its audience. Küng performs both theological tasks in singularly ecumenical fashion. As displayed in his theology, the dogmatic-ecumenical principle evidently informs and shapes the apologetic principle, inasmuch as the latter is simply another species of ecumenically-oriented theology.

The suitability of the historical enterprise for theology may be evaluated independently of ecumenical theology, but the reverse is not true, for ecumenical theology is quite difficult to envision apart from the historical point of view. There are many possible epistemological combinations possible in theology (for example, dogma-faith instead of faith-history), and a theology with a different starting point will not necessarily eventuate in an ecumenical hermeneutic. But historically-oriented theology is at least potentially ecumenical, since it is able to regard doctrinal and historical developments more as relative accretions to the tradition than as elements which must be maintained in the present. The ecumenical vision sees "all things being one in Christ" despite a plurality of beliefs and practices. And being able to live with theological and confessional pluralism requires assigning a relative value to respective doctrines and practices; here ecumenical theology is well-served by the historical perspective.

It is well-known that Küng is an active and vocal ecumenist; some critics have even voiced the objection that he tailors facts to fit his fancy, his fancy being that of ecumenical re-union.[51] Better put, and removed of its negative connotations, one may say that Hans Küng's over-arching hermeneutical principle is _ecumenical_. The 'dialectical'

relationship of faith and history culminates in the formation of this hermeneutic which has, as we have seen, two complementary features: apologetic
and dogmatic. One might at this point be tempted to designate Küng's whole
methodology "ecumenical" instead of "theological" (as in the title of this
dissertation) in order to indicate one emphasis in his theological interpretation. It would be as misleading to specify his methodology as
"historical-critical," for this would overlook the priority he assigns to
faith. For once a methodology is qualified by any term besides "theological" (such as "transcendental" or "liberation"), then the impression is
given that the theologian who practices the method is manifestly and perhaps
even disproportionately biased towards ecumenism or transcendentalism or
some other view. Because "ecumenical methodology" is something of a mis-
nomer, it is more accurate to describe Küng's as a theological methodology,
that is, a theological means of arriving at an interpretation.

Küng's starting point, then, is the first major 'moment' in a methodology which seeks to be both contemporary and biblical, both scholarly and
pastoral, both historical and systematic, both apologetic and dogmatic. It
is a theological methodology which seeks always to have Jesus Christ at its
center, determining its direction, guiding its formulations, measuring its
results.

Critical remarks concerning Küng's methodology will comprise Chapter V.
We may now turn to the second 'moment' of methodology: the sources which
are ordered in light of this starting point.

CHAPTER TWO

SCRIPTURE: THE <u>NORMA NORMANS</u>

"Sacred Scripture is the <u>norma</u> <u>normans</u>."[1] From the standpoint of theological methodology, this principle plays the crucial role in Küng's theology and methodology. His view of Scripture arises out of the theological
hermeneutic explained in Chapter I, and so it reflects most powerfully the
combination of the faith-and history-perspectives. At the same time, Scripture is also the chief source of the Küngian hermeneutic. Thus in the case
of Scripture it can be seen how interdependent the first and second methodological 'moments' really are.

It has been pointed out that the application of the historical-critical
method to the Bible may lead to a destructive exegesis, a thorough-going
relativism, even an unintended reductionism, in which the Bible emerges as
one document among others, but one certainly not containing in itself a
special normativity or critical value.[2] Clearly there is a theoretical consideration in Küng's starting point which would preclude this, namely, his
theological modification of historical principles. And so, it is the task
of this chapter to trace the emergence of the historical-critical method in
Küng's writings, to see the application of this method to Scripture and the
view of Scripture which results, to investigate various ways in which Scripture is <u>norma</u> <u>normans</u>, and therewith to have illustrated where the provenance of historical criticism ends and where the other epistemological component (faith) enters in and renders Küng's methodology theological.

The Historical Word of God

One of the most remarkable features of Küng's theology and methodology
is the extent to which his position on Scripture changed. The first task

before us, then, is to trace Küng's inauguration into historical criticism
and its profound impact on him.

The Shift from Pre-criticism
to Historical Criticism

In Hans Küng's first major work, Justification. The Doctrine of Karl
Barth and a Catholic Reflection, in the context of an examination of
Barth's teaching on justification and prior to formulating a Catholic
response to Barth, Küng wrote a pivotal chapter on his own methodology.
Therein Küng reiterates Catholic teaching of that time on Scripture, Tradition, and their relationship.[3] His statements concerning Scripture,
although brief, could not be clearer nor more traditional. For example, he
writes,

> The well from which Catholic doctrine and Catholic theology draw is
> the Word of God. The Word of God, in the strictest sense, is Sacred
> Scripture alone. (J 111)

> Only in (Sacred Scripture) do we possess the outright and unmediated
> testimony of God Himself, and in its original idiom and its primal
> source. That is why Sacred Scripture has an absolute precedence
> which no other theological argument can whittle away. (J 111)
> (emphasis mine)

Küng surveys several prominent Catholic theologians who, in one way or
another, support his own position. For example, he approvingly cites T.
Zapelena who says, "Scripture is formally the Word of God; tradition is not
formally the Word of God but contains the Word of God." (J 112)

Yet only five years later in a 1962 article,[4] Hans Küng rhetorically
posed to Karl Barth the bold question, "What is the Word of God?" Barth's
answer was to serve as a critical question to Catholic theology,[5] for as
Küng lamented, Catholic theology had no far-reaching (umfassende) definition
of the essence (Wesen) of the Word of God. Even though Catholic theology
spoke frequently of the Word of God in relation to revelation, inspiration,
Church, Christ, and Saviour, in each case what was missing was

a truly far-reaching, concentrated, deep and developed dogmatic
teaching on the Word of God itself in its manifestations (Holy
Scripture, Church proclamation), on its fundamental aspects
(mysterious word and deed of God: verbum efficax) and its essential
qualities (personal, spiritual, free, historical, limited,
infinite . . .), of its foundation in the incarnation of the Word
spoken by the Father in the Spirit from all eternity, and finally
in its eschatological function.[6]

Barth's own teaching on the Word of God as threefold (Jesus Christ; Scrip-

ture; preaching) is well-known and need not concern us here.[7] But it is to

Barth's pointed criticism of Catholic theology (namely, whether it is suffi-

ciently aware that the Church stands under the Word of God and that the Word

of God and the word of the Church are not identical, whether Catholic theo-

logy takes in earnest the uniqueness and radically Christian character of

revelation when it speaks of 'natural' as well as 'supernatural' revela-

tion), that Küng replies.[8]

Küng's answer to Barth in this essay is important for later considera-

tions in this dissertation, for one finds expressed here in germ the themes

and convictions which will continue to dominate his thought and method.

Küng answers Barth's attack on natural theology with a counter-question:

Catholic theology will affirm that God is unique, as is his revelation, and

even Vatican I did not propose two revelations, one Christian and one pro-

fane; still, "Is the good creation of the good God mute? Does it speak no

word?"[9] Here Küng was asking not only whether Barth had correctly under-

stood Catholic theology's teaching on the Word of God, but also whether

Barth had correctly understood the Word of God itself. This confirms not

only Küng's departure from Barth which had happened already, at least doc-

trinally, in Justification, but it also signals his more decisive departure

from Barth in terms of methodology. As Küng put it recently, his and

Barth's starting points were at variance in that Barth began "from above,"

from God and his free sovereign activity in Christ, whereas Küng began "from

below," from humanity and historicity.

> Right from the start this was a major point of difference between me
> and Barth, who indeed rejected any true knowledge of God that was
> not based on Christian revelation. My view on the other hand—and
> here I find myself in the great Catholic tradition and indeed that
> of the Reformation—is that even according to the Old and New
> Testaments, whose statements in this context Barth did violence to,
> it is necessary in fact to accept a knowledge of the one true God
> even among non-Christians, among "the heathen." Of course, along
> with Barth I am convinced that it is only with the Christian message
> that God is made manifest to me in his complete unambiguity with all
> the consequences that flow from this. (W&W 148; cp. EG 566-571)

Küng's reply charged that perhaps Barth had not taken sufficiently seriously

the Christological and hence incarnational center enunciated so strictly in

his own programme, in not insisting equally on revelation of the Word of God

in human words. That is, Küng wondered whether Barth diminished the

sovereign glory of the Word of God by reducing the triumph of this Word in

creation and by neglecting the question of "the relationship of one Word of

God to the other words, which in their creatureliness still are or can be

true words."[10]

What we have at this point, then, is not only the departure from

Barth's teaching on the Word of God, but also Küng's beginning dissatisfac-

tion with traditional Catholic teaching on the Word of God. Although in

early 1962 Küng had only framed the question of the Word of God and Scrip-

ture (perhaps in terms of Barth) he was only beginning to acquire the

tools he needed to answer it. It is interesting to see that although Küng

felt there to be a certain weakness in Catholic theology's teaching, inas-

much as it needed a deepened reformulation in historical, trinitarian and

eschatological terms, at the same time he found in traditional Catholic

theology the seed of an answer both to Barth's objections and to what he

considered weaknesses in Catholic theology. Insofar as, for Küng, Catholic

theology paid more heed to the "incarnational principle" in its theology

than did Barth, already included in Catholic theology, then, was the respect

for anthropology, for the human side of revelation and its human attestation in Scripture. It seems quite fitting then that Küng's insistence on the human element (against Barth), along with his desire to evidence (also to Barth) an equal insistence on the sovereignty of God and the distinction between the Word of God and the Word of the Church, should find a powerful opportunity for combination in the historical-critical method. For in this method, there would of course be the full incorporation of the human element in terms of its historicity <u>and</u>, by so classifying all human reality as historical, finite, changeable, the gulf between God and man would be widened in a way different from both Barth and from Catholic theology; simultaneously, the principle would be established whereby God and man would truly be related, but again in a way different from both Barth and much of Catholic theology.

It is in fact the case that, owing to the growing impact of historical-critical studies on his theology and methodology, Küng's understanding of the relationship between Scripture and the Word of God evolved a great deal. But before we trace this development further, we wish to stop momentarily at a very important methodological decision Küng makes regarding the Canon of Scripture. As the remainder of this dissertation will evince, this largely unnoticed decision of Küng's had far-reaching implications for his whole theological enterprise.

The Canon of Scripture

As a result of a rather extensive dialogue with several prominent Protestant scholars on the subject of the unity of the Church and the New Testament Canon, we find Küng on two separate occasions in 1962 (EC; SC 135-151) reporting his deepening historical position on Scripture. In the essay "Early Catholicism in the New Testament as a Problem in Controversial Theology," which was the first fruit of Küng's historical-critical research into Scripture,[11] Küng enunciates the common ground he shared with Ernst

Käsemann and Hermann Diem, yet also his departure from each on "Catholic grounds." (W&W 158) In the debate Küng shrewdly pits his two Protestant Tübingen colleagues against each other. The exegete, Ernst Käsemann, is from the Bultmannian school; the dogmatic theologian, Hermann Diem, is from the Barthian school. In contrast to and as a corrective of their respective positions, Küng's own is clearly to be seen.

The central concern of the debate is to determine the foundation of the unity of the Church and its relationship to the unity of the New Testament Canon. The exact relationship between them hinges on how one views "early Catholicism" in the New Testament. Harnack had traced back early catholicism to the beginning of the second century, and the Bultmannian school had pushed it back even farther, to the New Testament itself. This raised difficult hermeneutical problems, especially for Protestant theologians, for how could one accept the whole of the New Testament, then, without also accepting Catholicism?[12]

The Positions of Käsemann and Diem

Ernst Käsemann's position is that the New Testament Canon cannot be the foundation of the unity of the Church but only a basis for the multiplicity of sects, because of (1) the variability of the New Testament kergyma itself;[13] (2) the variety of theological positions in primitive Christianity; (3) the apparent incompatibility among theological positions in the New Testament itself. (EC 239-243) For Käsemann "the different confessions in existence today all appeal to the New Testament--and they are right, for even in Christianity as it was at the beginning there was a multitude of different confessions alongside each other combined with each other, over against each other." (EC 244) This leads him to distinguish between spirit and letter, between Gospel and Canon; the Canon is the word

of God only when, in the power of the Holy Spirit, it becomes the Gospel.

(EC 245) The Gospel alone founds the unity of the Church.

The Scriptures must be understood and interpreted by this Gospel

itself, through a "discernment of Spirits," which leads Käsemann on the

middle road of the Reformation, somewhere between

> . . . pseudo-mystical Enthusiasm on the left . . . which tries to
> get beyond Scripture so as to seize hold of the Gospel, and Catholic
> traditionalism on the right . . . which regards the Gospel as simply
> available and accessible in Scripture without measuring it constantly
> by the critical standard of the Gospel. (EC 245)

Käsemann's middle road is somewhere between the Scriptures and the Gospel,

between the Canon and the Gospel. Protestant theology's task is continually

to apprehend anew the Gospel within the Scriptures. In and of themselves

the Scriptures are only historical documents, but for the believer, "the

Gospel," the center of the Scriptures, is the justification of the sinner.

(EC 247) Ecclesial unity, then, rests on this Gospel, the core of Christian

teaching and proclamation which is justification. Küng adds in a sympathet-

ic vein that Käsemann's honest desire is the unity of the Church, despite

what may seem a rather tenuous way of basing the unity. Küng makes a state-

ment here that, although brief is penetrating in its implications for our

discussion. He remarks of Käsemann's solution that it advocates "a unity of

the Church which rests upon the Gospel, and as such is never plainly detect-

able but only present to faith." (EC 249)

The other discussion partner, Hermann Diem, likewise sees as untenable

the position of a "dogmatic unity" in Scripture. In fact for Diem, the

Reformation churches which taught such a unity by making Scripture into a

sort of summa of theology instead of a text for preaching, who asserted the

verbal inspiration and divine character of Scripture,

. . . ceased to be content with the mere fact of the Canon as
something given in practice, and made a principle of its being
finally closed. This has done damage to preaching and to faith.
(EC 250)

Diem attributes to historical-critical scholarship the current healthy re-

examination of the doctrine of Scripture. He points out that recent studies

have stressed the kerygmatic character of the New Testament, against modern

Protestantism which has made dogmatics the guardian of Scripture.

Yet Diem also departs from Käsemann by countering, "No Canon within

the Canon." (EC 252) For Diem, Käsemann's use of the doctrine of justifi-

cation as a hermeneutical criterion is not a solution which can claim to

have returned to Luther's interpretive principle (the preaching of Christ)

and thereby to have overcome its distortion in modern Protestant dogmatics.

Although justification is certainly an event more than a teaching, an event

to which Käsemann asks that we submit ourselves and our histories, Diem asks

of Käsemann the damaging question,

. . . whether he really does or can submit to the power of this
self-proclaiming history, or whether he paralyzes and must paralyze
the authority of this event conveyed to him through the preaching of
Scripture by the fact that he makes of it a history with a compelling power only after first testing it critically and asserting to
it subsequently. (EC 253)

In contrast, Diem holds that the Church's role in the formation of the Canon

cannot be superseded by a sub-canon. Küng quotes Diem who says,

This compelling process of self-proclamatory history consists in the
fact that the Church has exclusively heard, in the proclamation of
these witnesses, the Word of God, and we must therefore continue to
proclaim and hear just as exclusively through these witnesses. This
fact can only be recognized; it cannot fundamentally be justified.
(EC 254)

The self-evidencing power of Scripture as it is preached is for Diem the

only possible theological justification. Hence Diem argues for the unity of

the Canon on the basis of the "self-testifying character of the Scripture as

proclaimed, in whose testimonies Jesus Christ proclaims himself and is

listened to by the Church." (EC 254) The variety of New Testament witnesses

is the result of the different situations in which the proclamation is made;
still,

> . . . the Canon of Scripture must be recognized as the text which in
> any event is permanently binding, and that all our attempts at
> exposition, on the other hand, are only commentaries, which with
> their constantly changing conclusions cannot take the place of the
> text itself. (EC 255)

This, Diem believes, protects the exegete from arbitrary subjectivity and
hence is the basis for the unity of the Church. (EC 255f.)

Yet, the two Protestant positions are in sharp disagreement. Küng
writes, "For Käsemann, Diem's 'Canon' can never become 'the Gospel', while
for Diem, Käsemann's 'Gospel' can never become 'the Canon'." (EC 256) What
is Küng's critique of each and what does he suggest as a happier solution
(and as a Catholic position)? How does Küng ground the unity of the Church?

Küng's Position

Küng accepts from Käsemann certain historical-critical findings such
as: (a) the non-unitary character of the New Testament Canon; (b) the variability in the New Testament kerygma; (c) the hearing, in faith, of the
Gospel which justifies the sinner. (EC 257) And from Diem: (a) that the
New Testament is not a dogmatic system; (b) the importance of considering
the situation in which the proclamation is given, in terms of both (i) the
different theological and dogmatic intentions of the original proclaimers,
and (ii) the different people and situations to which the message must be
preached today, hence of the possibility of setting some testimonies in the
foreground while others recede; (c) the practical nature of the New Testament Canon and its unity as it is given in practice (preaching). (EC 258)

Küng also grants Käsemann that the New Testament Canon lies at the root
of the multiplicity of confessions. But for Küng, despite the absence of
unity in the Canon, the Canon is one thing and has been received by the

Church as one thing. (EC 260) "And the various testimonies in it have been understood not as some sort of dogmatically rich negative programme contrasting with the Gospel, but as an expression and crystallization of the Gospel, positively proportioned to it." (EC 260) Why, then, is there a multiplicity of confessions?

> The answer is unavoidable: By choice, that is by not seriously accepting the Canon as one thing, for all its lack of unity; by not striving through all the difficulties confronting each other in it, to reach a comprehensive understanding of it. By using the lack of unity in the Canon to make a selection from the Canon. This can, in certain circumstances, lead to an impressive concentration of the kerygma, but at the same time it means a reduction of the kerygma, made at the expense of the New Testament and of the unity of the Church, who stands behind the Canon. (EC 260f.)

What is implied in this disregard for the wholeness of the New Testament is "nothing less than the abandonment, fundamentally, of catholicity in the understanding of Scripture in favor of heresy." (EC 261) The absence of unity in the New Testament is indeed a "necessary presupposition and occasion for confessional multiplicity, but not strictly its root or cause." (EC 261) The actual cause of multiplicity is not the Canon which, understood in a 'catholic' way, is a basic condition for the unity of the Church, but hairesis, which dissolves the unity of the Church.

Küng faults Käsemann and Diem for the "hairesis" of each: selection as a matter of principle, and selection as a matter of practice, respectively. Käsemann's "discernment of spirits" is really "a formal principle of interpretation which turns out to be at the same time a material principle of selection." (EC 263) Only those texts which herald the sinner's justification belong to the 'Gospel'. "This involves an abandonment in principle (even if the word 'principle' is avoided) of catholicity in the understanding of Scripture, and Käsemann consciously accepts this as 'Evangelical'." (EC 264) Even Diem criticizes Käsemann for supposing that he himself can judge when and when not we have the Gospel. Diem reminds us that the Church always stands behind the New Testament Canon, then and now, and that even if we give prominence to some witnesses and neglect others in our preaching today, still all witnesses "in fact bear witness to Christ . . . and did find a hearing in the Church, and thus spoke under the inspiration of the Holy Spirit." (EC 266) The exegete who is not bound to the Canon risks doing violence to the texts in the name of exegesis and may impede their proclamatory value. Küng pushes the critique to its logical and devastating end:

> There is nothing objectionable in pointing to a 'central core' in the Gospel. But we may ask on what basis Käsemann finds himself so confronted only in these texts and not in others, able to hear only these texts and not others as 'the Gospel'. Certainly the New Testament cannot be the foundation for this; for the New Testament, according to Käsemann himself signifies something more than his Gospel. Nor simply 'exegetical findings', with the 'central Pauline line' imposing itself as 'the Gospel'. And it would only be to push the problem back if it were any other particular 'central line'. For the question is precisely why Käsemann can see only this 'central line' as 'the Gospel'. Can Käsemann appeal here to anything more. than some basic Protestant understanding of the matter preceding all else (unconsciously due, perhaps, to philosophical premises, or to some presentation of the Catholic position, in history or at the present time of a kind unworthy of belief)? Or, at a deeper level, to some kind of ultimate choice, perhaps of the kind in which one simply finds onself placed (the Lutheran tradition?) rather than one that one adopts oneself? But in any case, a choice made previous to any exegesis? Is it possible, in this position, to give any reasons such as could restrain anyone else from making a different choice and, because of a different traditional understanding adopted beforehand, discovering exegetically a different centre and a different Gospel? It is surely not possible to appeal to the New Testament as a whole, after letting its catholicity go by the board. (EC 267)

In Küng's opinion, Käsemann's "bold programme" of a Canon within the Canon amounts to a 'demand to be more biblical than the Bible, more New Testament-minded than the New Testament, more evangelical than the Gospel, more Pauline, even, than Paul." (EC 269) Such "heresy" cannot escape becoming also hubris, Küng writes, whereas the contrasting Catholic attitude "strives to preserve a full openness and freedom towards the whole of the New Testament." (EC 269)[14]

Nor is Diem spared Küng's razor. Although Diem rejects "the application to the New Testament of any formal principle of interpretation, which
turns out to be a material principle of selection," Diem's selection as a
matter of practice fails to do justice to particular testimonies that are
present in the Canon. (EC 269) Diem rejects "early Catholicism" with its
episcopal office and apostolic succession as a "deflection from the New
Testament" and assumes that the New Testament has nothing to do with early
Catholicism. (EC 270) Küng sides in this instance with Käsemann who pushes
catholicism back to Luke-Acts (EC 270-275), hence both he and Käsemann
regard the Catholic principle as indisputably present in the New Testament.[15] It is not unimportant in this regard to note that probably the
latest document in the New Testament is II Peter wherein the statement is
found, "First of all you must understand this, that no prophecy of Scripture
is a matter of one's own interpretation." (II Pet, 1:20) (RSV) The document is clearly Catholic because of the normative character assigned to tradition for the interpretation of Sacred Scripture.

Given the presence of catholicity, ". . . the position of a Protestant
theologian (is made) very difficult, if he wants fundamentally to take the
whole of the New Testament seriously and still not become a Catholic." (EC
277) The choice is either to go Käsemann's route and consistently declare
New Testament Catholicism as un-evangelical, or, to go the Catholic way
which takes seriously New Testament Catholicism as evangelical. Both
Käsemann and Diem lack full freedom and openness towards the New Testament
as a whole, Küng declares;

> Their tacit, taken-for-granted a priori position is Protestantism.
> And what this means is that it is laid down from the outset that
> within their exegesis and theology there is to be no road towards
> 'Rome' . . . . Then what is to be done when one has to recognize
> (what for a Catholic involves nothing surprising) that even in the
> New Testament, in the end, all roads lead to 'Rome'? (EC 280)

Each starts with the same New Testament, but Käsemann's

> . . . fundamental choice so lays down the lines of interpretation in
> advance that highly important lines in the New Testament are never
> seriously considered at all; so that, in particular, the road of
> 'early Catholicism', which must lead inevitably to 'late
> Catholicism' is blocked in advance . . . . (EC 280)

Even Diem, who is in principle free to follow all New Testament lines,

aborts the analysis when "Rome" comes onto the distant horizon.

Küng counterposes the Catholic attitude which he characterizes as an

openness in principle to every New Testament witness. To be Catholic means

to be open towards the whole, all-embracing truth of the New Testament.

Käsemann's and Diem's failure (and unwillingness) to do likewise is more

than a protest against early Catholicism—it is a protest against

Catholicism in general.

> This protest—which is not in truth simply unfounded—is directed
> against the Catholic Church. But not only against what is
> uncatholic in the Catholic Church; that would be a Catholic protest.
> Against what is Catholic in the Catholic Church as well; and this is
> Protestant. But, as a Protestant protest, the protest against the
> catholicity of the Church inevitably turns into a protest against
> the catholicity of Scripture, which was meant to have been the one
> and only basis for the protest against the catholicity of the
> Church. From being corrective (which is how it was meant by Luther
> originally) the protest becomes constitutive (which is how it is
> meant by Protestantism in its various forms). The protest goes
> rigid and cancels itself out, itself demolishing the foundation upon
> which it took its stand. (EC 283)

And, Küng continues, "A false understanding of sola scriptura leads to a

sola pars scriptura and this again to a sola pars Ecclesiae . . . " (EC

283)

It is not enough merely to say "To be catholic is to be evangelical."

The Catholic task is to strive ever more ardently to solve the weighty

exegetical and dogmatic problems which result from present biblical studies.

(EC 285f.)[16] One way of doing this is through historical-critical methods

of biblical research. Previous Roman Catholic interpretations of Sacred

Scripture have not always been 'catholic' in the best sense of the word,

inasmuch as Catholics often have overstressed the Pastoral Epistles as
against the more charismatic Pauline Epistles.

But truly 'catholic' exegesis, Küng contends, is more difficult than
selective (Protestant) exegesis. Greater precision and discernment is
required to highlight the overall unity of the New Testament, not in the
sense of a false harmonizing but in interpreting all witnesses in light of
the whole. (TC 17ff.) One means of doing this is to distinguish between
original and derived testimonies in the New Testament. Original testimonies
(e.g., Romans) are those which stand in greater temporal proximity to the
message of Jesus Christ, and hence take precedence over derived testimonies
(e.g., Epistle to James) which bear less temporal proximity hence less
inner objective proximity to the New Testament message.[17] In II Peter,
then, we have a derived testimony, hence, II Pet. 1:20 cannot be "the decisive document determining the interpretation of the whole New Testament."
(EC 288)

> The more derived a testimony is, the more both exegetes and dogmatic
> theologians will have to be careful of the way in which it treats of
> the event of salvation in Jesus Christ; of what factors are at work
> in each particular situation in which it is proclaimed; promoting or
> constricting it; strengthening or weakening, intensifying or
> softening. Hence every testimony in the whole of the New Testament
> has to be understood in terms of the message of Jesus and the
> original emphases." (EC 290)

"Originality" can be divided further into chronology (I Corinthians is
earlier than Ephesians), authenticity (I Corinthians is genuinely Pauline),
and relevance (in content I Corinthians is nearer the Gospel of Jesus than
is James). (TC 19)

It is the Church, Küng emphasizes, which transmitted the Canon to us,
the New Testament as a whole. And the Catholic Church proclaims its catholicity by the fact that it made room for both Paul and James, Paul and Acts.

An individual exegete can hardly do better than to trust the Church's "discernment of spirits" in making the whole New Testament canonical. The exegete who discerns contrariwise, who submits the Church's discernment of spirits to his or her own discernment of spirits, has an un-catholic attitude and a questionable understanding of the theologian's concrete relationship to the Church. Küng writes,

> We Catholics are convinced that we should go along with the early Church in regarding the whole of the New Testament as a true testimony to the event of revelation in Jesus Christ; to let each individual testimony really count, but differentiate it according to its relationship in theology and in practice. (EC 291f.)

In ecclesiology, then, where Catholic-Protestant roads diverge, the methodological course towards reunion has to do above all with each one's fundamental disposition towards the New Testament. Catholics must strive to do more justice to the New Testament with evangelical concentration, and Protestants must strive for catholic comprehensiveness. (EC 292) Only in this way will the path towards unity be paved. (Cf. Chaps. IV and V below)

The Historicity of Scripture

Küng's study with Käsemann had consequences which reached far beyond those just described regarding the New Testament Canon. In this section it will be seen concretely in what ways his gradual appropriation of the historical-critical method modified his previously held traditional Catholic dogmatic view of Scripture.

Composition of Scripture

In Justification, as we discovered already, Küng regarded Scripture as the only text containing the "unmediated" testimony of God Himself, a testimony "inspired" by God and, we may now add, ". . . as God's word, Sacred Scripture is a source free of error, valid for all times and places, and most important of all, inexhaustible."[18] This "pre-criticism" statement is

perfectly contrary to Küng's position of even five years later.[19]   As W.
Kasper correctly observes,[20] in The Church Küng no longer equates Scripture
with the Word of God, but makes a sharp distinction between the word of God
and the word of man.   The word of man is thoroughly historical, thus it is
conditioned, finite, imprecise; the word of God is alone complete and fully
true, since God is its source.   Only the divine word, even though it be
intractably encased in the human word, can claim "freedom from error."
Scripture consists of human words through which God's word of revelation is
originally testified.   (TC 15f.)

Due to the unmitigated historicity of all things, there can be no
exception claimed for the Bible.   The Bible, Küng writes, did not fall from
heaven, nor was it the product of "ecstatics filled with a divine madness,"
nor were its writers simply puppets of the Holy Spirit.   Rather, the Bible
is the very human product of "real men in all their humanity, historicity
and fallibility," whose testimonies are fundamentally historical."   (TC 16f;
cf. OBC 463)

It is in The Church that Küng elaborates some of the best-known and
most commonly accepted fruits of historical research concerning the composition of the Bible, especially of the New Testament.   It is generally agreed
that the Bible came into existence through a long historical development
during which different oral testimonies were collected and eventually united
into what we now possess as the Old and New Testaments.   Historical research
distinguishes in the New Testament three different strata: tradition history (Traditiongeschichte), which pertains to the historical Jesus' words
and deeds; form history (Formgeschichte), which discerns the community's
memory of Jesus preserved in different literary forms; and redaction history
(Redactiongeschichte), which analyzes the evangelist's redaction into
written form.   (OBC 158)[21]

The New Testament accounts of Jesus are not biographical, historio-
graphical, objective, un-involved reports; rather they are "committed testimonies of faith meant to commit their readers." (OBC 153) They are kerygma
set down in a post-resurrection perspective. The authors of the New
Testament did not willfully falsify information about Jesus, but "they were
simply convinced that they now knew better than in Jesus' lifetime who he
really was and what he really signified." (OBC 154) Moreover, biblical language is not scientific language; its concepts are set in different literary
forms which do not violate historical fact but serve to interpret it in
light of the author's faith. (OBC 412ff.) But the New Testament is not for
these reasons "un-historical." The question for us today is, Küng points
out, which elements are historical and which are proclamatory? Which are
Jesus' actual words and deeds, what is augumentation and supplementation?
What comes from Jesus and what is only attributed to him?

It is here that historical criticism is eminently useful, in distinguishing the actual course of composition; the various levels of interpretation and the manifold layers placed over the original event by the earliest
community and by the New Testament authors; the various modes of expression.
It is precisely here too, however, that the limitations of historical
research clearly emerge. For the whole New Testament yields both kerygma
and history and, in principle, historical scholarship is unable to interpret
the meaning behind the historical event, that is, to interpret the event in
light of what we have been calling the faith perspective.

In Küng's opinion, based on "the far-reaching agreement in principle
even between the more progressive German scholars and the more conservative
Anglo-Saxon and French scholars," the gospels contain both testimonies of
faith (along with Barth, Bultmann, and Tillich), yet they also contains historical information. (OBC 154) Yet the kerygma is not understandable except

in light of the historical Jesus of Nazareth. "Between the pre-paschal
Jesus and the proclamation of the post-paschal community there is not only a
break, but also a connection: a continuity despite all discontinuity."
(OBC 157)

Küng labels "uncritical" the assumption that because one piece of
tradition is reliable, the whole content of the Gospels (and of the Old
Testament) is therefore entirely historically factual. Similarly, a
hypercritical reader would also wrongly assume that because one piece of
tradition is not historical, then nothing in the Gospels is reliable as
fact.

> The truth lies between shallow credulity which is closely related to
> superstition and radical skepticism which is frequently linked with
> an uncritical belief in hypotheses. If we examine the state of the
> New Testament sources without prejudice, we shall describe the Jesus
> tradition historically as relatively reliable. (OBC 157)

As pointed out in Chapter I, historical knowledge is not certain
knowledge, indeed not in the sense of mathematical certainty. History
always approaches only probable knowledge; certainty pertains to faith.
(OBC 159) But historical knowledge can reconstruct "the typical basic
features and outlines of Jesus' proclamation, behavior and fate." (OBC 159)
This suffices for the believer, "even though what we call the authenticity
of every individual saying of Jesus or the historicity of every individual
narrative is not proved." (OBC 159) What does emerge, despite disagreement
over small exegetical details, are the "ruling tendencies, the peculiar
forms of behavior, the typical basic trends, the clearly dominating
factors . . . the 'open' total picture." (OBC 159)

The historical picture of Jesus is not intended to be separated from
the faith perspective of Jesus the Christ. The historical Jesus is not the
whole Jesus, nor can theology cease its investigations at the historical

level. The Jesus of history and the Christ of faith are, after all, united
in the one and same "Jesus Christ" who is the object of both theological
reflection and of faith.

Truth and Error in Scripture

The pervasive and unavoidable historicity of the Bible in its course of
composition, its modes of expression and modes of thought, modifies
accordingly the idea of error in the Bible and thereby also of the traditional conception of inspiration. Because of the historicity of human
words, biblical propositions are just like other propositions: they are
limited, fallible, even potentially erroneous. The thorough-going historical conditionedness of the Bible means that ". . . errors of the most
varied kind cannot a priori be excluded . . ." (Inf 215) What, then, is
the meaning of biblical 'inspiration'?

Just as there is for Küng no a priori infallible teaching office, there
is also no infallible 'paper pope'. (Inf 209) He traces the development
of the theory of verbal inspiration to Protestantism which linked together
the sola scriptura and infallibility of biblical propositions. 'Inspiration' became equivocated with 'inerrancy'. "The Bible (was) thus declared
to be in every respect--linguistically, stylistically, logically,
historically--the perfect and infallible sacred book. Infallibility, complete inerrancy belongs a priori to the word of the Bible as such." (Inf
210)

The Enlightenment and the historical-critical exegesis which resulted
called into question the very foundations of such a theory of verbal
inspiration and inerrancy. "Thus, at the same time, the capacity for error
of the biblical authors became more than clear." (Inf 210) Still, much of

Protestantism retained its theory of inspiration and substituted belief in

the Bible for belief in Christ. (Inf 210; OBC 163)

On the other hand, Catholic theology, even at the time of Trent, had

not linked together verbal inspiration and verbal inerrancy. "It was toward

the end of the nineteenth century, under the pressure of a destructive cri-

tical exegesis, that the popes took over--with a remarkable switch of

phases--the theory of verbal inspiration worked out by Protestant ortho-

doxy." (Inf 212) As the Englightenment heritage pushed on in the form of

Modernism, Catholic theology began explicitly and systematically defending

the complete and absolute inerrancy of Scripture.[22]

> It was thought possible to tackle the destructive efforts of
> rationalism only--as in the case of ecclesiastical infallibility--by
> applying the rationalistic concept of truth (under Cartesian
> influences) and asserting a propositional inerrancy also to
> Scripture even in matters of natural science and history. (Inf 212)

The Second Vatican Council marked a turning point in the whole ques-

tion, despite Curial attempts to reaffirm prior Catholic teaching. At

Vatican II the biblical author

> . . . is no longer described as 'instrument' but as 'true author'
> and God no longer as 'principal author' but simply as 'author'.
> Inspiration does not mean the exclusion, repression, or replacement
> of the human activity of the hagiographers. (Inf 213)

The negative term 'inerrancy' came to be replaced by the positive term

'truth', especially at the urging of Cardinal König who said "that the

Scriptures in matters of history and natural science are sometimes lacking

in truth." (Inf 213)

> An unhistorical attitude in these matters does not save the author-
> ity of the bible, but only renders exegesis incredible. Today a
> deviation from the truth in historical and scientific questions in
> no way endangers the authority of Scripture. In theological terms,
> this would rather be evidence of divine condescension. God takes
> the human author with all his weaknesses and failures and still
> achieves his aim of teaching man the 'truth' of revelation. (Inf
> 213)

The final form of Article 11 in the Constitution on Revelation retained both something of the old theory of inspiration and something of the new historical thinking,[23] but it left the future open for post-conciliar theology to examine the problem further.

Küng's own position, one which he sees as deserving of Catholic-Orthodox-Protestant agreement is this: (a) "God himself acts with us and on us through the human word of Scripture, so far as he thereby stirs us to faith and makes the word of man in proclamation the instrument of his Spirit. . .," and (b) "The Scriptures are at the same time thoroughly human writings, by human authors with their gifts and limitations, possibilities of knowledge and of error, so that errors of the most varied kind cannot a priori be excluded . . ." (Inf 215; OBC 464f.) Both (a) and (b), seemingly conflicting, can be maintained simultaneously in view of the epistemological principles discussed above in Chapter I.

> . . . God gains his end, without doing any violence to men, through human weakness and historicity. Through all human fragility and the whole historical relativity and limitation of the biblical authors, who are often able to speak only stammeringly and with inadequate conceptual means, it happens that God's call as it finally sounded out in Jesus is truthfully heard, believed, and realized. (Inf 215; OBC 466)

Not only the particular New Testament writings, but also "the whole course of the origin, collecting, and transmission of the word, the whole process of accepting in faith and handing on the message in proclamation, is under the guidance and disposition of the Spirit." (Inf 216; OBC 465) In this sense the whole pre- and post-history of Scripture is 'inspired', that is, Spirit-effected and Spirit-filled. (OBC 465) The divine power and human historicity work in tandem, and neither one attenuates the reality of the other. For Küng, God acts in and through humanity and historicity, never contrary to it in "miraculous" ways. He writes, "The Scrptures are not themselves divine relevation." (OBC 466)

By the time Küng wrote Infallible? An Inquiry (Unfehlbar? Eine
Anfrage, 1970) the relationship between Scripture and the Word of God
acquires another nuance. He writes that Scripture really attests revelation
when in faith the proclaimed gospel is received in faith as truth,
experienced as Gospel.[24] Moreover,

> . . . the human weakness, autonomy, and historicity of the biblical
> writers remain completely untouched. They are never at any time made
> inerrant, almost superhuman, which would mean that they were not
> really human at all, but tools, without will and without
> responsibility. The operation of the Spirit excludes neither
> defects nor faults, excludes neither concealment nor dilution,
> neither limitation nor error." (Inf 217)

Recalling Chapter I, it is in Scripture where the interplay of the two
elements, history and faith, may be seen as God is active in each. God uses
the human element to achieve his work and will--this is perhaps the greatest
thing that can be said for humanity. At the same time, God uses it not
coercively but awaits our free decision in faith.

The operation of the Spirit in "unrestricted human historicity"
warrants biblical, textual, literary, historical and theological criticism
so that the variety and diversity of testimonies may become apparent. (OBC
155) Still, Scripture is the Church's original testimony; as such it has
"lasting normative authority." But the Church does not believe in the Bible
but in He whom the Bible proclaims.

> I believe then, not--as it were--first in Scripture or still less
> first in the book's inspired character, and then in the truth of the
> gospel, in Jesus Christ. But I believe in the Jesus Christ origin-
> ally attested in Scripture, and, by thus experiencing Scripture
> as gospel in faith, I become certain of Scripture as Spirit-
> effected and Spirit-filled. (Inf 218; OBC 456f.)

Thus infallibility--in the sense of inerrancy--cannot be attributed to the
Bible (or to the Church) but only to God, and to his gospel message "which
is the inerringly faithful testimony of this salvation-event." (Inf 219)
And Scripture, although not infallible because restricted by human
historicity, nonetheless faithfully announces "the truth" of the gospel,

which is Jesus Christ himself. (Inf 219) The uniqueness of Scripture comes
from the one whom it announces:

> By speaking of him it exercises a living authority in virtue of its
> content (power of truth), by which faith is constantly subdued
> afresh. Both to the person who proclaims the message and to the one
> who hears it, in decisive matters, it is always freshly clear and
> accessible (perspicuity). It provokes assent and rejection and
> thus, in a completely unmagical and elusive way becomes truly
> effective (efficacy). And its unity in the context renders intelli-
> gible precisely that salvific action of God which was shown in Jesus
> (unity). (Inf 220)

The truth of Scripture does not consist in an a priori propositional
inerrancy,[25] "but certainly in the sense of a testimony to Jesus Christ
that, through all defects in detail, is sound and faithful as a whole. And
even though there are no propositions in the Bible which are a priori free
from error, nevertheless there are in fact true propositions attesting the
gospel." (Inf 220) And beyond even all specific true propositions, truth
of Scripture means fidelity: the fidelity of God to his word and promise.

> There is not a single passage of Scripture that speaks of Scripture
> as not containing any error. But every passage of Scripture
> witnesses in its narrower or wider context to this fidelity of God,
> who never lies, who remains faithful to himself and his word and
> thus also to men, who finally made his word definitively true by
> fulfilling all words of God in the one Word: in him who is 'the
> Word' and '14:6). In this sense Scripture
> which is by no means free from error, attests unrestrictedly the
> truth as the perpetual fidelity of God who cannot deceive or be
> deceived. In this sense Scripture attests the infallibility of God
> himself. (Inf 221; OBC 466-467)

Küng's understanding of the Word of God was further modified by the time of

On Being a Christian (Christ sein, 1974). He writes,

> The Bible is not simply God's word: it is first of all and in its
> whole extent man's word, the word of quite definite individuals.
>   The Bible does not simply contain God's word: there are not
> certain propositions which are God's word, while the rest are man's.
>   The Bible becomes God's word: it becomes God's word for anyone
> who submits truthfully and in faith to its testimony and so to the
> God revealed in it and to Jesus Christ. (OBC 467)

Furthermore, due to the changes in his definition of the Word of God,
we may note another shift in Küng's phraseology from "Scripture is the norma

normans" to "Jesus Christ is the norma normans." As the Word of God becomes
more closely identified with the person of Jesus, he comes to replace
individual historical scriptural words in terms of theological normativity.
(W&W 164, OBC 238-248)[26] Thus, from the writing of Justification to the
near-present, then, Küng's understanding of the extent to which Scripture
could be called the Word of God, changed from being a strict convertability
to a positive potentiality. In Justification what was the unmediated word
of God later becomes the thoroughly mediated divine word, the mediation
being that of historicity.

The far-reaching application of historical-critical principles to the
norma normans affects, then, not only Küng's understanding of the Word of
God but also of the truth and error of Scripture. There are two senses in
which one may speak of error in Scripture; first, the Bible contains simply
untrue propositions.[27] The second sense of "error" requires a brief introduction, for it hinges on Küng's theory of truth. It was primarily in connection with the topic of infallibility that Küng spelled out his understanding of truth, but it may be noted here that for Küng, truth is primarily contextual, which means that the unique (historical) context in which
a proposition is uttered, has a determinative influence on the truth of that
proposition. Thus, truth is not simply facticity. (cf. T; OBC 415ff.) A
corollary of this view is that there is a hierarchy of truths determined
according to historical context; some propositions are more true, others
less true. And so, propositions in Scripture are no exception; just as
there are elements which stand at the very center of the Gospel, there are
others which take their place at the farthest outside circle, the center
being the truth of the Gospel. These peripheral elements do not affect the
central truth of the Gospel.[28]

To summarize: Scripture is _norma_ _normans_ for three reasons. First, from the standpoint of history and historical principles of interpretation, the New Testament witness to Christ is the original document, hence it is normative, binding and obligatory. Second, from the standpoint of faith, it is only in Scripture that the Gospel of Jesus Christ is experienced by faith _as_ Gospel. And third, from the standpoint of ecumenism, Scripture is the only basis common to all ecclesial communions, for it is in Scripture that Jesus Christ—who is the foundation of Christian life and unity—is made accessible. The interplay among these perspectives is reflected in the following set of juxtaposed statements:

(1) Historical scholarship shows that the New Testament writings contain a variety of emphases, perspectives, purposes, theologies, which result from the complex development of the New Testament itself, spanning several decades and varied geographical and cultural locales. This fact rules out a reading of the New Testament as if it were composed of a single theory or proclamation, and precludes a falsely-rendered solution to its tensions and contradictions.

Yet, there is a real unity of the New Testament Canon which is based on the Church's delimitation, not on uniformity in doctrine. Hence _all_ testimonies must be regarded as authentic, not only those singled out by any arbitrary hermeneutic.

(2) Historical-critical interpretations of Scripture enable distinctions to be made among different historical strata in the New Testament. According to this, the interpreter is enabled to determine which testimonies are closest to, which farthest from, Jesus' own words. There are the criteria of chronology, authenticity, and relevance.

Yet, the 'center' of the New Testament is not a Gospel within the Canon, not a central doctrine, but has to do with the saving event in Jesus

Christ himself. All testimonies must be judged by their pertinence to this
event.

(3) The New Testament contains doctrine, morals and history.

Yet, the New Testament is always kerygma.

(4) The modes of expression and of thought in the New Testament partake
in the same historical limitations which accrue to all other human arte-
facts. Biblical words and concepts are fully historically conditioned,
fallible, imprecise. Error cannot a priori be excluded from the Bible.

Yet, because of the Holy Spirit's effect on Scripture, the many human
words give voice to the one Word of God who alone is infallible.

The Normativity of Scripture

The preceding sections have laid the groundwork leading up to the
second theme of this chapter: to see the concrete ways in which Scripture
functions for Küng as the norma normans non normata. Literally this means
that Scripture is the norm measuring all other norms, itself not measured by
any norm. For theological methodology and for the life of the Church this
principle is enormously significant.

Scripture is normative for the Church in three ways: (a) Church theology; (b) Church councils; (c) Church renewal and reunion.

Church Theology

The relationship between scripture and theology is quite straightforward for Küng: all theology must be based in, centered on, and measured
by Scripture; the starting point for all theology (dogmatic; systematic;
conciliar; moral; practical) can be none other than Scripture.[29] In
Justification Küng had argued that since only in Scripture is there the
direct testimony of God Himself, ". . . that is why from time immemorial
Scripture has been the first font of Catholic dogmatic theology." (J 111)

But even at that time he did not consider Scripture the starting point in the sense that one could merely collect isolated passages from its pages; "Sacred Scripture is not just a mine of arguments for theologians, or an instrument panel for orthodoxy, but rather is the foundation of theology and the taproot of its power." (J 113) As Küng has said elsewhere, only a theology that is "backed by the Gospel of Jesus Christ itself" will in the long run be representative of the Church. (Th&Ch 57)

Concretely the normativity of Scripture for theology means to Küng that the biblical Christology is more correct, more fitting and even more intelligible today than the speculative Christology of Hegel or of classical dogmatics (Protestant and Catholic). The same holds true for ecclesiology; a biblically-based presentation of the Church is also in his opinion more correct, more fitting, and more intelligible today than an ecclesiology which begins with a platonized, juridicized or other concept of the Church. (Cf. TC 15ff.; OBC 478ff.)[30]

It is clearly within the logic of Küng's insistence on Scripture as norma normans that it be normative for theological terminology as well. In Justification he had written,

> (Scripture) is the theologian's primary norm, even when it irks him. And that is true for theological terminology too. Not that the use of extra-biblical categories should be forbidden to theologians. Even biblical utterance is determined by certain well-defined Hebrew and Greek categories, though these two languages are in no way absolute prototypes (as the medieval grammarians thought). Theology is not just a repetition but rather an elaboration of revelation, and there was never any theology witout some kind of philosophy. Yet it must be borne in mind that once it is agreed that Sacred Scripture must be the primary source of theology and that, consequently, theological elaboration is concerned not with just any teaching whatsoever but precisely with what Sacred Scripture teaches, then all theological and philosophical categories must necessarily be conformed and oriented to the Word of God itself. (J 113; cf. also J 180f.)

What Küng understands by "theology orienting itself to the Word of God" shifts as his understanding of "Word of God" shifts. To illustrate this we may refer to the Christological example given in Chapter I concerning his

suggestion in _Menschwerdung Gottes_, _On_ _Being_ _A_ _Christian_ and again in _Does_

God _Exist_? that the biblical terms "man" and "God" be used in place of the

Aristotelian-scholastic "nature" and "supernature." In the span of these

three publications, Küng's notion of the Word of God underwent a deepened

historical imprint, for the divine Word was eventually said to be altogether

limited by the human words in which it was expressed. And so, the

methodological normativity of Scripture for theological terminology evolved

from being more of an emphasis on individual words, to being the more

general judgment that the fundamental testimony of the Bible is

historical.[31] Consequently, Küng believed, theology--if it is truly

biblical--unavoidably will be historically oriented. To put it another way,

what was significant for Küng was no longer that the Bible uses 'these'

particular words--which could be equated with the Word of God--but the fact

that 'these' particular words remain a thoroughly human product, even though

tranformed by the Spirit into the Word of God.

Taking biblical terminology seriously, then, means investigating it on

its own terms. And, Küng writes, scholars have now developed the tool which

best achieves this. "Modern historical-critical method provides the

theologian of today with a scholarly instrument for investigating the

origins of the Church which an earlier generation of theologians did not

possess." Küng continues, "Only with methodical historical thinking has

it become possible to gain, to a limited extent at least, an overall view of

the changes in the Church and in theology since New Testament times, of the

shifts in the perspective and emphasis, the improvements and deteriorations,

the gains and losses." (TC 201; see also J 214; CRR 89-92, 103-110, 163; SC

187ff.; 114f.; OBC 155ff.) A respect for biblical terminology does not

promote fundamentalism or literalism, for both are un-historical approaches;

rather, the historical approach emphasizes that the Holy Spirit's effect on the Bible has to do with the whole of it, including, as we saw above in another context, its pre- and post-history. Because Scripture is Spirit-effected within the confines of human historicity, Scripture not only "is subject to" exegesis (TC 16), it even, Küng later wrote, "requires" it. (OBC 465) Theology, he declares, is only good theology if it makes use of sound exegesis. Theology cannot return to a pre-critical stage; the historical-critical method is seen by Küng as warranted by Scripture itself.

> The modern Church needs good exegesis; exploration, at once humble and alert, perceptively attentive and critically intelligent, of that original and, for that very reason, unique and uniquely binding, testimony to God's saving word and saving work proclaimed to us in the Old and New Testaments. What is needed today is an exegesis that does not dodge problems, either from the fear that means lack of faith or the 'tact' that is mere timeserving, but grapples with them boldly, purposefully and concretely; an exegesis that does not explain away the multifariously human and fragmentary character of the biblical witnesses, but perceives the Word of God precisely in that human and fragmentary character; which does not slide into unhistorical harmonization of texts nor, on the other hand, delight in hypercritical dissociation of them; which is neither a prop for lazy-minded, hidebound unbiblical 'orthodoxy' nor leads to skepticism (sometimes marked by a sense of superiority, sometimes merely resigned to itself, but always involving the abandonment of hope); an exegesis in which what is derivative is distinguished from what is original, but which is nevertheless capable of hearing the one Word uttered by all the various witnesses. (Th&Ch 9f.)

Theology, then, in its orientation, concentration, even its terminology must have its foundation in Scripture. All theology (dogmatic; conciliar; pastoral) that is not scripturally oriented is attacked by Küng for being too 'speculative', too 'dialectical', too 'unhistorical'. That Küng's own theology has been the enduring attempt to formulate an ecclesiology, a Christology, and, most recently, a theology from the Scriptural perspective can be easily affirmed; whether he carries out this task in ways acceptable to the majority of theologians is a judgment that cannot be made at this point in our study.

Church Councils

In his very insightful book, Structures of the Church, Küng wrote,

For ecclesiology an ecumenical council is like a prism. Filtered through a triangular glass prism, white, visible-invisible sunlight discloses its rich, multicolored spectrum, its inner nature and mode of being. In an ecumenical council the pure, visible-invisible Church reveals the image of her mysterious, manifold nature to the eye of the believer . . . . Whoever reflects upon ecumenical councils reflects, expressly or not, upon the Church herself. (SC 1)

Because of this very explicit relation that obtains between Church and council, to say that Scripture is normative in and for the Church means also that Scripture is normative in and for Church councils. The specification of the ways in which Scripture is normative for the Church determines, in its turn, how Scripture is normative for Church councils.

It is interesting to note that Küng claims to derive his theological understanding of ecumenical councils from Scripture itself. On the basis of an etymological study of ekklesia and concilium which have the same root, Küng concludes that the Church is the ecumenical council convoked by God Himself, and that the ecumenical council by human convocation is a representation of the Ecumenical Council by Divine Convocation (the Church). Bearing in mind his ecclesiological principle, it must be said that since Scripture is normative for Church theology, and since the Church is the ecumenical council by divine convocation, the particular Church activity which best reflects the essential structure of the Church (the ecumenical council by human convocation) must also have Scripture as its theological norm.

Because Scripture alone is "inspired" (in the sense defined above), ecumenical councils are not 'inspired' but are 'assisted' by the Holy Spirit. Conciliar definitions are thoroughly human statements and are not

the Word of God; they testify only indirectly to the Word of God. "Hence
ecumenical councils do not stand above Holy Scripture but--precisely as
serving to explain and interpret it--below Holy Scripture." (SC 53f.) That
is why council teachings have as their exclusive purpose the expounding,
proclaiming and interpreting for the Church the Gospel of Jesus Christ as it
is recorded in Scripture.[32] "Therefore ecumenical councils--especially in
their exegetic and explanatory role--do not stand above, but below Holy
Scripture. From this it follows that Holy Scripture is the primary norm for
councils." (SC 105)

Küng's emphasis on the normativity of Scripture for conciliar
definitions proves very important in the later infallibility and Christological controversies. Although Chapter IV examines in detail the first of
these, we may condense in the present context Küng's fundamental position.

Küng adjudges that many definitions of councils, ranging from
Chalcedon's two-nature doctrine to Vatican I's dogma of papal infallibility,
are not biblically-based. Most notorious is the 1870 dogma about which he
writes, "it rests on foundations which for a modern theology and perhaps
even for that time could not be described as secure and unassailable." (Inf
111, also 96ff.) In his view, dogmatic definitions are only as strong (and
as true) as they are biblical.[33]

Although the relationship between Scripture and Tradition is not under
discussion at this point (see Chapter III below), we may note here it is
Küng's opinion that no part of Tradition may come to dominate Scripture,
whether it be by doctrinal interpretation or by practice. Rather, since
Scripture is the norma normans, every aspect of Tradition--especially the
conciliar tradition--must stand under the Word of God. Councils which, in
his judgment, have failed to subordinate themselves to Scripture have
produced tremendously thorny problems for the subsequent Church.[34]

Küng also recommends that not only doctrinal decisions, but all council
activities should be regulated by Scripture.

> It is not enough merely to display the Bible before the council.
> What will be decisive is whether the Gospel at the council will play
> the dignified role of an 'honorary presidency', honoured undoubtedly
> but practically without influence . . . or whether it will actively
> set the tone and effectively guide this assembly even in its
> details, . . . in the preparatory work of the commissions, for
> example, in the (so important) selection of speakers, in the order
> and direction of discussions, in the mode and manner of debates, in
> the definitions and decrees. All this should 'breathe Holy
> Scripture'! (SC 57f., 105f.)[35]

Church councils, then, must be evangelical in both doctrine and practice.
The earliest councils, and some later councils, Küng tells us, were faithful
to Scripture in both doctrine and practice (SC 55-57), and it was Küng's
fervent hope that Vatican II would proceed entirely according to the Gospel.
(Cf. CRR) His post-conciliar dissatisfaction is a result of the fact that,
in his opinion, in many ways Vatican II did not unqualifiedly "stand under
the Word of God."

Church Renewal

The ecclesiology of Hans Küng was formulated even in its earliest
stages in such a way as to allow ample room for reform of doctrine and practice. The lengthiest treatment of the topic of renewal is found in Council,
Reform and Reunion, a book published just prior to Vatican II. It is surely
a tribute to Küng's powers of insight and foresight that the theological
explanation of Church reform and the concrete programme suggested therein
were, in fact, adopted by Vatican II only a few short years later.

The ancient adage, ecclesia semper reformanda, has been taken most
seriously by Küng. "Insofar as the Church is deformed, she has to be
reformed: ecclesia reformanda." And "Insofar as the Church is constantly,
repeatedly deformed, she has to be constantly, repeatedly reformed:
ecclesia semper reformanda." (CRR 36)[36] In fact, reunion, which was

expressly acknowledged by John XXIII as a priority of the Second Vatican Council, was to be contingent on a Catholic renewal and reform within its own house. It is interesting to see that Küng's theological reasoning for arguing that the Roman Catholic Church needed reform was not based in Scripture per se, as if one could find in the New Testament any statement to that exact effect. Rather, the normativity of Scripture enters in when the what of reform, the concrete, practical programme for renewal, is proposed. (Cf. CRR; TC 337-341, 276-296) Reform and renewal have as their end the restoration of the essential structure of the Church to its essential and normative historical form, its original New Testament form.

> There is no ordinary human norm which can measure every institution in the Church, Pope, bishops, priests and laity, the whole Church of yesterday, today and tomorrow. The norm to which we can keep looking, in all our action, is Jesus Christ, the Lord of the Church, who speaks to the Church of every century in his Gospel, making his demands upon her . . . . We can be fearlessly confident that the vox Evangelii, being the vox Dei, will also be the best possible answer to the vox temporis. Neither opportunist modernism nor opportunist traditionalism but fidelity to the Gospel of Jesus Christ is the right frame of mind for a renewal of the Church. (CRR 56; cf. CRR 12-36; TC 337-341)

Thus Küng's overall ecclesiological programme consists of systematic historical-critical research into the original form of the Church, not so we can copy it today, for even the earliest structures were historically conditioned. But only the Church of the New Testament can show us the original design, the essential structure, the indispensable form. (TC 24; CRR 56)

If Church renewal proceeds according to Scripture, it will be, in Küng's mind, ecumenical in orientation. Without going into the specific areas which he recommended be reformed, the guiding principle may be noted here. As a consequence of Küng's ecumenical hermeneutic, Scripture is interpreted in such a way that only those historical developments which are in accord with it are acceptable; all others which presently prohibit reunion are to be discarded, or at least not made absolute.[37] Thus in saying that reform and renewal must proceed according to the Gospel, Küng is in effect also saying they must proceed ecumenically, and **vice versa**. For renewal of Church practices often hinges on doctrinal renewal, which itself is to be guided by the original testimony of Scripture. Doctrinal renewal usually happens officially through councils, and not infrequently unofficially through theologians. Thus in these three interrelated areas—theology; councils; ecclesiastical reform—Scripture is to be absolutely normative.

Consequences For Methodology

This chapter has been designed to show how historical criticism and faith are combined methodologically and applied to the first source and final norm of theology: Scripture. Neither an unhistorical (biblicist) exegesis, nor an historical-skeptical (rationalist) exegesis has been promoted by Küng, rather, a biblical and rational exegesis which are cogently united in a ecumenical exegesis. The methodological principle, "Scripture is the norma normans" is thus the first foundation of the ecumenical hermeneutic. This ordering has profound methodological consequences, the most important of which pertains to the matter of the Canon and its ultimate bearing on ecumenism.

In the previous discussion on the unity of Scripture it was seen that a theologically defensible understanding of the Canon is essential for both ecclesiology (to secure the unity of the Church) and for hermeneutics and exegesis (to affirm the unity of the Canon). It is very important to note that the unity of the Canon and the unity of the Church go hand-in-hand, so much so that one is not possible without the other. We saw that Käsemann denied the possibility of either, while Diem claimed that the fact that the Church has heard the Word of God in all the New Testament witnesses "can

only be recognized; it cannot fundamentally be justified." (EC 254) Hans
Küng, however, in contradistinction to this Protestant hermeneutic, has
linked together in his own hermeneutic the indispensability of the Church
(the catholic principle), with the necessity of letting Scripture interpret
Scripture (the Protestant principle); he has combined these 'dialectically',
as it were, in identifying the one Canon as the foundation of the one
Church: the ecumenical principle. Küng's insistence on the oneness of the
Canon (which, with all its divergent voices, attests the one Jesus Christ)
as the foundation of ecclesial unity preserves Scripture as norma normans
yet also insures that Tradition always be considered along with Scripture
(Cf. Chap. III below). Küng stated that the false understanding of sola
scriptura leads to a sola pars scriptura and ultimately to a sola pars
Ecclesiae. We might add in parallel fashion, the correct (catholic) understanding of sola scriptura leads ultimately to sola una scriptura and this
again to a sola una Ecclesiae.

The previous argument on the unity of Scripture followed the lines that
a return to ecclesial unity could be based only on accepting the fact of the
"oneness" of the Canon itself, not on an erroneously postulated oneness of
its teaching or proclamatory value. It was, after all, the Church which
received and handed on as one thing the New Testament Canon. (EC 261; 290)
And the Canon was not chosen by an a priori principle, but pragmatically, by
the early Christian community's "discernment of spirits." (TC 15f.)

Hence it is accurate to say, as does Küng, that "Without the Church
there would be no New Testament." (SC 149) And in this sense there is a
certain priority of the Church over Scripture. But how can this be
explained in order to maintain also that Scripture is the norma normans?
For, strictly speaking, if it was the Church which decided the Canon, in

what way did the _norma normans_ avoid being itself measured, that is, determined by the Church?[38]

It is possible to suggest here that the Church is prior to Scripture in
the two-fold sense that the Church established the limits of the Canon
(twenty-seven books), and the Church also decided the content of the Canon
(_which_ twenty-seven books). But the Church did so on the basis of the
not-yet-delimited Canon itself. That is to say, although the Church did not
find in currently circulating written testimonies a _formal_ hermeneutical
principle by which it could select which books authentically preserved and
attested the message of Jesus, the Church did find in its practice (both by
listening to the Holy Spirit's guidance and by reflecting on its life in
light of the very proclamation itself), that certain writings verified what
it knew already in practice.[39] The decision on the Canon clearly was not
made on the basis of any historical-critical methods, nor any hermeneutical
principles _per se_,[40] but on the basis of Scripture itself as interpreted
through the Holy Spirit and the Church. In this sense, what came to be
known as the Canon was already normative and operative _in practice_ in the
Church's faith.

For Küng, then, there can be no Canon within the Canon, in Käsemann's
sense of a sub-canon consisting of an interpretive principle. There are
only different strata in the New Testament, some closer to, others further
from, the center of the Gospel. Küng's historical-critical principles take
him as far as distinguishing among the different strata, but no further.
Why? Why is Küng not willing to follow Käsemann's (and others') route and
supply an ultimately extra-scriptural hermeneutical principle for theology
to follow? Why does Küng accept the Canon as is? The answer can only be
the one Küng himself has proposed: a catholic (hence correct) regard for

Scripture leaves no alternative. That is to say, the catholic stance vis-à-vis Scripture must always recognize not only in principle (as Diem does) but also in practice that the Church and its Tradition stand behind the Canon. Not to do so destroys not only the integrity of Scripture but, ultimately also the unity and catholicity of the Church. In such a view Scripture could no longer really be the norma normans, since an arbitrarily chosen hermeneutical principle would have replaced it: the subjectivity of the exegete would have been put in place of the Church's decision on the Canon.[41] The sola scriptura principle originally intended by Luther also would be eroded: a sub-Canon would have been substituted for the whole Canon. In both instances, the basis for ecclesial unity also would have been destroyed in the process. Clearly, a theological methodology which is at base ecumenical could never follow an un-Catholic interpretation of Scripture, because of this very result.

Viewed from the side of Scripture, then, the methodological choice Küng makes concerning the Canon has far-reaching implications. Indeed, as our next chapter will show, this decision was positively crucial for his quite controverted view of Tradition.

CHAPTER THREE

TRADITION: THE NORMA NORMATA

Both as a source and as a norm for theology, the subject of Tradition raises in a most trenchant way the problem of theological methodology. For example, one may claim that Scripture is one's highest or even one's only norm and source, but Scripture needs always to be interpreted, and when an interpretation is rendered, one therewith takes a stand, willingly or not, about the Tradition of the Church. Luther's and Calvin's sola scriptura is no longer naively or polemically claimed to exempt one from Tradition, nor to obviate the intrinsic connection between the two.

But even if a consensus is reached that Scripture is the unique and authoritative locus of revelation, the question persists about God's continuing agency in the Church. The Roman Catholic Church has understood this to be a continuation in terms of a teaching authority through which, it is claimed, the Holy Spirit helps the Church rightly understand what God accomplished in Christ. Protestants generally view this as an attempt to supplant the absolute authority of Scripture, while Catholics counter that Tradition is the indispensable and authoritative interpreter of Scripture, not itself able to supersede Scripture, but apart from which many heretical interpretations are possible.[1]

It is on the subject of Tradition that the most vigorous protests against Küng have been registered. This will be taken up from different perspectives in subsequent chapters. In this part of our study, we are interested in the methodological problem of Tradition, that is to say, how Tradition is ordered as a source. Following Chapter I's assertion that theological sources are ordered according to hermeneutical principles, we will explore what it means for Küng to call Tradition norma normata (in contrast to the norma normans which is Scripture).

95

It may be noted at the outset that one of the fundamental problems with Küng's theology and methodology is that he gives no clear definition of Tradition. From time to time he explicitly mentions three components of Tradition: the Canon; decisions of councils; past theological thought. At other times he evidently means to include also past ecclesiastical and ritual practices. However, cataloguing elements in Tradition plainly falls short of supplying a theological definition of Tradition and the place one envisions for it in one's theology. Since the purpose of this chapter is restricted to a methodological elaboration, the task of extrapolating Küng's _theological_ understanding of Tradition is reserved for Chapter V. Presently, however, in order to work around this fundamental defect in his theology, while at the same time not wishing to impose on his works an extraneous definition, we may broadly describe Tradition as consisting of diverse "expressions of faith." These would be sub-divisible into _professions_ of faith, and _practices_ of faith. And so, based on the material discussed in Chapter I, this chapter will ask and answer in light of the Küngian hermeneutic two questions: how does historical criticism undergird Küng's understanding of Tradition, and second, how is Tradition ordered as a source in relation to Scripture.

Expressions of Faith

Practices of faith are cultural expressions of faith which reflect various dogmatic teachings or theological opinions. It is common today to recognize the historical conditionedness of practices of faith, hence their intrinsic relativity and in some cases dispensability.

Professions of faith are those components of Tradition which pertain directly to dogmatic, doctrinal, catechetical or credal teachings. Among these Küng differentiates three basic types of professions: (1)

abbreviating–recapitulating, (2) defensive–defining, and (3) tendentious–
explicating propositions. (Inf 144–149) The first are summary statments
of faith, such as are found in creeds. This type of profession may take
several other forms (such as doxology; blessing; et. al.), but each form
expresses diverse aspects of the one faith. The second, defensive–defining
propositions, are "polemical demarcations from what is unchristian," or,
positive and explicit demarcations of faith. The third, tendentious–
explicating propositions are, Küng writes, unnecessary and pre–disposed
formulations. Since the two latter types are expressly related to the
magisterial side of Tradition, and so belong to the more disputed area of
dogma, they will be the focus of this discussion. The extent to which historical contingency pervades the teachings of faith (some of which are
promulgated by the Roman Catholic Church as being universally binding,
infallibly true and necessary for salvation) is by no means unanimously
agreed upon by theologians and magisterium. Thus the remarks of this
section are made principally with respect to professions of faith; however,
what holds for professions holds also for practices.

The Historicity of Professions of Faith

Unlike the shift in Küng's understanding of Scripture, there did not
occur as dramatic a change in his view of Tradition. If we begin with
Küng's statements in Justification, we find him already quite attuned to the
expressly historical structure of Tradition, and especially of dogma. Karl
Rahner's influence is readily apparent in Küng's summary of the Catholic
teaching on tradition.[2] In Justification, Küng proposed to identify and
clear up what he felt to be Barth's misunderstanding and misrepresentation
of Catholic teaching on (Scripture and) Tradition. He charged that Barth
had misunderstood the nature of Tradition (and the Catholic Church's
teaching on Tradition) in three ways.

First, Barth had not at all taken into account the historical context
of the Tridentine decree regarding justification when, unlike the Catholic
Church itself, he regarded the Church's official statements as ". . . rigid
and frozen formulations . . . (instead of) as living signposts for continued
research into the inexhaustible riches of the revelation of Jesus Christ."
(J 101) Barth's disregard for the historical nature of Trent's decrees
accounted for his second blindspot: lack of understanding of the polemical
and defensive character of Trent's statements. Both these, Küng remarked,
reflected an inadequate sense of the historically conditioned development of
dogma--a subject to which we shall return shortly. Third, Küng observed
that Barth culled his summaries of Catholic teaching from textbooks. (J 108)
Although one can find Catholic teaching in these manuals, it is
". . . utterly wrong . . . simply to equate the full and living Catholic
teaching with the theology found in modern textbooks--let alone equate it,
as Barth does, with the one textbook by Bartmann which, after all, even in
the Catholic camp is by no means the most prominent." (J 110) Barth's
unhistorical reading of Trent led him to interpret its statement which
reads, "with the same sense of devotion and reverence (the Council) also
accepts and venerates traditions" (Denz. 783) to mean that Tradition, like
Scripture, could claim divine inspiration.[3] Küng counters,

> There was never any tampering with the fundamental truth, that is,
> that even the most important documents of tradition such as
> infallible papal and conciliar definitions--despite all the positive
> things that can be said about them for example, the negative
> assistance of the Holy Spirit--still constitute no more than a human
> account of divine revelation. (J 111)

Still, the importance assigned Tradition is what specifies and differentiates Catholic theology. Küng summarizes the Catholic position (at that
time) as follows:

(1) "To define tradition correctly as a source of revelation, we must
eliminate all purely human and ecclesiastical traditions (apostolic as well

as post-apostolic)."[4] (J 113) For, "It is quite apparent that tradition is
of radically reduced value as a font of faith." (J 114)

(2) "Tradition is not simply coordinate with Sacred Scripture."
(J 114) It is neither a residual concept nor entirely independent of
Scripture. Tradition "revolves around" and "gravitates towards" Scripture.
(J 116)

(3) "This tradition--carried forward by the total Church of all
centuries in the obedient consciousness of faith given it through the power
of the Holy Spirit--is deposited in the various ecclesiastical documents and
monuments (creeds, papal, conciliar, and episcopal decisions, the writings
of the Fathers of the Church and of theologians, in catechisms, liturgies,
ecclesiastical tradition and art)." (J 116) Yet none of these--even an
infallible document--represents divine tradition; they are merely human
ecclesiastical aids which preserve tradition. Tradition is not the Word of
God but contains it.

(4) "Official ecclesiastical doctrinal documents in particular
represent an extremely valuable aid (since they are not subject to
discussion) to the Catholic theologian who is examining the tradition of the
Church." (J 116)[5] The Catholic theologian, Küng warns, must take care lest
he or she make Barth's mistake, and regard the Church's official statements
as 'petrifications' of truth.

Küng is clearly anxious here to demonstrate that there is no Catholic
"two-source" position; he does this by emphasizing not merely the thoroughly
historical nature of dogmatic decrees but their 'derived' or 'secondary'
relationship to Scripture. That is to say, Tradition is different "in kind"
from Scripture, thus dogmatic decrees, which exist only to serve Scripture,
cannot be a second source of revelation. Küng's statements after 1957

differ from this only insofar as they exhibit the more thorough and stringent application to Tradition of the principle of historicity.

Küng's next publication, The Council, Reform and Reunion (1960), evidenced his growing utilization of this principle. (CRR 112ff.) In 1962, in Structures of the Church, he showed that the same historical-critical principles enunciated with respect to Scripture (see Chapter II) pertain also to various types of professions of faith.

To summarize: Just as in Scripture there are various testimonies but only one essential message pertaining to the one Jesus Christ, so in Tradition there are various ways of formulating the one faith. Faith and the formulations of faith are not to be confused, nor is their intimate mutuality to be underrated. "Christian faith has a historical character and is expressed in ever-new formulations." (SC 344)[6] In order to highlight the unchangeability of the essential truth of the formulation despite its recast terminology, Küng uses the example that the Councils of Nicaea and Sardica asserted one hypostasis in God, whereas Constantinople asserted three hypostases in God. (SC 345)[7]

Second, just as in Scripture the different formulations were molded by distinct historical and personal factors, so also behind diverse formulations of faith there stand distinct conditioning factors. (SC 345f.) Thus exegesis of Tradition (especially of councils) becomes most necessary. Küng recently wrote, "Exegesis that is grounded in the historical-critical method calls for a dogmatics that is likewise historically-critically grounded." (CIT 8)

Third, although Scripture is historically conditioned, it cannot ever be superseded by Tradition. Scripture expounds and attests the message of Jesus Christ; Tradition is at the service of Scripture.[8] "The preaching and teaching of the Church, despite all progress, must remain with Jesus, with the revelation of God promulgated for all time. Every formulation of the faith by the Church must be oriented to that." (SC 347) Yet formulations of faith contained in Tradition can supersede each other, for as the history of dogma shows, there have been factual corrections of one council by another. Küng explains, "The christological definition of Chalcedon overrode and actually replaced the Christological definition of Ephesus." (SC 347; Inf. 204ff.; OBC 129ff.)

The Special Nature of Dogmatic Professions

The historical conditionedness of all professions of faith, including dogma, may be explained further in terms of two specific characteristics of dogma: (1) its polemical nature, and (2) its developmental character.

The Polemical Nature of Dogma

Küng makes a great deal of the fact that dogmatic definitions are unavoidably polemical (he calls them defensive-defining propositions). (Inf 131ff.) Because of the problematic nature of propositions in general, (Inf 182ff.) it is clear that the polemical character of dogmatic formulas has to do with the special problematic of ecclesiastical definitions. "If every human statement of truth, as humanly limited, borders on error and easily turns into error, this holds in a special way for polemical ecclesiastical definitions." (Inf 170) Since most dogmatic definitions have been drawn up against specific heresies and errors, the definition is directed against what is untrue in a particular position. But since every error or heresy, no matter how un-christian, still contains within it some element of truth, the dogmatic definitions attack not only the untruth but also the kernel of truth in the heresy. (SC 350; TC 244-249) Hence the statement of truth is then a half truth--what it asserts is right, as is what it passes over in silence.

> From the speaker's viewpoint, such a statement of truth confronts
> the error; from the viewpoint of the person addressed, it takes the
> core of truth. The first one rightly regards his statement as true,
> the second--not without reason--as false. In short, because half-
> truths can also be half-errors, one fails to understand each other.
> (SC 351, Cf. Inf 172; Chap. IV below)

Hence dogmatic definitions always risk one-sidedness because any one

definition can omit important aspects of a related revealed truth.

"Definitions and decrees are simply not intended to say everything that

there is to say about the truth in question. They are not intended as

balanced, detached, learned treatises but as corrections of particular,

definite errors." (CRR 113f.) Just as heresy both strengthens and weakens

the Church (strengthens because it deepens the dogmatic consciousness by a

sharpening of conceptual categories and distinctions; weakens because of the

danger of one-sidedness, with "theologians helping to petrify and

foreshorten" revealed truth and with "heretics contributing to the

impoverishment"), so too with a dogmatic definition: "It gains in

theological precision only at the risk of loss of vitality." (J 103)

To use Küng's example, consider the statement, "The just man lives by

faith." Spoken unpolemically by an Evangelical Christian, no shadow of

error attaches to the statement. Spoken polemically by the same person,

against perhaps a legalistic, good works-minded Catholic, the shadow of

error, the hidden meaning which may obscure the bare truth of the statement,

emerges: "The just man lives by faith (and does no works)." The converse

is also possible. If a Catholic Christian polemically asserts against a

quietist Protestant who overstresses faith, "The just man does works of

charity" there may come to the fore the unexpressed second meaning, "The

just man does works of charity (and does not live by faith)." (Inf 170; SC

350) Particularly with ecclesiastical definitions, then, great care must be

taken since every proposition may be true and false[9] depending on its

context. The history of the Church is replete with instances where

sufficient care was not taken to respect the truth in another's formulation
of it.

> If a theology, if a Church, does not take seriously this dialectic
> of truth and error, then it is inevitably on the way from dogma to
> dogmatism; the functional character of a definition and the way it
> is tied to the matter in hand are then overlooked; the concept of
> dogma is overtaxed, overcharged, overstretched; the particular dogma
> is forced into an undialectical and uncritical isolation and
> acquires an absolute status . . . . (Inf 172f.)[10]

The Development of Dogma

The phrase "development of dogma" refers to the theological counterpart
of the new idea of history which was introduced at the Enlightenment. When
the pioneers in studies of the history of dogma began to see that even
official church statements were permeated with human historicity and so with
time-conditionedness, hence that even ecclesiastical definitions could
'develop', the very foundations of a rigid ecclesiastical authority seemed
to be threatened. In whatever forms the 'development of dogma' proponents
have expressed their convictions, official Roman Catholic reaction has been,
until most recently, markedly negative.[11] However, this concept has gained
currency for better or ill in contemporary Roman Catholic and Protestant
theology alike.

The phrase "development of dogma" is at times an amorphous concept.
From what or to what does dogma develop? A first assumption is that dogmas
may develop because they are by nature fragmentary, partial, in need of
improvement. The further supposition is that dogmas develop from either
their adumbrations in Scripture or from previous dogmas. And dogmas develop
to a more rarefied or relevant understanding of revelation, not to a new
truth hitherto unknown. Küng understands the development of dogma to be an
unfolding, an explicitation of what is already contained implicitly
elsewhere, in another dogma or in the teaching of Scripture. (T 24-36) Yet
there are two restrictions on the ways in which dogmas may develop. For

one, dogmatic development is not organic. Küng explicitly rejects a
processive or Hegelian-idealistic notion of development; he said to W.
Kasper concerning past Christological definitions that,

> The primary criterion of Christology (the biblical Jesus Christ) is
> often overdone, it seems to me, by the secondary criterion (the
> teaching of the Church) with the help of an ecclesiastical-
> idealistic theory of development. (A 173)*

That is to say, there is no necessary improvement in dogmatic understanding
through time, as the Hegelian scheme would have it, because the Holy Spirit
is not Hegel's Absolute Spirit. Consequently, the Church--even its
magisterium--cannot be identified with the Holy Spirit, for insuperable
difficulties ensue concerning the limitations of dogma. In Küng's view, the
development of dogma proponents tend to overlook the very fragmentary and
limited character of all professions of faith. Since in his opinion there
have been many false and erroneous developments, the Holy Spirit's activity
in the Church is not necessarily one of progress in dogma, but the maintenance of God's will in the Church, or what he later comes to call the
indefectibility of the Church.

Furthermore, since a specific characteristic of a dogma is its
polemical orientation, dogmas may not be defined by the Church "at will" so
to speak, simply for the sake of defining. Küng writes,

> Dogmas indeed can lead to a certain rigidity of faith. In any case
> it would not be desirable if the opinion developed that faith could
> be brought to bloom by defining a dogma. If this were the case it
> would be entirely incomprehensible why the early Church did not
> define more dogmas. But at that time the correct conviction was
> already held that faith unfolds itself through the preaching of the
> Gospel, through the Sacraments, through prayer, love, suffering,
> etc., and that dogmas are no more and no less than emergency
> measures which the Church was forced to adopt because of heresies.
> (SC 349; see also J 103 passim; CRR 113f.; TC 289ff.; Inf 169 ff.)

And dogmatic development cannot be planned, following on "tendentious-
explicating" propositions. Küng pointedly adds:

Seen in the light of this almost two-thousand-year-old, common Christian tradition, which is supported by the New Testament itself, it must be regarded as an aberration when a Church—without being compelled to do so—produces dogmas, whether for reasons of ecclesiastical or theological policy (the two Vatican dogmas of the pope) or for reasons of piety and propaganda (the two Vatican dogmas of Mary). The aberration is all the greater when it deepens the division of Christendom. (Inf 149; emphasis mine)

The second restriction is that one dogmatic formulation cannot be replaced by another chosen at random. Again, the necessary guidance of the Holy Spirit in "bringing the Church into all truth" can never be obviated. And, "the intellectual refinement achieved through centuries and the univocal general use of many such formulas warn against any frivolousness in this matter." (J 102) To put it another way, development of dogma is not to be mistakenly thought of as a reform of dogma. Reform presupposes some sort of deformation. (CRR 112f.) Still, dogmatic definitions, by virtue of their historicity, are finite statements and never exhaust the mystery and fullness of revelation.

They too originated in specific historical settings and must constantly be prized out of their historical setting and put in wider (but of course still finite) historical perpsective, so that we can appreciate them correctly, more fully, more truly. (TC 270; cf. CRR 113; J 102)

Furthermore, development of doctrine, even in the limited sense that Küng employs it, does not mean the relativistic dissolution of individual dogmas, for one doctrinal statement always presupposes and builds on another; any deepened explicitation of the Church belongs again to the course of Tradition and cannot happen outside the aegis of the Church.

Küng is not unique here in distinguishing between 'implicit' and 'explicit' content. Just as the living infallible perfect Word of God finds expression in human erring words (in Scripture), and just as there is one faith despite its many expressions, so there is in dogma an implicit and irreformable content cast in explicit and reformable forms. The irreformable constants of faith are given by God through Jesus Christ in the

Holy Spirit (for example, the godhead and manhood of Jesus Christ), but the human, ecclesiastical formulations of such abiding constants are thoroughly historically conditioned (for example, the two-natures doctrine), and so in principle are reformable. (TC 287ff.; CRR 115f.; MG Chap. VI; OBC; A) Still, any reform or re-interpretation of dogma must occur under the aegis of the Holy Spirit, for it is the Spirit who guarantees the indefectibility of the Church despite individual errors in detail.

Extraordinary cases. Küng makes note of the conditions in which dogma may develop in our day, that is, in what he terms "extraordinary" or "emergency" situations. Because of the defensive nature of dogmatic propositions, and because the faith of the Church continues to be threatened by heresy, superstition and unbelief, the Church on occasion finds it necessary to reassert its adherence to Jesus Christ through a formal proclamation.[12] According to him extraordinary definitions may be made not only by Church leaders against theologians who have ceased to teach the Gospel correctly, but even by theologians when Church leaders obscure or betray the Gospel. (Inf 214f.) In order for such a status confessionis to exist, three conditions must be met:

a. "In the conflict of faith there must be involved a causa major, where it is a question in one way or another of the existence of non-existence of the Church (articulus stantis et cadentis Ecclesiae)." (Inf 132)

b. Other means (discussion, exhortation, challenge) must have been exhausted already. (Inf 133)[13]

c. The definition cannot be understood as a final judgment or damnation but as a temporary measure which restores the peace of the Church. (Inf 133; TC 191-203; 244-257)

The binding character of such an emergency definition would prevail not so much because of an obedience required by ecclesiastical law, but because of the way truth based on the Gospel in itself elicits assent and imposes a type of moral obligation. However, for Hans Küng, such definitions are still limited and fallible.

> Even if they have a definitive and obligatory--and to that extent, dogmatic--character for a particular situation, it is a question in the last resort of a ruling, not on principle and for eternity, but of a practical ruling on terminology conditioned by the situation. (Inf 133)

An example of dogmatic development: Extra ecclesiam nulla salus. To see quite clearly the historically conditioned nature of a dogmatic statement and the way dogma develops in understanding, an illustration is apposite: extra ecclesiam nulla salus. The fact that this axiom is a profession of faith but not a defined dogma, does not lessen the aptness of such a choice. This axiom has been firmly ensconced in Catholic Tradition since the early Patristic period, thus it belongs to what is generally called the teaching of the 'ordinary' magisterium. Another attractive feature is that the axiom clearly has everything to do with ecumenism--a fitting choice in a study of Hans Küng.

Küng offers three possible modes of interpretation of the teaching,[14] the first two of which are, for him, unacceptable and untenable. First, in a positivistic interpretation, professions of faith are taken literally and verbally. No regard is given the context of the statement (the axiom in question was formulated when the 'whole' of the world was rather restricted), how it has changed (Vatican II compared to Boniface VIII), how it might be better formulated ("salvation in the Church" instead of "no salvation outside the Church"). Dogmatic positivism regards official ecclesiastical documents as the beginning and end of theology (for example, Denzinger-type theology) and fails to regard the historical situation in which the propositions were formulated. Doctrine becomes a law of faith, unyielding and unproductive.[15] But one way out of such unhistorical positivism is to turn to a speculative interpretation.

In this second, _speculative_ interpretation the axiom would still be interpreted literally, but the 'tenor' of the words is changed. In what he admits is a 'caricature', Küng shows the undesirable results of the dialectical, speculative approach wherein "the formula remains but the content is recast."

> . . . the axiom _extra ecclesiam nulla salus_ should not be under-
> stood primitively, verbally, literally, it must rather be understood
> intelligently, pneumatically, speculatively, dialectically. And
> then it means 'really' also _extra ecclesiam salus_. It means
> 'really' therefore also its opposite. In this dialectical operation
> it is really not at all important which word of the axiom is dis-
> tinguished, 'differentiated': what is decisive is the result.
> (T 145f.)

Thus, Küng continues, _extra_ means not really outside but also inside (all those who were outside for the early Church are now inside the Church). Or, _ecclesia_ really means not only Church but also all people who in good faith live according to their conscience; even those who deliberately reject being Church members are made secret members of the Church.[16] And _salus_ does not mean only salvation but also damnation (outside the Church there is not damnation but only salvation more difficult to achieve). And _nulla_ does not mean only 'no' but also 'some' (people outside the Church have 'some' salvation since they lack Christian preaching and sacraments). (T 145f.) Clearly, the speculative approach, taken too far, renders the meaning of a proposition other than was originally intended. Yet such an approach does correct the rigidity of a strict positivism.

The middle road (and the correct one, in Küng's view) is the _historical_ interpretation which takes seriously both form and content, and is not afraid to admit the fact and consequences of error. The historical and theological situation which shaped the teaching, the Church in which it

lived, the politics, civilization, personalities and other factors which
affected it--all these must be considered. Even the present axiom, despite
its problematic nature, can be reinterpreted historically.[17] Küng suggests
moreover that the use of the teaching should be restricted; in dogmatic
theology the phrase should be commemorated with respect as having been an
authentic expression of Tradition, while at the same time its limitations
should be frankly acknowledged. In preaching the axiom should be used as
infrequently as possible, since only misunderstanding and contradiction
result. (TC 318; T 149)[18]

These convictions concerning the historicity of dogma continued to play
a key role in Küng's later writings. By the time he wrote Infallible? An
Inquiry, the idea of historical conditionedness had not only extended well
into Scripture, as we saw in Chapter II above, but his dogmatic analysis in
Infallible? would be unthinkable apart from the tools of historical
criticism by which he analyzed Vatican I as he did. In addition, the
outlines of Christology enunciated in Menschwerdung Gottes and the actual
Christology finally elaborated in On Being a Christian, both depend on the
relativization of dogma which goes along with the historical view. That is
to say, in Exkurs I ("Der Weg zur klassischen Christologie") in the book on
Hegel and again in Chapter B. of On Being a Christian, Küng was able to
formulate some of the deeper consequences of the views expressed already in
Structures of the Church and The Church. Not only are all formulations of
faith partial and incomplete, including those of, say, Chalcedon or Vatican
I, they also have a diminished value with respect to the present. Past
formulations are, as he says, worthy of respect, but to the degree that they
are largely the product of another era, another conceptuality, they are not
directly transferrable or applicable to the present. The substance of their
affirmation still binds the Church, but the exact propositional form does

not. To see this in greater detail, we now turn to the chief producers of dogmas: Church councils.

Church Councils

It was said earlier that dogmas have their ultimate foundation in Scripture, and that what the Church presumably accomplishes in defining a dogma is an interpretation of some portion or theme of Scripture, or a refinement of a prior dogmatic formulation. Among the questions which arise, then, are those which concern whether and to what extent various ecclesiastical definitions are based on Scripture, and simultaneously, if there is an agent or structure in the Church which is a reliable index for establishing this. To use an example from Christology, how does one know whether the Chalcedonian two-nature formula is an authoritative and binding interpretation of biblical Christology, unless one has already a set of criteria on the basis of which one considers Chalcedon an authoritative council? Hence, the subject of dogma invariably involves one in a fundamental ecclesiological question concerning the nature of Church councils, their bindingness and authority.

The Importance of Ecumenical Councils

Interpreters of Scripture and Developers of Dogma

In Chapter II it was seen that ecumenical councils by human convocation represent in a special way the essential structure of the Church which is the Ecumenical Council by Divine Convocation. No human council is ecumenical unless it reflects this structure which may be characterized as one, holy, catholic and apostolic. To be sure, this accords ecumenical councils an extremely important role in Tradition; they are a sign of the Holy Spirit's activity in the consensus of the Church, thus such councils become not only the most reliable interpreters of Scripture, they are also binding interpreters of Scripture. This is not to say that councils are the only interpreters of Scripture; it must be remembered that in the intervening periods between, leading up to, and during councils, the Holy Spirit may work in theologians and the faithful who bring to the Church's interpretation of Scripture their own sometimes Spirit-effected views. But a truly ecumenical council is indisputably the authoritative interpreter of Scripture as is no other Church synod, papal bull or encyclical, theological position or popular understanding. Küng writes in Structures that,

> In the Catholic Church it is taken for granted that Holy Scripture . . . may not be interpreted by individual believers in isolated and self-glorifying intellectual certainty . . . . The doctrine of a council, as regulated by Scripture, becomes a norm for the individual Christian for the correct understanding of Scripture. (SC 54)

Also, owing to the relation between the ecumenical council and the Church, an ecumenical council is the 'ordinary' means of dogmatic development. This means (a) that teachings promulgated by an ecumenical council would be more binding than (though still as fallible as) other teachings from other organs in the Church; and (b) that dogmas which are promulgated as infallible yet which were not defined by any council, much less by an ecumenical council (the two Marian dogmas), are immensely problematic, to say the least. It is hardly coincidental, thinks Küng, that these two dogmas, plus the two papal dogmas, seriously and persistently divide Christendom.

All this could leave one with the impression that non-ecumenical councils, lesser papal statements, and theologians cannot interpret Scripture correctly, or cannot better reformulate Church teaching. In no way is this true. But the fundamental difference among these different magisterial elements is their binding character. In Küng's opinion, only definitions which have behind them the Holy Spirit and the whole ecumene are binding. And their bindingness stems from the divinely guaranteed infallibility (indefectibility) of the Church—a subject to which we shall turn momentarily. But first there is another consideration to be made.

Catholicity in Space and Time

Councils are important in a second way, as a medium of continuity through Church history. Küng wrote in 1957 that "Scripture can be rightly understood only in light of the Church's documents," whose function lies in their being a means of defense against heresies, or an index of what is contained in Scripture and Tradition. (J 118) And so, Küng declared, even a theology which concentrates on Sacred Scripture includes an obligation to the Church's authoritative teaching:

> Church tradition, and in particular Church documents, are for us not signposts in the history of dogma which simply help a man find his way, but signposts which help him decide which way he is going to take. The Catholic theologian feels bound at this point not only in a relative but in an absolute way. Hence he does not begin by investigating Scripture as an independent Christian individual and subsequently consulting the Church's dogmatic proclamation (as a negative norm). Rather, he carries on his investigations into Sacred Scripture while remaining at the same time positively aware that he is absolutely bound to the teaching of the Church. Nevertheless—and there is no getting away from it—he is searching Sacred Scripture, around which as the immediate, tangible Word of God, all other things must revolve. (J 118)

The obligation to Tradition on the part of the theologian was formulated eventually by Küng in terms of catholicity. A theology which bypassed Tradition—especially the conciliar tradition—could not be considered catholic.[19] In The Church Küng had investigated the original and derivative meanings of 'catholicity', and determined that the original usage of "catholic" meant the "all-embracing" Church, the whole Church. (TC 297f.) But within centuries, due to the emergence of various heretical groups, the word took on polemical nuances and came to mean the orthodox Church: "instead of the reality of catholicity there develops the claim to catholicity." (TC 298) At the same time, the unprecedented growth of the Church added to "ecclesia catholica" a new idea: geographical catholicity (extension over the whole earth) and numerical catholicity (largest number). Vincent of Lerins added the sense of an orthodoxy believed always and everywhere: temporal catholicity. With the Protestant Reformation, Küng writes, "the 'Catholic Church' was not the same as it had been before that division, and . . . its catholicity, in whatever sense, appeared to have been destroyed along with its unity." (TC 386) Küng concludes that identity is the basis of catholicity: identity with the essence of the Church. Despite changes in historical forms, the Church's divinely established essence perdures unchanged. (Cf. TC A.I.)

According to the original sense of the word, then, the catholic theologian is one who feels obliged in his or her theology to the catholic--and that means the whole--church. (F 337)[20] This involves two dimensions.

Catholicity in time. The theologian is catholic if he or she is bound to the church of all times. He or she will not qualify a priori certain centuries as "unchristian" or "unevangelical" but believes there is in all centuries a faithful community of believers reached by the gospel. Küng writes that in contrast with this is "Protestant radicalism" which is in danger of restricting tradition to mean the periods from Jesus to Paul, Paul to Augustine, then jumping to Luther and Calvin. The catholic theologian proceeds from the view that the gospel in no period has been unknown, and so he or she will try to learn from all previous periods. The catholic theologian is interested in the continuity of Christian faith despite all disruptions. (F 337)[21]

Catholicity in space. The theologian is catholic if he or she is bound to the churches of all nations and continents, and believes the gospel of Jesus Christ is heard across the entire world. In contrast to "Protestant particularism," which is often very nationalistic and provincial, the

catholic theologian is interested in the <u>universality</u> of Christian faith,
evidenced in its many different groups. (F 338)

Küng continues, precisely <u>because</u> one wishes to be a catholic theologian, one cannot simply restrict his or her catholic faith and catholic
theology to Roman achievements of the eleventh century onwards. (F 339, 342)
Küng testifies, "I am a Catholic theologian if I am really considering the
whole of tradition of the two thousand years."[22] In this connection Küng
remarks in his own defense that he has done more in this area than many
other theologians, for he has consistently tried to gain a positive understanding of the great but lesser known conciliar tradition.[23]

The Fallibility of Councils

Ecumenical councils reflect the essential structure of the Church which
is one, holy, catholic and apostolic. And if 'infallibility' or 'indefectibility' belongs in some way to the essence of the Church, then ecumenical
councils must also share in it. This is related to a second factor: the
'infallibility' of the pope. But precisely what such 'infallibility' consists in must be clarified as it is applicable to councils.

The Relationship Between Council and Pope

It may be noted at the outset that the papacy, papal primacy, and papal
infallibility are not the focus of the present discussion—this is reserved
for a later chapter. But from the viewpoint of ecclesiology, conciliar
theology has everything to do with the Petrine office. As Küng remarks,

> All difficulties of a theological-dogmatic and practical-existential
> character that stand in the way of the reunion of separated
> Christians <u>and</u> in the way of a general council of the <u>whole</u> of
> Christendom converge and are rooted in the Petrine office. Here too
> lies the cardinal problem with respect to a <u>theology</u> of ecumenical
> councils. (SC 201)

And so it will be necessary ever so briefly to record Küng's understanding
of the relationship between pope and council, viewed in this section from
the side of the council. And because of the nature of ecumenical councils,
the relationship between pope and council is the same as that between pope
and Church. Küng writes,

> This results directly from the fact, which we Catholics believe,
> that the Church according to Matthew 16:18f; Luke 22:32, John
> 21:15-19, and according to the attestation of the Acts of the
> Apostles and the events of Church history has--and still has today--
> something to do with the Petrine office. According to the Catholic
> understanding of the faith Christ founded the Church on the rock of
> the Petrine office (and also the apostolic office)--the ecumenical
> council by divine convocation. If an ecumenical council by human
> convocation truly aims to represent the ecumenical council by
> divine convocation, it accordingly must reflect the basic structure
> of the Church and therefore make present--in whatever form--the
> Petrine office. (SC 205; emphasis mine)

A delimited papal primacy at Vatican I. Küng cites Canon 228 #1 which
reads, "An ecumenical council holds supreme power over the universal
Church." In competition is Canon 218 #1:

> The Roman Pontiff, the successor to the primacy of Saint Peter, not
> only has the primacy of honour but the supreme and full juridical
> power over the universal Church in regard to faith and morals as
> well as in what pertains to discipline and government of the Church
> which is spread through the whole world. #2: This power is truly
> episcopal power, ordinary and immediate, over each and every
> individual church as well as over each and every one of the pastors
> and faithful, and independent of any human authority. (SC 206)

These canons clearly are grounded in the definitions of papal primacy given
at Vatican I. (Cf. Denz. 1827; 1831) Given these canons, is there any room
for "an ecumenical council that is more than an advisory or an applauding
organ of the pope?" (SC 207)[24]

As a matter of fact, Vatican I did circumscribe papal primacy: papal
authority is neither absolute nor arbitrary. (SC 209) Concretely this
means: (a) the pope cannot abolish the episcopate, nor usurp the rights of
bishops, nor substitute his authority for theirs; (SC 210-213) (b) the pope
cannot interfere with the orderly exercise of office by the bishops

(principle of subsidiarity);[25] (SC 213-218) (c) papal primacy should edify the Church and should serve ecclesial unity and not its own greatness and glory; (SC 218-220) (d) papal office should be "non-arbitrary, non-inopportune, non-exaggerated, non-irregular." (SC 221)[26]

Pope vs. Council at Constance. These four strictures are clear enough, but what about a conflict between pope and Church, pope and council? In the last resort, which--pope or council--has final say? Can anything be said beyond Canon 1556: "The first see is under judgment of nobody"? "We can give a satisfactory answer to this question only if we dare to look at the facts of Church history soberly, without embellishments of any kind." (SC 224)

Church history is not lacking in instances where popes have resigned or have been deposed by councils. In general, popes lost their office in five ways: through death, resignation, mental illness, heresy, and schism. (SC 230-236) In such cases the Church (ecumenical council) has the duty to take action against the pope.

> But there is the difficult question: Who judges? We have heard the answers that the canonists in general give: An ecumenical council; the bishops (formerly one also named the College of Cardinals); in any case it must always be a representation of the whole Church which effects a remedy. (SC 236)

But if such a pope refuses to convoke a council--what then? If a regional synod is not sufficient to solve the problems, then, according to Suarez, for instance, an ecumenical council must be convoked by the bishops or cardinals and be obeyed. (SC 237) Thus, "On the basis of both historical facts and canon-law theory it has become obvious that the principle Prima sedes a nemine iudicatur has in fact its internal limits." (SC 237)[27] This internal limit "inheres in papal authority as a finite-human authority established by its Lord." (SC 328)[28] When an ecumenical council, then, pronounces its legitimate and authoritative sentence on the pope,

> . . . this authentic sentence is merely a <u>declarative</u> sentence. It
> is a verdict which does not, as such, effect or bring into being the
> fact that has been judged; rather, as such, it merely makes public
> and authoritative declaration thereof. Hence it does not <u>effect</u>
> that this man, who was pope, is now no longer pope. Rather, it
> <u>establishes</u> that this man, who was pope, is now no longer
> pope . . . . (SC 239)

This careful distinction permits Küng to speak guardedly of a council's

"superiority" over the pope, without it becoming also an independent, higher

legal authority "which the pope would face simply as its subject." (SC 240)

The classic case of conflict between pope and Church is the Council of

Constance. Only Küng's two conclusions merit our present mention: the

Constance decrees <u>are</u> <u>binding</u> (on Catholics), and the Council <u>did</u> <u>define</u> a

kind of superiority of the council (it did not define a radical

conciliarism). (SC 254-258) But 'superiority' may be misleading: the

relationship between pope and council still should be understood as a

"reciprocal ministerial relationship in the service of the Church under the

one and only Lord." (SC 258)

As these two brief sub-sections have illustrated, Vatican I and the

Council of Constance exhibit contrasting views along the spectrum. "Both

are councils of the same Church; both teach what is necessary and exhibit

the essential structures of the Church." (SC 279) Yet each can be mis-

understood by being referred to exclusively. An ecclesiology based on

Constance alone "does not end with the Petrine office in the sense of Holy

Scripture, but at best with the chief official of a democratic-

parliamentary Church association." (SC 280) And an ecclesiology built

solely on Vatican I "glimpses the Church not as the great council of all the

faithful, who according to Scripture are filled with the Spirit (Rom. 8) and

are a royal priesthood (I Pet. 2:5-10), but at best an ecclesiastical

subject people ruled in a totalitarian fashion by an absolute monarch (or his apparatus of officials)." (SC 280) Only the middle path will disclose the complex essential structure of the Church.[29]

The Infallibility of the Church and the Fallibility of Councils

It is clear from the foregoing that whatever one decides about the infallibility of pope or of councils (or, similarly, even of Scripture) is ultimately based in a decision about the infallibility of the Church. And so, it falls within the purview of a discussion of Church Councils to make a few remarks about the infallibility of the Church and how this pertains to councils.[30]

Both Luther and especially Calvin held that councils are fallible because of the prior and superior position of Scripture. Councils have been known to contradict and correct one another,[31] wrote Calvin, and only on the basis of Scripture is it possible to determine a council's orthodoxy. Even though the presence of the Holy Spirit at councils does not preclude (human) error, still, a council is the best means of settling dogmatic disputes. (SC 305-313) Küng considers differences between Calvin's understanding and Catholic doctrine to be minimal today, for in the Catholic view, too, (1) the Church is always composed of sinful human beings, thus it is forever plagued by false prophets and teachers against whom it must defend itself; (2) office-holders are servants of the Church and are bound to the Word of God in the Holy Spirit through whom they hold office; and (3) the Church cannot formulate definitions arbitrarily; it must adhere to the Word of God in Scripture. (SC 313) But the real point of controversy is not the continuation of the Church in truth but the continuation of individual councils in the truth. "It concerns the infallibility of councils which Calvin contested and which the Catholic Church upholds." (SC 313)

Beyond the objections of Luther and Calvin, Küng argues that the quintessential structure of the Church is what is variously called infallibility, indefectibility, indestructibility, perpetuity. According to Scripture certain promises have been made to the Church that attest God's will to keep the Church alive, despite its infidelity and sinfulness (Mt. 16:18, 28:20; Jn. 14:16, 16:13; I Tim. 3:15). The Church's essence is indestructible, permanent and infallible only because God does not abandon it.[32] The Church may fall away from the truth in individual matters, but the "Spirit of all Truth" has been promised to it, hence the Church as a whole will perdure in the truth. (SC 336ff.; TC 342ff.; Inf 173ff.) Using the beautiful biblical metaphors Küng writes,

> (The Church) will never cease to be what it is: the communion of saints, the people of God, the creation of the Spirit, the body of Christ. It will never become a different Church, a pseudo-Church. As the Fathers explained, it can become a beggar-woman, set itself up as a trader, sell itself as a prostitute; but through God's preserving, saving and forgiving mercy it will always remain the bride of Christ. It may wander through the world poor, hungry and helpless, but the Father will always run to embrace and kiss it on its return. It may lose its way in the desert, but the shepherd will always go out after it. It may roam through the town, but the bridegroom will always find it. It may desert him, but he will never desert it. The Church goes on its pilgrim way through the ages, along a road not of its own choosing, along the way to which it is irrevocably called. It may lose the way, make detours, take wrong turnings, it may stumble and fall, it may fall among thieves and lie half-dead by the roadside. But God the Lord will not pass by on the other side; he will pour oil on its wounds, lift it up, give it a lodging and provide for its healing even that which it could not have foreseen. (TC 344)

At the same time, Küng urges that errors in the Church be frankly acknowledged.[33] Because such errors have occurred, either the promises made to the Church are unreal, or, errors cannot be admitted, or, as Küng proposes, "The Church will persist in the truth IN SPITE OF all ever possible errors!" (Inf 175)[34] From this 'solution' the following may be concluded: (1) infallibility, or indefectibility despite all errors in detail, belongs indisputably to the essence of the Church as attested in

Scripture; (2) the organs which reflect the structure of the Church
(ecumenical councils and pope) are likewise infallible; (3) the thoroughly
human element at ecumenical councils is not attenuated by this infallibility; (4) the infallibility of councils is not an a priori guaranteed
immunity from error.

Regarding the fourth point, the same difficulties that inhere in all
human propositions (including those of Scripture) apply also to the
decisions of ecumenical councils. That is, an a priori certainty about the
infallible and irreformable truth of conciliar definitions is simply
impossible; judgment about the truth of a definition can be rendered only a
posteriori by the Church.[35] Thus Küng writes:

> . . . ecumenical councils can be an expression of the infallibility
> or indefectibility of the Church. But they are not so a priori in
> virtue of the will of those who convoke them or take part in them,
> as if the latter were granted infallibility a priori by the Spirit
> of God in response to their desires and prayers: this is exactly
> what cannot be substantiated from any source. Councils are an
> expression of the infallibility or indefectibility of the Church
> rather a posteriori, if and in so far as--that is--they
> authentically attest the truth of the gospel of Jesus Christ. Hence
> there are not indeed a priori infallible conciliar statements. But
> there are certainly factually true, conciliar statements: those,
> namely, which are in harmony with the original Christian message and
> are also recognized by the Church as being in harmony with it. (Inf
> 207)

It is possible, then, to speak about the fallibility of councils, not so
much in Calvin's sense, but inasmuch as conciliar definitions are subject to
the vagaries of history. Hence it is true both that there can be no a
priori certainty about the truth of definitions, and, that councils do enact
true (and binding) decrees.

The continuation in truth of the Church in the Holy Spirit extends also
to ecumenical councils. However, the ecumenicity of councils is not an a
priori certainty either. More importantly, Küng notes with Calvin, councils
have not only contradicted one another but have corrected one another.
Besides obvious Christological examples, in The Church Küng devotes an

excursus to an ecclesiological example of such a supersedure. (Cf. TC 439f.) The examples show only that the Church cannot know a priori which of its definitions are universally true and applicable, because historically conditioned elements invariably enter in, tying down the definition to a particular, restricted point in time and in the history of ideas. There is for Küng no such thing as an infallible proposition, not even in Scripture, but obviously there are true ecclesial propositions by virtue of God's promises of indefectibility (infallibility) to the Church.

Errors in Tradition

The subject of error arises because of Küng's emphasis on the pervasiveness of historical conditioning in Tradition. He has frequently encouraged the Church to admit freely the so-called errors committed by its teaching office, and mentions the following among the "classical errors" of the ecclesiastical teaching office: the excommunication of Photius; the prohibition of interest; the condemnation of Galileo, the condemnation of new forms of worship in the Rites controversy; the maintenance up to Vatican I of the medieval secular power of the Pope; the condemnation of modern historical-critical exegesis of the Bible; the condemnation of religious freedom; the condemnation of modernism. In Infallible? Küng added to the list of errors, Humanae Vitae. Among other errors (in practice) would be: the restriction of priestly ministry to celibate males; the condemnation of theologians and imposition of inquisition-like methods of censure; the condemnation of worker-priests; the failure to condemn Nazism; the insistence on the Latin Vulgate translation; some forms of Marianism; and many others (Inf 31ff.; T 24-26)

The criterion Küng employs for determining error is, on first sight, straightforward: Scripture. Küng differentiates among developments secundum, contra or praeter evangelium.[36] An evolutio contra evangelium must not in any case be tolerated. An _evolutio praeter evangelium_ is an "actual development alongside the gospel which, even if it is not forbidden by the gospel, is at any rate not authorized by it." (T 93) Such a development may be tolerated, but not turned into an absolute. An _evolutio secundum evangelium_ is in accord with the gospel, even required by it. (T 96f.; Inf 112)

There seems to be an incipient "theology of history" here, which shares two features common to any other "philosophy of history": a "present standard" and a "future hope" which are used to read the past. The present standard for Küng is the strictly historical framework which replaces traditional metaphysics. (Cf. espec. MG & EG). He does not entertain a notion of history in which there occurs an inexorable progress or advance, for he rejects Hegel's speculative identification of God with the world. In theological terms, the effects of sin and infidelity are far more pervasive than such historical optimism would allow. Küng's view that the Church, like the individual, is _simul justus et peccator_ means that _a priori_ error cannot be excluded from, nor an _a priori_ infallibility or inerrancy be attributed to, either the teachings or practices of the Church.

Further, God's Holy Spirit, unlike Hegel's Spirit, cannot and must not be identified with any one aspect of humanity, not even with the Church itself. (TC 173-176) If the Spirit were so identified, God would no longer be free, hence, God no longer would be God. Consequently, regarding the matter of error in the Church, if the Holy Spirit is too closely identified with the Church (or with one organ in the Church, such as the hierarchy), it becomes simply impossible to account for or admit to past errors, deviations, aberrations, unless, that is, one wants to saddle the Holy Spirit with such mistakes. In Küng's view, faith that is truly confident in God's promises need not hesitate to admit either the Church's past guilt, or errors it is bound to commit in the future. As long as God rules the Church, it will not perish, yet as long as men and women constitute the Church, it will go astray.[37]

Secondly, errors are identified on the basis of a "future hope," namely, ecumenical reunion. The methodological key to the door of reunion is carved by Küng's ecclesiological principle which designates ecumenical councils as the authoritative interpreters of Scripture and the developers of dogma. This priniciple effectively establishes the grounds for ecumenical rapprochement, because those formal dogmatic teachings which presently prevent reunion (Mary; Pope) are demonstrated by Küng to have been reached not by ecumenical consensus but by Roman Catholic councils. Therefore they must be relatively low on the scale of authority or bindingness on Christendom as a whole (regardless of their bindingness on Roman Catholics). Moreover, lesser doctrinal teachings (for example, justification; sacraments) which have hindered reunion in the past can be exposed in their polemical historical encasements (by means of contemporary exegetical tools) and reformulated with more sensitivity to other points of view. Admitting error in past interpretations is therefore not fatal or destructive but historically honest! Just as the recognition of error in Scripture does not destroy either Scripture or its absolute authority and normativity, similarly, the recognition of errors in Tradition cannot destroy the Church but perhaps only render it more credible today. (SC 26ff.)

An example would be the Petrine office. Küng has striven at great length to show the biblical sanctions for a Petrine ministry. He has argued simultaneously that several of the 'trappings' associated with the papacy are not therewith authorized by its origins in Scripture. These latter items are relative historical accretions; they are also those which continue

124

to divide Christians and even make a full and unreserved Protestant
recognition of the Petrine ministry (which up to now has happened only
theoretically) at least more difficult if not impossible.

Summary

The purpose of Tradition, as Küng sees it, is to expound faithfully the
revelation of God already attested in Scripture. The Church best
accomplishes this when, under the guidance of the Holy Spirit, it meets in
ecumenical council and interprets God's revelation. Ecumenical councils,
which represent the essential structure of the Church, are infallible in the
sense that the whole Church is infallible, but infallibility does not mean
inerrancy, or exemption from historical conditioning, or immunity from
error. The limitations of historicity extend to all aspects of Tradition,
even to the so-called infallible definitions. But the historical conditionedness of a dogmatic decree, for example, does not necessarily detract
from its truth nor from its bindingness on the Church. Just as in Scripture
the Holy Spirit works through the human factor, taking into account its
fragmentary and fallible character, it is no different in principle with
respect to Tradition. Because the Spirit works in "unrestricted human historicity" in the Bible, critical exegesis is warranted; because the Spirit
works the same way in the Church, exegesis of Tradition is likewise
warranted, especially exegesis of councils.

Scripture and Tradition, then, are similar in many ways in Küngian
methodology. Both are thoroughly historically conditioned, yet both
attest--in varying degrees of immediacy--the revelation of God. Yet the
irrefragable difference between Scripture and Tradition lies in the
normative and authoritative status of each: Scripture is norma normans and
Tradition is norma normata. In Chapter V we shall investigate the serious

theological and methodological implications of Küng's radical subordination

of Tradition to Scripture.

CHAPTER FOUR

INFALLIBILITY: A TEST CASE

Hans Küng begins the section entitled "The Petrine Power and the Petrine Ministry" in his book The Church with the caveat, "Readers who begin reading at this point are making a mistake. Some people . . . are constantly on the lookout for this one point: is the writer 'for' or 'against' the pope?" (TC 444) A similar warning might be invoked here, for what follows is not the taking of a position 'for' or 'against' the pope, nor really even 'for' or 'against' Hans Küng. The more modest purpose of the present chapter is two-fold. First, an analysis of Küng's position on infallibility is chosen as a concrete illustration of the methodological principles described in the preceding chapters. The prehistory of his position is included to indicate the consistency of application of the method as described above; the following analysis of Infallible? An Inquiry and accompanying commentary are best understood in terms of the groundwork covered above.

This so-called test-case is not chosen in the false hopes that the complex problem of infallibility can hereby be solved, and even less because it is a pregnant topic and certain to evoke feelings of both approval and disapproval. Rather, it is in the notorious problem of papal authority and papal infallibility that the strands in Küng's theological methodology converge in a precisely identifiable way. Recently his Christology has also attracted a great deal of controversy, and it, too, easily could have been used as a test-case. But it is to our advantage that nearly ten years have elapsed since the publication of Küng's Inquiry, which, it may be hoped, grants us something of a perspective on the issue.

The second purpose of this chapter follows closely on the first. The volume of material which followed Küng's Inquiry and which comprises the so-called "Infallibility Debate," is remarkable not only for its breadth, variety and unusual passion, but also in its not infrequent failure to understand his central thesis.[1] This is due to a considerable degree to a dissent (sometimes only implicit) from the theological methodology which guides Küng to his central thesis and solution. Consequently we have devoted the final section in this chapter to an inventory of the major methodological objections registered against him on this topic, as well as his replies to his critics.

Our intention is not to enter the infallibility debate as such, if that means taking a position for or against either Küng or his opponents, but to call attention to one concrete application of his methodology, and to the resultant methodological debate. Accordingly, we have made every effort to refrain from polemics and inaccuracies on our own part, since such conduct did not seem to further the debate substantially [2] but illustrated how arguments based on inaccuracies only clouded the issue.[3]

The Pre-history to Infallible? An Inquiry

When Küng published Infallible? he certainly expected a negative reaction from the Vatican, considering that ever since the publication of Justification in 1957 a dossier had been compiled on his works. He probably expected also somewhat of a mixed reaction from various theologians. But what greatly took him by surprise was the shock registered by some of his reviewers about the 'radicalness' and 'newness' of his views, since many of the opinions expressed in Infallible? had been expressed already in previous works,[4] and no one had taken issue with them there. For our present methodological study it is important to review the pre-history to the

Inquiry to see whether the conclusions reached therein are in continuity
with or divergent from Küng's earlier determinations.

Continuity or Break?

In Justification, as we saw in Chapter III above, Küng used the tools
of historical criticism to turn the edge on Barth's criticisms of Trent.
Predominantly influenced by K. Rahner and others, Küng argued against
Barth's narrow conceptions by stressing the historicity of dogma and dogmatic propositions. He wrote, ". . . a truth of faith can always be arti-
culated in formulas which are (conceptually as well as terminologically)
more complete, more adequate, and more perfect." (J 102) At the same time,
he drew attention to the risk (Gefahrlichkeit) involved in dogmatic definitions, for there is "the danger of one-sidedness and particularity, with
theologians helping to petrify and foreshorten revealed truth and with heretics contributing to the impoverishment." (J 103) Küng later says of this
clear adumbration, "If dogmas . . . are historical, incomplete, imperfect
and inadequate, why then in a single instance can they not be also possibly
in error?" (F 313)*

Just before Vatican II Küng published in 1960 his next book. Here he
was influenced by Y. Congar, yet wished to surpass the latter's distinction
between true reform, meaning reform of the Church's life (Catholic reform),
and false reform, meaning reform of the Church's teaching (Protestant
reform). (F 314; W&W 151f.) Küng wrote that dogma "expresses at the same
time both the irreformable divine revelation and what is human and reformable. There are . . . certain abiding constants . . . but there are not,
properly speaking, any irreformable areas in what is of human, ecclesiastical formulation." (CRR 116)

Küng's next work, Structures of the Church (1962) contained significant new research on infallibility and is a sort of capsule form of Infallible?[5] In Structures he asked the question about a possible conflict between pope and church, as in the case of a heretical or schismatic pope. In addition, in Chapter VII, entitled, "What Does Infallibility Mean?" Küng identified the real point of controversy between Catholics and Protestants as "the infallibility of councils which Calvin contested and which the Catholic Church upholds." (SC 313) He goes on to say, "For Catholic doctrine the infallibility of the Church and the infallibility of ecclesiastical office (of the pope and of the councils) are essentially connected." (SC 314) God promised to preserve the Church as a whole from apostasy, from a substantial error that would destroy the gospel. The infallibility of the Church is based exclusively in the promised assistance of the Holy Spirit.

With respect to papal infallibility, Vatican I clearly set certain limits. (SC 314-336) (1) Absolute infallibility is ascribed to God exclusively, not to the pope; (2) the pope is not separate from the Church, and is infallible only insofar as he represents the whole Church; (3) the subject of infallibility is pope and council; (4) But: "Can it not also be said that ultimately and finally the pope exclusively can define without the episcopate and Church, and that therefore he can define arbitrarily?" (SC 333) At least as far as what was said at Vatican I, there is no way to prevent a pope from defining arbitrarily; "if the pope merely wills it, he can do so ultimately even without the Church." (SC 333; cp. Inf 105)

Küng then notes certain problematic aspects of the term Unfehlbarkeit, which in German has undesirable moral overtones, and which the Latin infallibilitas does not have. Also, immunitas ab errore means that in ex cathedra decisions the pope in principle cannot err, not only does not err. Küng suggests that Irrtumsfreiheit (freedom from error) or Irrtumslosigkeit (errorlessness) be substituted for the ambiguous <u>Unfehlbarkeit</u>. Yet the

theological problem is not overcome merely because of a linguistic change.

(SC 334-336)

Already in 1962, then, the question was formulated:

Let us have no illusions on this score: whether the infallibility
of the pope is exclusive or whether he shares it with the
episcopate, whether or not he has to depend on support from other
sources, whether infallibility extends only to matters of faith and
morals or also to other areas, whether the infallible definition of
the pope needs the consensus of the Church, and so on, are all very
secondary questions indeed for the Protestant Christian. To put it
more sharply, it suffices that during the thousands of years of
Church history one single pope at some particular moment pronounced
with absolute certainty a single dogma of the Church as a pope
infallible from the outset to see the whole significance of the
problem: is a man who is not God infallible? (SC 337)

The same question applies to ecumenical councils:

. . . it is of little use to base oneself on the charism of
infallibility in discussions with Protestants. For them this is a
mere postulate which despite the scriptural proof adduced by
Catholic theology is without scriptural foundation. They regard it
as a merely legal contrivance based on a specific biblical text ("if
Peter is to be the rock, then he must also be or have this or that,
or be able to do this or that, and so on"). (SC 337)

Küng adds, Protestants can affirm the Church's essence to be indestructible,

permanent and infallible. (SC 337; cp. Inf. 193ff.) But for them "the

postulate of human infallibility is an expression of a lack of faith in the

power of the Holy Spirit in the Church." (SC 339; cp. Inf. 176f.) "For

Protestant Christians the continuity and indestructibility of the Church

does not depend upon the infallibility of certain utterances." (SC 339)

Again pre-figuring <u>Infallible</u>? Küng wrote in <u>Structures</u> that the

Fathers of Vatican I were not aware of certain systematic difficulties. He

briefly describes the <u>Sitz im Leben</u> of the Council:

They were concerned with the extirpation of Gallicanism root and
branch. Most of the main discussions revolved around certain
modalities of infallibility and around opportuneness of a definition
of infallibility. On this point the views of the Reformers were not
at issue and infallibility as such was not directly discussed. The
theology text-books also, written wholly within the scope of the

problems posed by the First Vatican Council, and the few modern investigations of these problems do not furnish a comprehensive answer to the difficulties that have just been outlined. (SC 340; cp. Inf Chap. II)

Finally, in striking similarity to Küng's later position, he wrote in the concluding pages of Structures on the relationship between faith and particular dogmatic formulations of faith. (SC 344ff.) Although there is only one faith, formulations may be not only different but contradictory. Because of their historicity, "as human--and as historical formulations--the definitions of the Church are inherently capable and in need of improvement." (SC 347) Moreover, Küng made a statement that was repeated in Infallible? and became very controversial: "Every statement can be true and false--in accordance with its aim, structure and its intent." (SC 351; cp. Inf 169)

In the next years Küng was busy with the Vatican Council which, he happily notes, refrained from making any infallible statements. In 1964, one slim volume in the Theological Meditations series (which he edits) appeared, entitled, The Theologian and the Church. This work commented upon the relationship between the theologian's adherence to the Church (kirchliche Bindung) and his or her critical perspective (kritische Sichtung). He wrote,

> While loyally holding to his Church's confessions of faith and definitions, the theologian has the right and duty to use all means to investigate, at once humbly and without constraint, how far these confessions and definitions bear witness to the Word of God in Scripture . . . . (Th&Ch 24)

The question of infallibility was also raised in this book.

> Catholic theology has as yet given no adequate answer to the question of what is implied for it by this imperfect, incomplete, enigmatic, partial, fragmentary character of all our formulations of faith. The word 'infallible' does not express all this, but obviously it does not deny it . . . . Perhaps there will at last be found some more comprehensive concept that will express, better than the concept 'infallible', at once the strictly binding character and the profoundly fragmentary character of the Church's formulations of the faith. (Th&Ch 30)[6]

In 1967 Küng published in the series "Ökumenische Forschungen" the massive work The Church. Here, too, he devoted an excursus to nuances of the words Unfehlbarkeit, Untruglichkeit, and Fehlerlosigkeit.[7] He wrote, "God has promised and granted to (the Church) infallibility. Despite its errors and misunderstandings God will preserve it in the truth." (TC 342) Infallibility, then, means that "the Church, in so far as it is humbly obedient to the word of God, has a share in the truth of God himself, "who can neither deceive nor be deceived." If it is obedient, then all lies and deceits and deceitfulness are removed from it. 'Infallibility' therefore means a fundamental remaining in the truth, which is not disturbed by individual errors." (TC 342) And, Küng continued, "This infallibility is scriptural, and even the Reformers never questioned it. Whether on the other hand it has as a necessary consequence the a priori, unquestionable and verifiable infallibility of particular statements is something that is not directly demonstrable from the New Testament." (TC 342)

Küng later pointed out that despite these numerous and explicit statements on infallibility, no one disputed him or took up the questions he raised. (F 322f.) Then Humanae Vitae was published, which was perhaps the "straw that broke the camel's back." Humanae Vitae gave Küng the opportunity to connect his thesis on infallibility with a specific case, to show precisely how far the "Roman" theory of infallibility extends in practice. Apparently also in some despair over the post-conciliar reactionary course of the Church (F 323f.) he decided to "sound the alarm." The gentler style of his earlier works had not roused those in responsible positions in the Church, so Küng decided to write his Inquiry in a different way. He wryly notes that when his style changed, many in the Church "woke up suddenly and complained loudly," not about the failure of leadership since Vatican II, the Church's loss of credibility, the mass exodus from the priesthood, questionable birth control, marriage and celibacy regulations, but about his "outspoken language." "There are cases, and this is one of them, where it is expedient to engage in polemics. The replies to my fair polemics have been polemical enough in themselves and I do not accept that serious polemics are necessarily unscientific."[8]

As these citations from Küng's previous works show, the Inquiry was decidedly in continuity. "This means no break with the author's previous theological work, but is rather a sign of continuity . . ."[9]

A Methodological Analysis of Infallible? An Inquiry

In this section we propose to comb the pages of Küng's Inquiry, section by section, in order to call attention to the several instances where his theological methodology (as defined in Chapter I above: starting point; ordering of sources) is clearly operative.

The fundamental question Küng poses is whether the infallibility of the Church (which he plainly upholds) is dependent on a priori infallible propositions. His answer is that the Church will persist in the truth despite all individual errors.

"A Candid Preface"

Küng cites the post-conciliar standstill as the context for his Inquiry and the reason for his change in style. Despite the open doors of Vatican II, centralism, juridicism and absolutism continue to prevail in Rome. Paul VI has failed to continue in the line of credibility established by John XIIII. The central inquiry pertains to "the complex of questions relating to the ecclesiastical teaching authority."[10] It seems, writes Küng, that the more the Pope attempts to take his office seriously, it happens at the expense of the credibility of the teaching office and the unity of the Church. (24) Various documents issued by Paul VI are criticized by Küng because of their "defective biblical substantiation" (Ecclesiam Suam, 1963; Sacerdotalis Coelibatus, 1967); "text-book theology" which evidences neither sound exegesis nor historical study (Mysterium Fidei, 1976; Humanae Vitae, 1968); theological naivete (Papal Credo, 1968), and un-ecumenical attitude (1970 Decree on Mixed Marriages). (25)

That Küng should take issue with the post-conciliar Church in just this fashion is not surprising. The material in the documents he mentions reflects a theology and methodology quite dissimilar to his own. Specifically, by their supposed "defective biblical, historical and exegetical" foundation, the documents contravene what is most important to Küng: the absolute priority of Scripture. This makes ecumenical consensus on these matters all the more difficult; if they were biblically grounded, in Küng's opinion, ecumenical agreement would be more easily attained. Also, the loss of credibility which is furthered by such documents inhibits effective apologetics both inside and outside the Catholic Church.

Küng goes on to make one of the most important statements in the book: "Let it be known that the writer of this book is and remains for all his criticism a convinced Catholic theologian." (26) He writes that his intention is not to bring unrest and uncertainty, but to speak courageously about the way the people of God are being deprived of the fruits of the Council. No Imprimatur was sought for the book, not because it is not Catholic, Küng writes, but because it is Catholic even without an Imprimatur.

Küng therewith sets the stage in his preface for bringing to bear on the question of ecclesiastical authority a passion born of intense disillusionment, but the firm resolution to speak as a Catholic. This had numerous implications, as we shall see below.[11]

Chapter I: "Infallible Teaching Office?"

The opening sentences of this chapter fittingly express the fundamental concern of Küng for ecumenical reunion. "The assertion of an 'infallibility' of the teaching office in the Catholic Church has always been unacceptable to non-Christians and to Christians outside that Church. In recent times, however, it has become to a surprising extent at least questionable even within the Catholic Church." (31) It is significant that what follows is a list of the errors of the ecclesiastical teaching office.[12] When in the past an error could no longer be denied, past theology simply adjudged it not to have been an infallible decision in the first place. The most recent error, in Küng's opinion, is _Humanae Vitae_, which is "extraordinarily revealing in regard to the problem of infallibility." (33)

Küng is not especially interested in the encyclical itself;[13] his main reason for examining _Humanae Vitae_ is to take up the _formal_ question of teaching authority. He asks why Paul VI decided in favor of the minority conservative position formulated by the study commission. The first reason he gives is what the pope felt to be his strict obligation to the centuries-old doctrinal tradition and that of his three immediate predecessors.[14] And, "according to his own testimony, the Pope plainly did not consider more closely the original biblical message. Presumably he was convinced that no arguments against contraception could be drawn from that source." (48) Küng remarks that the weighting of sources in the encyclical leans obviously towards Tradition; about twenty-five times "there are references to the 'teaching of the Church' and the 'magisterium', while 'gospel' appears only twice and then as 'law of the gospel' (as if Paul had not contrasted 'law' and 'gospel')." (49) About thirty times ecclesiastical law is mentioned, but not the "freedom of the children of God." Papal statements are cited forty times, Vatican II thirteen times, while Scripture is quoted sixteen times "but in a moralizing connection and never in any instance in order to substantiate the main thesis." (49) Then comes the statement that reveals once more how differently from "Roman" theology Küng himself would order theological sources:

> All these are clear signs that in this document the law counts for more than Christian freedom, the ecclesiastical teaching office for more than the gospel of Jesus Christ, papal tradition for more than Scripture. (49)

This brings Küng to what he calls the neuralgic point: the question of error in the teachings of Tradition. (50) Contraception could have been permitted only at the expense of admitting error in the teaching of the last three popes.

The progressive majority, which was even prepared to admit error on the part of the teaching office, was unable to convince the pope. Here Küng analyzes the arguments of the majority which dealt more with moral theology (material aspect), and of the minority, which argued from fundamental theology (formal aspect). (51-63) Because the prohibition on contraception, though never defined ex cathedra, had always and everywhere been taught by the ordinary magisterium (pope, bishops, supported by theologians), it therefore "belongs to the universal, infallible Catholic faith." (57) The teaching of Humanae Vitae is therefore factually infallible. Consequently the pope had no option but to reaffirm in Humanae Vitae past teaching on contraception; he could not admit any error on the part of the Church in its past teaching, and simultaneously maintain the Roman Catholic doctrine of infallibility. Küng writes there are only two theological possibilities: either treat past teaching as infallible and irreversible and adhere to it despite all difficulties, or, simply question the whole theory of infallibility. (67f.)

Küng's methodology has come to light already, then, in his situating the problem of infallibility in the ecumenical arena and in his rejection of

the 'dishonesty' of dialectical theology which tries to show how errors are
not really errors. He also takes issue with the "Roman" way of subor-
dinating Scripture to Tradition. In this connection he isolates the fundamental problem as that of admitting error in Church teaching. The impossibility of admitting error is what happens, he reasons, once Tradition
becomes a theological norm on a par with Scripture. This clearly is incom-
patible with Küng's own perspective on Scripture and Tradition.

Chapter II: "Firm Foundations"

Here Küng begins with a strict textual analysis of the teaching on
infallibility contained in the dogmatic manuals. Infallibility is defined
as the impossibility of falling into error, and is ascribed to the pope, and
to the episcopate in union with the pope. (68ff.) Little scriptural
argumentation is provided amidst the manuals' assertions; equally rare are
patristic quotations. "The whole question is therefore, whether the
presupposition here is rightly made or whether the same Scripture texts
permit also another presupposition." (69)

Küng turns to Vatican II's documents. His textual analysis yields the
conclusion that Vatican II simply adopted the teaching of textbook theology
on infallibility. (69-74) Lumen Gentium reads, "This infallibility with
which the divine Redeemer willed his Church to be endowed in defining a
doctrine of faith or morals extends as far as extends the deposit of divine
revelation, which must be religiously guarded and faithfully expounded."
(73) The statement actually applies to the infallibility of the Church,
Küng notes, but who in the Church, or what structure or office in the
Church, "religiously guards" and "faithfully expounds" divine revelation?
(74) Does the infallibility of the Church precede the infallibility of
Pope and bishops, or vice versa? (Cf. SC 331f.) Article 25 continues:

But when either the Roman Pontiff or the body of bishops together
with him defines a judgment, they pronounce it in accord with
revelation itself. All are obliged to maintain and be ruled by this
revelation, which, as written or preserved by tradition, is
transmitted in its entirety through the legitimate succession of
bishops and especially through the care of the Roman Pontiff
himself. (Inf 75f.)

Küng attacks this statement on the grounds that it lends some weight to the

objection of Barth and others that the Catholic Church identifies itself

with revelation, "that Scripture is played down by tradition and tradition

again played down by the present-day teaching office, which decides what is

tradition and therefore also what is Scripture." (76) In Küng's opinion,

Vatican II did not neatly define the relationship between Scripture and

Tradition, Scripture being the _norma_ _normans_ of ecclesiastical Tradition

which is therefore _norma_ _normata_. Vatican II, in Küng's estimation, too

closely aligned the two as equally normative theological criteria, hence the

question of the supreme norm was left undecided. (78)[15]

Although Vatican II attempted to balance Vatican I's definition by

emphasizing collegiality, "the arguments are partly drawn from presupposi-

tions which today can no longer be regarded as historically sound," namely,

(a) that the bishops in a definite, direct and exclusive way are the suc-

cessors of the apostles, and (b) that the apostles claimed to be infallible.

(81) Here Küng's previous historical-critical research enters in. He

argues, as he had in The Church, (cf. section D. IV.1) that according to the

New Testament, especially the synoptic gospels, there is no lack of mention

of the weaknesses and failings of the apostles. The apostles had no special

a priori incapacity to err, but were thoroughly human individuals. (81f.)

And, as we saw in Chapter I, to all things human attaches the possibility of

error.

Second, it is equally impossible to prove an apostolic succession which

applies to the bishops only. Küng argues as he has elsewhere[16] that the exegetical, historical and systematic details are more in favor of apostolic succession of the whole Church, inasmuch as the whole Church in its confession and faith is the apostolic Church. (82ff.) Based on exegetical and historical research Küng concludes that the tripartite division of offices is not to be found in the New Testament but begins with Ignatius of Antioch. Moreover, it is not possible to prove that the bishops are the sole authentic teachers in the Church. According to the New Testament, he avers, there is also a special succession of (prophets and) teachers. (84) (cf. TC E.II.2) Finally, then, despite Vatican II's new pastoral orientation, "the statements about an infallibility of the college of bishops, based on the traditional, unhistorical theory of a direct and exclusive apostolic succession of the bishops, exegetically, historically, theologically, have feet of clay." (86)

Because Vatican II depended for its definition on Vatican I Küng shifts his attention to an analysis of that Council.[17] He maintains that one cannot simply analyze the texts of Vatican I and therewith suppose one has understood it. Rather, "the definition of papal infallibility was largely decided before the Council itself voted for it." (89) That is to say, Küng analyzes the decades preceding the Council in terms of political, ideological and social factors (anti-clericalism; liberalism; rationalism; "the desire to maintain the old order and hostility toward the new") which are viewed as among the general historically conditioning factors. Moreover, there were specifically Vatican factors: Pius IX himself pressed hard for a definition of papal infallibility. Simultaneously the pope managed to generate sympathy for his person and office; "the dogmatic bond of Catholics to the pope now acquired a sentimental touch." Also, Küng refers to the "Roman Question" as the Vatican's anxiety over the status of the city of

Rome in face of the Italian unity movement. (90-94) This confluence of historical factors can be cited, according to Küng's methodology, to explain
why the definition of Vatican I was so well-prepared for and subsequently so
widely accepted. Winding up his historical analysis, Küng writes a crucial
sentence which demonstrates exactly how very formative he thinks historical
context is, not only on expressions of truth but on truth itself:

> . . . the problematical historical background of the definition of
> infallibility belongs not merely to the prehistory of the
> definition, but to the history of the definition itself. But it is
> not sufficient to expose this background critically and frankly--as
> Catholic historians do today--while at the same time refraining from
> any critical reflection on the definition itself. The historical
> problematic revealed here does not affect merely the 'opportuneness'
> of the definition of infallibility--as it was often innocuously
> formulated in the past--but its very truth. (94; emphasis mine)

Having given the historical context, Küng focuses on Vatican I's Constitution, Pastor Aeternus. He distinguishes here between the definition of
papal infallibility, and the definition of papal primacy. (94) With respect
to primacy, which is supposed to be petrine, perpetual and Roman, Küng notes
that (a) Vatican I admitted certain limits (largely moral) to papal primacy,
(b) Vatican I (and II) omitted a discussion of the possibility of a heretical or schismatic pope, thereby circumventing many of the real implications of papal primacy, (cf. SC Chap. VII) and (c) Vatican I's entire argument on a petrine, perpetual and Roman primacy presents "serious difficulties from the standpoint of contemporary exegesis and history, which no
Catholic theologian has been able to resolve up to now. They make the
possibility of a convincing proof of a historical succession of the bishop
of Rome in a primacy of Peter seem extremely dubious." (97); (d) the
absence of exegetical-historical proof of succession does not mean that the
primacy of one individual is contrary to Scripture, as long as it is succession in the Spirit; a primacy of service. (97) (cf. TC sec. E.II.3)

The definition of papal _infallibility_ is unambiguous both in what is allowed and denied to the pope. (100) (Cf. SC Chap. VII.2; TC sec. E.II.3) Still, "the relationship in principle between the infallibility of the Church and the infallibility of the pope remains undefined in the formula of Vatican I." (101) Accordingly, the possibility of conflict between pope and church also remains undefined. And so, Küng says, "the problem is still papal absolutism," that is to say, "the pope, of himself, at any time, without necessarily bringing in the Church or the episcopate, can claim ecclesiastical infallibility and with finality decide alone any question of theory or practice that is important for the Church." (101) But even though the pope is obligated to revelation, and may be only morally required to investigate a question by appropriate means (councils, synods, bishops, cardinals, theologians and others), Küng formulated the matter this way (which was quickly seized upon by critics): "the teaching of Vatican I really amounts to this: if he wants, the pope can do everything, even without the Church." (105) And again, regarding the possibility of conflict, if the pope can define _without_ the consensus of the Church, can he also define _against_ the _consensus Ecclesiae_ (as in _Humanae Vitae_)? (107)

The critical counter-questions Küng now directs at the points covered thus far even more clearly reveal his methodological premises and priorities. He argues that the same difficulties which plague the primacy of jurisdiction plague also the primacy of teaching (this is Küng's term): that it be petrine, perpetual and Roman. (108) Vatican I, in Küng's opinion, does not substantiate--except juridically--its own position on this point.

> Since--as Vatican I itself says--no new revelation and no new inspiration are bestowed on the pope, then neither are they granted to the Council; and since Vatican I describes its infallible definition of infallibility as divinely revealed dogma, then it must indeed be found--according to the view of the Council itself--in the testimonies of this revelation. Hence the Council too cites such

testimonies. But we are involved here--if it were possible--in even greater embarrassment than in connection with the primacy. (108)

There immediately follows Küng's verdict: in Vatican I's whole chapter on infallibility Scripture is quoted only once (Lk. 22:32) (apart from an indirect quotation of Mt. 16:18).

Küng rebounds to repeat what he has said frequently: no one in Christendom would object to a petrine ministry carried out in evangelical spirit and faith. What is objectionable is a "historical and formally legal succession of a papal teaching office with a claim to infallibility." (109) To prove this one would need to show (a) that in Lk 22:32 (and in Mt 16:18, Jn 21:15) it is a question of both an infallible and of a teaching office (and why someone whose faith does not cease needs immunity from individual errors in order to strengthen others in faith); (b) that in Lk 22:32 (Mt 16:18, Jn 21:15) there is any mention of Peter or other successors; (c) that the Bishop of Rome is meant to be such a successor. Küng also takes issue with uncritical catholic exegetes who argue more from dogma than from Scripture. Moreover, historically speaking, Mt 16:18f. was not used to substantiate Roman primacy until much later in time. (109f.)

Küng's attack on the (lack of) Scriptural foundation comes as no surprise. But then, as if to turn "Roman" theology back on itself, he argues that Vatican I's definition rests also on sparse testimonies of Tradition. Of course, "no ecclesiastical tradition may be accepted without examination, but must be judged critically in the light of the original Christian message," (112) to determine whether a particular development is secundum, contra or praeter evangelium. Küng then gives a brief historical survey of the development of papal primacy. Until about the eleventh century, the pope was not generally regarded as infallible. The "monstrous forgeries of the Pseudo Isodore Decretals of the ninth century" were used to bolster papal claims. Even Thomas Aquinas relied on the forgeries so that his

theses on papal authority also laid a foundation for Vatican I. (112-120)
According to these and other testimonies of tradition. Küng remarks,

> . . . it will be understood why Vatican I was content to
> substantiate the definition with brief, general statements: 'this
> the Holy See has always held' and 'this the perpetual usage of the
> Church confirms'. The historical reality looks different. The
> papalist overcharging of the teaching authority in theory and
> practice may be based on what today have been proved to be forgeries
> and the decretals based on these and also again on the theologians
> 'proving' these decretals, but certainly not on Scripture nor on the
> common ecumenical tradition of the Church of the first millennium.
> (120)

This is what is greatly responsible, writes Küng, for the schism with the
east and with the churches of the Reformation. Finally, recalling what was
said in Chapter III above concerning the importance of ecumenical councils,
Küng deals the final blow to Vatican I's scant use of tradition: none of
the three lengthy texts cited in Pastor Aeternus comes from a universally
recognized general council. (121)

In the course of Küng's chapter "Firm Foundations" he has examined both
historical, theological and extra-theological reasons for the definitions of
Vatican I. He closes with the thought:

> But one thing must have become clear . . . : the traditional doctrine
> of ecclesiastical infallibility, however precisely described in the
> textbooks, at Vatican I and II, rests on foundations which for a
> modern theology and perhaps even for that time could not be
> described as secure and unassailable. (124)

What should also have become clear is how distinctly and concretely
Küng's methodology guides his path and structures his critique in this
section. He plainly shows in his analysis of Vatican I and II how the tools
and methods of historical criticism can be used equally well of councils as
of Scripture. At several junctures Küng carefully reconstructed both the
proximate and more remote historical contexts of the text in question; he
identified specific features of the text (or of other outside sources) which
bear the imprint of historical factors. More important, he analyzed the
meaning of the text itself as an historical product and thereby measured the

meaning in terms of its historicity. All this enabled Küng to acutely direct the critical question to Vatican II, whether it had sufficiently understood what precisely it was adopting from Vatican I, namely, whether (a) in the process it was jeopardizing the priority of Scripture over Tradition as a source and norm, and (b) whether it did not entertain an unhistorical (and therefore untenable) notion of historical succession.[18]

The same critical historical principles enabled Küng to focus on the numerous problems affecting Vatican I. As he sees it, its definitions were largely a backlash to the increasingly oppressive political situation, which led it in the direction of papal absolutism, hence to the dual definitions of papal primacy and papal infallibility. But in Küng's judgment neither definition is substantiated historically, exegetically, or theologically.

Finally, in terms of theological sources and norms, Küng excoriates both Vatican I and II for their inadequate biblical argumentation. Ironically, Küng even criticizes Vatican I for its unconvincing use of Tradition. All this, of course, flows from the determination in Chapters II and III above that for him, Scripture is norma normans and Tradition is norma normata.

Chapter III: "The Central Problem"

This part of Küng's Inquiry proposes to ascertain where the fundamental difficulty lies regarding infallibility and error, especially in light of the promises given to the Church (that the Lord will remain with his disciples, that the gates of hell shall not prevail, that the Spirit of truth will lead the Church into all truth, that the Church is the pillar and ground of truth). (125)

From the negative side, one cannot argue, says Küng, that Vatican I was not free because of ideological conditioning and Pius IX's influence. (128-130) Nor, as ecumenical discussions with Old Catholics, Orthodox and Protestants have shown, can one confuse papal primacy and papal infallibility. That is, even if the primacy question were resolved, the infallibility problem would not necessarily be settled simultaneously. (132-134) Still less can one take refuge in the rights of conscience, because the objective question of papal infallibility would not be answered. (134-136) Nor can one place one's stock in the rather strict limitations to papal infallibility decreed by Vatican I. (136-139) Here Küng repeats what he wrote in Structures: "It is sufficient if even one pope at any time at all is able to pronounce, with absolute certainty, as a pope a priori free from error, a single dogma binding on the Church: a man, who is not God--free from error?" (138) Fifth, despite the infelicities of the term Unfehlbarkeit, no theological solution is rendered by a mere linguistic change. (139-141)

The focal point of the problem of infallibility is also not the truth and authority of the Church. "The Church's truth cannot be assimilated to God's truth. For this reason we must examine expressly and of course critically from both sides the ecumenical import of our question (a factor which underlies all our discussions)." (141) Küng records K. G. Steck's objections to Catholic teaching on infallibility and then answers in a fashion that strikingly exemplifies the principles of his methodology.

> The Catholic theologian will have to agree with the Evangelical when the latter protests against the assimilation of the Church's truth to God's truth, with the result that the ambiguous historical reality of the Church is set up as an unequivocal sign of the credibility of Christian truth, faith is tied to the self-confident judgment of the Church, even in regard to the disciplinary questions of entering or leaving the Church, and a system of ecclesiastical dominion is set up over souls and over biblical interpretation. (141f.)

He continues, "God's truth however may be attested by the Church in a mandatory and authoritative manner." (142) God's truth is certainly found in Scripture, but it also really needs the testimony of the Church; in fact, it is Scripture which attests the "authority" of the Church. All this is, for the Catholic theologian, historical evidence that "the alternative to the authoritarian Roman doctrinal system certainly cannot be a Protestantism which protests against all authority in the Church." (142) Rightly understood, authority in the Church is necessary because it is sanctioned by the New Testament.

Where, then, lies the central problem? "The central problem may be stated positively in this way: is the Church's infallibility dependent on infallible propositions?" (143)

Here the heart of Küng's argument takes on more noticeable shape. As we saw in our Chapter III above, he distinguishes among abbreviating-recapitulating, defensive-defining and tendentious-explicating propositions of faith. The acerbic observation Küng makes is worth citing again in its original context:

> Seen in the light of this almost two-thousand-year-old common Christian tradition, which is supported by the New Testament itself, it must be regarded as an aberration when a church—without being compelled to do so—produces dogmas, whether for reasons of ecclesiastical or theological policy (the two Vatican dogmas of the pope) or for reasons of piety and propaganda (the two Vatican dogmas of Mary). The aberration is all the greater when it deepens the division of Christendom. (149)

Despite the necessity of propositions in general, Küng continues, it has not been proved that faith is dependent on infallible propositions of faith, that is, on propositions which a priori cannot be erroneous; "to accept the binding character of propositions of faith does not mean having to accept also their infallibility." (151) Neither Vatican Council was able to substantiate either from Scripture or from a universal, ecumenical tradition that there are such a priori infallible propositions, nor was textbook theology able to demonstrate their necessity or even their possibility. Why could not the promises to the Church be fulfilled without a priori infallible propositions? (152) Both Vatican I and II passed over this basic problematic because both presupposed that infallibility--of pope or council--was unthinkable apart from infallible propositions. (152-156)

From the standpoint of methodology it is interesting to see how Küng plays off history and theology. On the one hand, from the standpoint of faith, one believes in the promises made to the Church. On the other hand, of all the historically conditioning factors one might adduce to explain Vatican I, Küng comments that none of them touches the heart of the problem: is infallibility contingent on infallible propositions? Since this cannot be substantiated from Scripture or from the universal ecumenical Tradition, why did Vatican I (and therefore also Vatican II) accept it? Küng has laid the groundwork for his forthcoming answer.

Chapter IV: "An Answer"

This last chapter of Küng's Inquiry brings him to the defense of his central thesis: the Church can live in the promises of God without infallible propositions.

Since articles of faith have the form of propositions, they participate "in the problematic of human propositions, in general." (157) Relying on the work of a student, J. Nolte, Küng summarizes the problem involved in propositions: they fall short of reality; propositions are open to misunderstanding; they can be translated only up to a point; propositions are in motion; propositions are ideology-prone. (158-162) These observations belong most decidedly to the epistemology described in our Chapter I above, where it was seen that all truth, divine and human, comes to expression in history and therefore is subject to the limitations inherent therein. In the same connection it was pointed out that for Küng, the truth, bindingness and infallibility of propositions are separate considerations. That is to say, the historicity of truth rules out in principle guaranteed a priori infallible propositions, but this affects neither their bindingness nor truth. Nor do the historical limitations which attach to language render it entirely incapable of truthful expression; "we do not mean that propositions are incapable of stating the truth, that all propositions are equally true and false . . ." (161) but simply that they are not always as clear as they seem. Küng attributes Vatican I's interest in infallible propositions to the rationalist, Cartesian heritage appropriated by neoscholasticism and therefore also by itself. (162-169)

If propositions are so conditioned that they can attain only a measure of clarity, why can they not also be erroneous? As Küng averred in Structures (SC 351) and repeats in his Inquiry, a proposition can be true and false, considered in light of its objective, its context, its intended meaning. (170f.) That is to say, as Chapter I above maintained, the historical context of a proposition determines the meaning and ultimately also its truth. Here the influence of Hegel is apparent. Küng writes, "If a theology, if a Church, does not take seriously this dialectic of truth and error, then it is inevitably on the way from dogma to dogmatism . . ."[19]

There are three possible solutions to the dilemma between errors and promises, according to Küng. First, choose one or other of the alternatives (either the promise has failed or certain errors can never be admitted; both are untenable for the believer); second, falsely harmonize one alternative at the expense of the other (this also is untenable). Consequently, the dilemma can be overcome only by raising the alternatives to a higher level: "The Church will persist in the truth IN SPITE OF all ever possible errors!"

(175)   Here Küng's methodological priorities distinctly impose themselves
once more; the solution, he writes, can be defended in light of Scripture
(which is not true of the "Roman" theory), and it does justice to the facts
of Church history (which also is not true of the "Roman" theory). (176)
And, as if this were not sufficient grounds for his dissent, Küng voices for
the first time in the book what is really his ultimate objection: "the
Achilles heel of the Roman theory of infallibility--contrary to the intention of its defenders, who talk so much about faith--is ultimately a lack of
faith." (Inf. 176, emphasis mine)   That is to say, the Roman theory
dangerously identifies the Church with the Holy Spirit, which renders
absolutely impossible the admission of error (unless one wishes to saddle
the Holy Spirit with error).   Hans Küng clearly believes that God's Spirit
rules and maintains the Church.   But fallible (historical) human beings can
deceive and be deceived, err and go astray.   But (confident) faith that is
placed in God, who alone can neither deceive nor be deceived, "will not
identify, but distinguish the Spirit of God and the Church.   Thus liberated,
it will be able to see without illusions that the Church's development
always includes wrong developments and her progress always includes set-
backs." (177)   The Church, like Israel, is "on the road to truth."   The
Church has received in Jesus Christ the final and definitive word of revelation, so that no threats or danger can finally destroy it. (178-181)   "So
far as the Church is humbly obedient to God's word and will, she shares in
truth of God himself, who can neither deceive nor be deceived . . . .
Infallibility, indeceivability in this radical sense, therefore, means a
fundamental remaining of the Church in truth, which is not annulled by
individual errors." (181)

Indefectibility is a truth of faith, perceived only by the believer.
(187)   The fact that after two thousand years of history Christ's Church has

not been destroyed is only an illustration, not an argument, to support
this belief. And nothing can be extrapolated for the future out of history.
God's promises simply must be trusted. Of course, "the gospel remains in
every case the source, norm, and power for the faith and for the perpetuity
and indefectibility of the Church in the truth." (190)

Küng then records some of the ecumenical consequences of his solution
(193-200) Although Protestant Churches object to papal and conciliar
infallibiity, they do affirm the indefectibility of the Church. (Cf. SC
337f.) This is the Church led by the Spirit and the Word of God, which is
"not simply identical with the official tradition and supposed apostolic
succession of ecclesiasticism . . ." (196) Küng concludes that ecumenical
agreement is entirely possible. (198)

With respect to the Orthodox Churches Küng declares that the identification of the infallibility of the Church with the infallibility of councils
is subject to the same difficulties as the Roman doctrine. First of all,
the ecumenicity of a council is not a priori certain, since councils con-
vened as such were not later recognized as ecumenical, and councils not convoked as ecumenical were later designated as such; second, councils have
corrected one another. (200-208) Ecumenical councils can be an expression
of the basic infallibility of the Church, but they are not so a priori, only
a posteriori "if and in so far as--that is--they authentically attest the
truth of the gospel of Jesus Christ." (206) This fallibility does not rob
council statements of their truth.

The same line of questioning may be directed toward the truth of Scripture. (209f.) We saw in great detail in Chapter II above how both truth and
error can be attributed to Scripture. The doctrine of inerrancy is one
manifestation of a priori propositional infallibility. But the words of
Scripture, however acted upon by God's Spirit, remain thoroughly human

152

words. And, as we saw, this "unrestricted human historicity" does not rob
Scripture of its unique authority and normativity. There are in the Bible
no a priori infallible propositions, but there are obviously true propositions. And "Scripture, which is by no means free from error, attests
unrestrictedly the truth as the perpetual fidelity of God, who cannot
deceive or be deceived. In this sense Scripture attests the infallibility
of God himself." (221)

    If, then, there is no theological confirmation for infallible proposi-
tions in Scripture, councils, and pope, what is the position of a teaching
office? Küng writes that the concept of a teaching office is both late (it
has no basis in either Scripture or in the older tradition, but became
common with Vatican I and the distinction between the teaching and taught
Church), and unclear. (221-223) All Christians are called to proclaim the
Word. (223-227) Church leaders are not necessarily the best teachers.
According to the New Testament there is a succession in different
ministries, including teaching; there is no monopoly of charisms in the New
Testament. (227-240) Church leaders should respect the independent ministry
of teaching and not play at being theologians unless so trained. Both
bishops and theologians have the same source and Lord, Jesus Christ.

    Küng's Inquiry ends with a description of "the Pope as he could be."
For our purposes it is necessary only to note that each of Küng's recommen-
dations emphasizes a biblically-based Petrine ministry of service and
humility, one which would touch not only Roman Catholics but other
Christians, as well as those outside the oikumene. (241-247)

                               Summary

    This last chapter of Küng's Inquiry also serves to illustrate con-
cretely the methodological elements described in our Chapter I. The central

theological premise of Küng comes fully to light: the confidence of faith
in God's promises. All the objections of Küng recorded in the remainder of
his book revolve around historical or exegetical matters. But the kernel of
his judgment, disarming for its boldness, is that the Roman theory of
infallibility has arrogated to itself not only that which belongs to God
alone (infallibility in the strict sense) but it has also restricted the
activity of God's free Spirit to a narrowly conceived set of propositions.
This is, he claims, an astonishing lack of faith. Although the historical-
critical epistemology exerts a great deal of influence in Küng's answer,
notably with respect to the repudiation of guaranteed a priori infallible
propositions even in Scripture, the central preoccupation of the solution is
that of faith. It is interesting to note also that the unmitigated historicity of the Church in terms of its practices and professions of faith,
serves in Küng's analysis to highlight the radicality of faith as confidence. That is to say, if confident faith need not hesitate to admit past
(and the possibility of future) errors in the Church, its attention is
turned more and more away from Tradition (as a supposedly infallible guide)
and towards Scripture which, as Küng has been saying all along, authoritatively attests "this Jesus Christ himself."

The decidedly ecumenical thrust to Küng's Inquiry, and the equally
definite ecumenical character of his answer, are hardly surprising. But in
light of what was described in Chapter I as Küng's hermeneutic, we can more
specifically identify the two basic hermeneutical tendencies which inform
his position.

First, the so-called dogmatic principle has been illustrated clearly
enough; by exegetical, historical and systematic procedures, one can remove
existing obstacles to ecumenical reunion, such as papal infallibility, and
show that these dogmas must be reinterpreted critically. Indeed, one need

only show that according to the Bible (which is one item common to Roman
Catholics, Protestants and Orthodox) there is attested a fundamental
remaining in the truth despite all errors, one of which is division (hence
another of which may be a dogma that promotes division). To aid the ecumenical effort, one may also restrict Tradition to mean the oldest, universal
ecumenical tradition common to all three communions. As a theological
source and norm, Tradition comes to mean something quite different than
Roman Catholic theology has understood it to be; Küng uses tradition to
obscure the differences among Roman Catholic, Protestant and Orthodox Christians.

Second, the apologetic principle is illustrated as well. The difficulties which attach to the Roman theory of papal infallibility find their
way to the practice of the office. If the papacy were conducted more like a
pastoral ministry of service, as its New Testament origins warrant, then it
would again become credible, both inside and outside the Churches. In
Küng's opinion, this near-universal credibility was something John XXIII was
able to accomplish. But as long as the papacy is trapped in an unscriptural
and authoritarian conceptuality, marked, moreover, by what Küng sees as a
monumental lack of faith, Barth's objection may hold valid also for
Küng: "I cannot hear the voice of the Good Shepherd from this 'Chair of
Peter'." (SC 326)

Methodological Areas of Dissent

The opposition to Küng was certainly more plentiful than praise.
Reviewers not only took exception to his presentation of complicated
theological realities; in the course of the debate fundamental methodological divergences were acknowledged by many to be central.[20] The Rahner-
Küng debate brings this out clearly. In Rahner's first scathing review, he
flatly stated that because of Küng's central thesis, one could carry on a

discussion with him "only as one would with a liberal Protestant for whom a council and also Scripture are not matters that make an absolute claim on him."[21] For Rahner, both Scripture and Tradition are norma normans. Küng replied that he had first learned about the historicity of dogma from Rahner and in fact had based the material in the crucial Chapter 20 of Justification on Rahner's pioneering work in this field.[22] Moreover, he wrote, Rahner should have seen that Küng's method was clearly a consequence of his own. In sharp contrast to Rahner's "speculative" interpretation of the historicity of dogma, Küng's is an historical interpretation.[23] Further, he wrote, Tradition is not norma normans in the same sense as Scripture. Only an unhistorical method such as Rahner's, Küng wrote, could confuse and equate the normativity of Scripture with that of Tradition.[24]

In Rahner's reply to Küng, he acknowledged the fundamental methodological divergence but he continued to deny there were grounds for an inner-Catholic discussion. He distinguished between the fundamental-theological and the dogmatic modes of argumentation. The dogmatic theologian, he wrote, accepts as true those articles of faith handed on by the magisterium, and does not accept them only after supplying his own historical and exegetical proof. The fundamental theologian, on the other hand, is required to substantiate each article of faith.[25] The basic methodological difficulty is thus "in the interpretation of the normative meaning of the actual faith-consciousness of the Church as it is expressed in her dogmas."[26] Küng's concluding "Postscript" concentrates on the differences which remain in methodologies, and wrote that Rahner's is really a neo-scholastic Denzinger-theology which is not able to do much with Scripture as norma normans non normata. In addition, Küng charged that Rahner resists a historical-critical analysis in lieu of a transcendental method which remains unable to substantiate its own position.[27]

There were also areas of agreement[28] and disagreement[29] concerning
Küng's presentation. But the general lines of the methodological controversy apply to what our previous chapters have elaborated concerning the
historical-critical ordering of theological sources. It is to these sub-
stantive methodological objections that we now turn.[30]

1. Humanae Vitae. There were two kinds of objections raised about Küng's
use of Humanae Vitae as a springboard for his Inquiry. The first type
claimed that such a controversial and unfounded rejection of Humanae Vitae
as erroneous could only cloud the main thesis Küng was trying to defend.[31]

The second class of objections to using Humanae Vitae is more apposite.
As we saw above, Küng argued that Paul VI had no choice but to reaffirm the
teaching of his predecessors, precisely because the condemnation of contraception had been universally taught by the ordinary magisterium and therefore it was, in practice, infallible. Rahner argues that first of all, Küng
failed to prove that Humanae Vitae is erroneous, and second, that Küng is
unsuccessful in proving that the prohibition of contraception is a dogma of
the ordinary magisterium.[32] According to Rahner, it is a question of a
binding proposition of the ordinary magisterium only when the proposition is
clearly proclaimed "as requiring an absolute assent of faith and as revealed
by God."[33] He attributes Küng's position (1) to a misreading of the papal
commission which does not speak of a dogma, and (2) to a malicious sort of
delight over ecclesiastical mistakes.[34]

Several contributors to Rahner's volume, Zum Problem Unfehlbarkeit.
Antworten auf die Anfrage von Hans Küng, objected for similar reasons.[35]
But Y. Congar more correctly interpreted him, Küng wrote, when Congar
acknowledged, "But Küng is well aware and even states that this document
was presented intentionally without any claim of being infallible."[36]

Küng answered Rahner by reaffirming what he had said already in Infallible?, "I hold that this doctrine is false and therefore not binding. Further, I consider it a regrettable consequence of a false understanding of the Church's magisterium. And therefore I chose the encyclical as a spring-board . . ."[37] He states why he considers Humanae Vitae an error, and why-- although like the minority of the commission he did not speak of a dogma-- the immorality of contraception is (according to Roman principles) an infallible truth of morals, though not defined as such.[38] Küng also declared in Fehlbar? that his opponents had as yet produced no counter-arguments to his contention that the encyclical is a "strict consequence of the Roman view of authority, irreformability, and even infallibility of doc-trine, when it is proclaimed unanimously and constantly by the ordinary magisterium as a doctrine of faith or morals that is to be held defini-tively."[39]

2. Pope Against Church? A fair amount of discussion was generated over Küng's bold statement, "but the teaching of Vatican I really amounts to this: if he wants, the pope can do everything, even without the Church."[40] This provoked the accusation that Küng's interpretation of Vatican I was "maximalistic."[41] As A. Dulles put it, "This interpretation of infalli-bility gives Küng a wide target to shoot at, but in the end it weakens his case, for moderate infallibilists will say that Küng has not hit the only target they would be interested in defending."[42] H. McSorley adduces a counter-argument to Küng, and writes that even though Gasser may not have said so explicitly, the pope is bound to consult the consensio of the Church prior to defining anything.[43] The majority of critics reminded their own readers that Vatican I established quite definite limits to papal authority and infallibility,[44] as Küng himself had already indicated in Structures (SC 326ff.) and again in Infallible?.

In _Fehlbar?_ Küng answers these objections. First he repeats what he wrote in _Infallible?_, namely that what is claimed for the pope is not an absolute infallibility, and that the pope is not to be separated from the Church. But, Küng continues, what his opponents fail to see is that according to both the Constitution of Vatican I and the official commentary: (1) the pope is to use his teaching office for the advantage of the Church, but it is the pope alone who must decide from case to case what benefits the Church (for example, the dogma of the assumption of Mary); (cf. F 360) (2) the pope is supposed to proceed carefully and judiciously, but no one can prevent him from acting willfully and arbitrarily; (3) the pope should use appropriate consultative means, but the pope alone decides if and to what extent he will use these; (4) there is not excluded a cooperation between pope and episcopate, but again the pope alone decides whether and how far he will cooperate. (F 358f.) And Küng considers _Humanae Vitae_ the latest illustration of this, as are the two Marian dogmas. Even if the pope is bound to the consensus of the Church, he continues, this consensus is in no case a pre-condition for a definition. (F 361) In any case, he is saying, if one takes the infallibility definition of Vatican I _as is_, then his _Inquiry_ (and conclusions) remain as is. (F 361f.)

3. Propositions: True and Binding? An area which engendered a great deal of protest and opposition concerned (a) Küng's "unsatisfactory" theory of propositions, their truth, falsity and general limitations,[45] and (b) the related question of the bindingness of fallible propositions.

(a) True and False Propositions. We saw above that eight years after _Infallible?_ Küng wrote that propositions can be true _and_ false, _in accord with_ their aim, structure and intent. (SC 351) In his _Inquiry_ Küng

repeated this and added the clarifying clause, "We do not mean that propositions are incapable of stating the truth, that all propositions are equally
true and false, that they cannot correspond to the reality which they claim
to express, that understanding is impossible." (Inf 161) Although in some
sense Küng was simply articulating the consequences of understanding propositions in terms of their historicity, Congar called his statements in this
regard "assez banale."[46] Rahner was much more irritated. He rejoined that
Küng's central thesis could be stated in this way: "Küng distinguishes
between 'remaining in the truth' and the 'truth of propositions'."[47] He
continues, "Basically nowhere does Küng give careful and extensive
consideration to the difference between the historical finiteness and ana-
logical nature of human statements on the one hand and what one can really
designate as error on the other." He leaves with the impression that for
Küng "all particular propositions, though in different degrees, are always
both true and false at the same time."[48] Rahner even grants that there does
not currently exist a theory which accounts for the co-existence of historicity and error in propositions (and he proceeds to give a transcendental
proof for the necessity of absolutely affirmable propositions), but then
decrees that Küng "should have been able to develop a theologically deeper
and more radical concept of truth in order to say what 'error' in theology
really means. He really had the obligation to do this in his research, even
though there is very little preparation for it in the traditional
theology . . ." and Küng should have "worked out a more precise theory of
the historicity of propositions as such."[49]

If Rahner's criticisms are somewhat one-sided, Küng later declared, it
is because he proceeded from an inexact formulation of his central thesis;
Küng contrasts remaining in the truth with infallible propositions.[50]
Further, Küng points out, he emphatically affirms that the faith of the

Church is dependent on propositions of faith.[51] But what cannot be shown, he repeats, is that faith is dependent on a priori error-free (infallible) propositions. In the second part of his reply to Rahner, Küng enlarges somewhat on his theory of propositions. In abstracto, he writes, any proposition is ambiguous and open to diverse meanings. But in concreto, a proposition is determined by its historical, space-time position to be true or false, more or less true or false, or obscurely true or false.[52] "There is no such thing as an a priori given infallibility of a proposition. A proposition has to be measured by reality to see whether and to what extent it is true."[53]

Küng's entire discussion of propositions, it will be remembered, belonged to his explanation of why Vatican I connected infallibility in general with the infallibility of propositions in particular. But M. Löhrer asks whether one can so readily attribute propositional error to magisterial propositions. He writes, "the decisive question seems to me: which type of infallibility is necessarily implied in the promises given to the church, in the sense that these promises would be nullified if such infallibility were questioned; and which type of infallibility is a necessary precondition for an act of faith?"[54] Others asked whether Küng had not misinterpreted Vatican I since not even according to it are there "a priori guaranteed infallible propositions."[55] Along these lines G. Lindbeck wondered aloud whether Küng had been "betrayed by the equivocity of the German word 'Satz'—which means both sentence and proposition—into a bit of sloppy thinking and bad argumentation."[56] W. Kasper expressed similar reservations. Küng's strict definition of "infallibility" as the inability to err was foreign to Vatican I, Kasper wrote. Neither witnesses of Tradition nor Vatican I even speak of infallible Sätze, but only of infallible Akte. Kasper says of Küng's position that "such propositions can

err, they are not a priori error-free. As a result Küng denies therewith
not only a priori error-free propositions but also a priori infallible
acts, which lead to a priori error-free propositions."[57] L. Scheffczyk
suggested that it would be better to speak of the truth of binding
teachings, than of their infallibility.[58]

Küng answers H. Fries that infallible propositions are by definition
those which not only are in error but which in principle cannot be in error.
(F 351; Inf 150) And because the assistance of the Holy Spirit is claimed
in this connection as the "Prinzip und Wirkursache" of infallible
definitions, it is correct to speak of "a priori guaranteed error-free
propositions." (F 352)[*] Küng takes Scheffczyk to task and notes that for
Vatican I there were not only infallible instances or acts, but also infallible Sätze. "For the Church then and now the infallible Dogma of the
Assumption of Mary is important, and the infallible act of 1950 of
infallible Pius XII relatively unimportant." (F 353)[*] He continues, either
the proposition in this infallible instance is infallible (so what purpose
is served by Scheffczyk's distinction), or, the proposition in this
infallible instance is fallible, meaning that an infallible act or instance
produces a fallible proposition. To continue with the example, "the dogmatic Pius XII and his act of defining were infallible, while the defined
Marian dogma itself is basically fallible, even possibly false!" (F 354)[*]
Vatican I made no such distinction between act and proposition, Küng continues, hence it is Scheffczyk, not himself, who has gone against the text
of the Council. (F 356)

(b) Binding Propositions. The question naturally arises, if there are
not any guaranteed infallible (true) propositions, how can there be binding
(true) propositions? Rahner was not alone in asking Küng for further clarification in this matter. In his second reply to Küng he asked how Küng

could leave room for a definitive "yes" or "no" from the Church yet deny such an answer the character of infallibility.[59] Although W. Kasper realized that Küng was not advocating a relativity of sorts when he held that even a binding definition is a temporary measure, how, he asked, can a temporary (vorläufige) formulation require a definitive (endgültige) yes or no?[60]

Küng's counter-argumentation runs thus. First of all, on the necessity of binding true propositions (F 373-379) he repeats what he wrote in Infallible? on the three types of professions of faith. (Inf 144ff.) Citing R. Schnackenburg (the only exegete in Rahner's volume, Antworten) Küng recaps six areas of agreement between them to the effect that there is no biblical basis for the infallibility of propositions of faith. The basic problem remains as Küng had formulated it already: accepting the binding character of propositions of faith does not mean also accepting their infallibility. (F 377; cp. Inf 151) If no exegetes can show that Scripture speaks of infallibility, what, Küng asks, is the systematic theologian to do? "Or should an exegete today wish to uphold a double-standard--the historical-critical method for the exegete and the positive-dogmatic for the systematician?" (F 378)*

Second, on the questionability of infallible true propositions (F 379-385) Küng writes that whether one places the question in terms of the Glaubenssatz, the Instanz, or the assistance of the Holy Spirit, it is a matter in each case of proving that there are infallibly true, preguaranteed propositions. (F 379-380) This, Küng retorts, no one--not Rahner, Brandmüller, Ratzinger, Vorgrimler, Mühlen and others--has been able to do.[61] Küng's conclusion: "No single theologian in the debate thus far has been able to furnish a proof of the possibility of guaranteed infallible propositions." (F 383)*

Third, questions were raised concerning the <u>continuity of propositions</u> <u>through history</u>.[62] Küng reaffirms that there are true propositions, held onto through time, especially by Christian faith and theology (which he calls "<u>Katholizität in der Zeit</u>"). Continuity in and of itself is not a criterion of truth, of course. The continuity of faith is bound to a continuity of verbal formulations. But as long as such propositions are capable of being improved (<u>verbesserungsfähig</u>), why are they also not capable of being in error (<u>Irrtumsmöglichkeit</u>)? (F 391) Küng adds that (a) a true proposition will remain true in history if it was an actually true proposition, when it really expresses reality. With respect to the infallibility question and the continuity of propositions of faith, "the impossibility of infallible propositions means that . . . they cannot be assumed a priori; a proposition is not true simply because it has been spoken in a certain instance under certain conditions." (F 391)* A proposition is not true because a council spoke it; it is true only because it expresses reality. And (b) a proposition will remain true if its new historical situation is similar or analogous. If the situation is radically different, the same proposition may be misunderstood, misleading or even false. (F 392ff.)

Fourth, how can propositions be both historically conditioned and binding?[63] Küng answers that <u>Situationsbedingtheit</u> does not necessarily mean <u>Situationsbeschränktheit</u>. He reminds that he affirms the possibility of a <u>status confessionis</u> ("and is thereby more conservative, if not more Roman, than Karl Rahner") (F 394)* in which binding definitions can be made. But no matter how binding, a proposition of faith is always limited by its place in history, just as biblical propositions are limited by their place in history. (F 395f.; MIT 59ff.)

Hence Küng's conclusion concerning the truth and infallibility of propositions is that no theologian in the course of the debate has shown the

contrary to his position to be true. "The assertion of an infallible proposition is unfounded. Yes, it is even less founded than the author had supposed two years ago." (F 403)*

4. Methodological Criteria. Certainly one of the most difficult methodological questions raised by Küng's Inquiry concerns the criterion for Christian truth. Apparently enough reviewers thought perhaps Küng had left this
question undecided--or at least had not decided it correctly--which induced
him in the final section of his balance-sheet to make some additional observations on theological method.

Küng wrote that not simply practice, nor reason, nor even the people's
faith, nor dogma, can be the final criteria of truth; the criterion for the
Christian Church is nothing other than the Christian message as originally
attested in the Bible, and ultimately Jesus Christ himself. (F 442f.) He
cautions, though, that not even the New Testament is a mine of infallible
propositions, but it is to be interpreted historically-critically at the
highest level of modern hermeneutics. (MIT 40)

Since Christian truth is not an eternal idea but is essentially
historical, he writes, there are two moments to the Verifikationsprozeß.
First, there is the moment of Gemeinschaft, in which truth is received and
in which it lives on today. One cannot prescind from this social context.
Second is the moment of Tradition. The Christian message was transmitted
through a two-thousand year history. This history can help both the
individual and the community guard against their subjectivity and to more
deeply comprehend the truth.

> The community and tradition of the Church have therefore an
> essential significance for the process of Christian truth-finding.
> That is what we meant above by catholicity in space and time.
> (F 443)*

Still, the incisive question has been asked by M. Löhrer, whether

historical criticism is given the last word in Küng's view, even over

Scripture. Löhrer wrote:

I do not know whether Küng wishes to set up simply the gospel as the
final criterion of theological work, to be normative for all statements of faith and even of the testimonies of Scripture. The critical question appears to me then to be how the individual theologian can make this criterion work. Which role does the present
faith-consciousness of the Church play, not only but also in
reference to Church office? Can the theologian abstract to some
degree from this faith-consciousness, and with the help of this
historical-critical method decide which testimonies of the Church do
or do not have value today with respect to the gospel? In that case
wouldn't each theologian de facto consider himself the ultimate
authority in matters of faith in spite of all willingness (which
Küng has surely granted) to provide the voice of the gospel in the
Church an "opportune inopportune" value?[64]

Küng answered Löhrer's critical question by saying, (1) the hermeneutical

circle is unavoidable in interpreting the New Testament. The theologian

always brings his or her subjective Verständnis to the text. But the text

should measure the theologian, not he or she the text. (2) There must be

trust that the Gospel live on by its own authority, despite all extreme or

erroneous interpretations. (3) Arbitrary subjectivity is always a danger

for the theologian, but even this is reducible if s/he takes care in the use

of the historical-critical method and strives for a real catholicity (in

space and time). In exegesis, then, the theologian would not be an isolated

individual but a member of the Church, remaining open to correction.

Historical criticism will not destroy but will expound clearly the

decisiveness of the message for Christians of today. (F 446ff.) And in

terms of what we have been calling the "ordering of sources," Küng writes:

Anyone who simply accepts as "super-criterion" either the "Church's
present sense of faith" or the ecclesiastical "magisterium" in one
way or the other becomes an apologist for the ecclesiastical system,
and forgets that even according to Vatican II the magisterium is
under the Word of God and consequently is open to criticism in light
of the normative criterion of Scripture. On the other hand, anyone
who neglects the Church's sense of faith and simply makes the gospel

the ultimate criterion is in danger of lapsing into an emotional
subjectivism, and with the aid of the historical-critical method
makes light of the ultimate authority of faith. (F 444)*

5. Küng's Catholicity. Küng's Inquiry touched off a significant debate on

catholicity in methodology.[65] In a class by itself stands the disapproba-

tion of the Sacred Congregation For the Doctrine of the Faith,[66] but in the

course of the debate there emerged additional specific criteria for catho-

licity from different reviewers. Karl Rahner denied outright Küng's catho-

licity because the latter no longer accepted as true the articles of faith

explicitly taught by Vatican I and II.[67] J. Ratzinger[68] and H. J.

McSorley[69] argued along similar lines. C. O'Grady wrote that Küng was too

Barthian and thus not Catholic, especially as he overlooked the requisite

"incarnational" emphasis in Catholic theology.[70] R. McBrien contended that

catholicity consists in a certain understanding of collegiality which must

be accompanied by infallibility.[71] In other cases, a positive judgment was

made in the absence of any stated criterion of catholicity (G. Baum; G.

Lindbeck; M. Barth; R. McAfee Brown).[72] The Protestant W. von Löwenich

authored an article entitled, "Is Küng Still Catholic?"[73] Because Catholics

had posed the question first, he felt justified in asking it also. He

wrote, "This much is certain, that even twenty years ago this question would

have been answered with an unequivocal no." (W&W 94) The decisive question,

he ended by saying, should not read, "Is Küng still catholic," but "Will

Catholicism succeed in struggling out of the constriction caused by a juri-

dical understanding of doctrinal authority to reach genuine catholicity?"

(W&W 95)

    The catholicity debate was furthered through the efforts of the German

Bishops' Conference. On Feb. 8, 1971 they issued a brief Declaration which

listed five requirements of catholicity, each of which pertained in one way

or another to <u>Tradition</u>.[74] In their lengthier, Feb. 17, 1975 Declaration
the Bishops formulated in greater detail what they saw as the point of
divergence between the Catholic view and Küng's view.

In brief, the Bishops insisted that the normative significance of
Church Tradition was indispensable for Catholic theology. "This is why,
in its function as interpreter of the origins, this binding transmission of
the faith has, even today, the significance of a norm."[75] Küng's books, the
Declaration continued, dangerously bypass Tradition in favor of Scripture,
but it is only with the help of the whole of Scripture and Tradition that
the gospel can be proclaimed in such a way as to avoid short-lived tendencies in theological thought. Second, on the relationship between the
teaching office and the theologian, the Bishops wrote that there is "no
place outside Scripture and the living tradition of the Church where with
regard to the whole tradition one can stand and play the part of a detached
and neutral umpire, <u>and</u> no place from which to construct at the same time a
theology that would be valid enough within the ambit of the Church."[76] No
Catholic theologian can stand outside a concrete believing community. Küng,
the Bishops feared, had placed himself outside by assigning the burden of
proof for the binding truth of dogmatic decisions on Rome, when this was, in
their opinion, the theologian's task. "It is, then, a necessary component
of theological method that the theologian should lean on the Magisterium of
the Church."[77] And finally, the Bishops once again objected to Küng's
narrow view of the historicity of propositions of faith, and remarked that
the definitive obligation to magisterial decisions is not adequately preserved in his theology.[78]

What emerges from the Bishops' and theologians' discussion is that
"catholicity" refers to a certain understanding of Tradition, which many
thought was not preserved in Küng's <u>Inquiry</u>. And, as Chapter III above

demonstrated, not only does the unique and problematic character of his conception of Tradition result from its historical-critical circumscription,
Küng also defines catholicity rather differently than those voices recorded
here.

The challenge to Küng's catholicity in the infallibility debate
impelled him to further analyze the meaning of the term. In Fehlbar? he
begins with J. Ratzinger's remark that the way he understands spiritual
office, his notion of apostolic succession and how he handles the authority
of councils, contradicts not only the scholastic type of theology (which
Küng attacks), but also the basic form of the original church and that which
always belonged to the idea 'catholic'. (F 331) Küng rejoins that he
opposes the Protestant view that the post-Constantinian or medieval churches
can be disqualified a priori as being unevangelical; at the same time, medieval theology is not the sole standard of catholicity. And even if the
Patristic period is closer in some ways to the New Testament, it, too, cannot be the absolute measure of catholicity. (F 333) "All this only makes it
clear that today it is no longer simple to determine what is uniquely
catholic and what isn't." (F 333)* But this is not an unfortunate matter in
Küng's opinion, not only because the term 'catholic' was not originally used
as a polemical differentiation, but also because there is clear evidence
that catholics and protestants have come closer in the last ten years. And
this ecumenical exchange has shown that papal infallibility remains the
cardinal problem standing in the way of reunion.

As we saw above, Küng's argument in Infallible? hinged on his view that
Vatican I's definition of papal infallibility was more "Roman" than
"catholic," and that the two are not necessarily identical with each other.
Indeed, Küng has said it often: "Roman-Catholic" is a contradictio in
adiecto.[79] In his opinion, the history of the term shows that an argument

such as Ratzinger's is simplistic when it uncritically identifies 'catholic' with 'the existing reality of catholicism'. "Think of everything one would have to swallow (schlucken) as being catholic!?" (F 336)[80]

With this, he takes up Ratzinger's question: "To what extent may I call myself a 'convinced catholic theologian'?" According to the original sense of the word, the catholic theologian is obliged to the Tradition of the whole Church, which Küng terms "catholicity in space and time." He continues, catholicity is not the inherited property of Catholics; catholicity becomes (Roman) Catholicism (Katholizismus) if the existing reality of catholicism becomes simply accepted, instead of being measured by the ultimate criterion: Jesus Christ himself. (F 339) Catholicity, Küng declares, must be understood critically, according to the gospel. The catholic theologian must be evangelical, and the evangelical catholic. An "evangelical catholicity" makes things more complicated, he remarks, but also more hopeful.[81]

Küng continues that precisely because one wishes to be a catholic theologian, one cannot simply restrict his or her catholic faith and catholic theology to Roman achievements of the eleventh century onwards. (F 339) Although there is much to be said for the Gregorian Reform, and for the popes, theologians and canonists of the thirteenth century, a critical stance is still necessary: evolutio contra evangelium cannot be tolerated. With respect to infallibility he writes that attributing a special position to Peter in the great Roman tradition of the Roman bishop standing among other bishops in a pastoral service to the whole Church, appears to be an element (if not the most important) of catholic tradition, and based in the gospel. (F 399; 346) But Roman centralism, absolutism and imperialism in teachings, morals and church discipline are not, in his opinion, based in the gospel nor in the great catholic tradition.[82] And it is these un-evangelical and un-catholic developments which are responsible for the schism between east and west and for the division between Protestants and Catholics. "It is this catholicism which in the name of the Catholicity of the Catholic Church is to be resisted and overcome." (F 340)*

Summary

The infallibility controversy displays the extent of divergence among theological methods. K. Rahner's transcendental method, with its primary commitment being vested in the magisterium, was entirely unable to countenance what Küng was proposing: that theology adhere primarily to Scripture and only secondarily to those parts of Tradition which belong to the universal ecumenical tradition and which are not in error. The Vatican and the German Bishops were equally unable to endorse Küng's theological views, again because of the radical subordination of Tradition to Scripture.

In the course of the debate, even amidst tremendous pressure from all sides, Küng relentlessly refused to "dialectically" or "speculatively" bend and twist Vatican I to get out of it a less unambiguous version of infallibility (Verbesserung durch Verwässerung). It is ironic in this connection that Küng was accused by the Vatican of not being sensitive enough to the 'nuances' of Vatican I's Constitution. It is also important to note that Küng did not say that in its definitions Vatican I erred, only that it was blind to other options. He contests the biblical and historical foundations of the definition of Vatican I, not the council's assistance by the Holy Spirit. Küng himself notes that the only thing worse than an infallible pope is a group of infallible theologians.

Küng wrote an Inquiry not only about papal infallibility, it turns out, but about theological method as well. His theological conclusions about papal infallibility certainly warrant further consideration and evaluation.

But in the present study we are limited to an evaluation of the theological methodology which accounts for this--and other--controversial results. It is to such an evaluation that we now turn.

CHAPTER FIVE

CRITIQUE AND CONCLUSION

The preceding chapters have endeavored to articulate the structure and
character of Hans Küng's theological methodology. In the Introduction to
this dissertation we pointed out that just as there would be no uncritical
defense of Küng, neither would there be an all-out attack on him. But there
can also be no passing over areas where critical questions must be asked and
where an evaluation of his theological methodology must be made.

The first part of this chapter will engage the principal theme of
Chapter I, namely, the tension between faith and history in Küngian methodology. In a catena of questions we shall be asking whether (as especially
the German Bishops wondered) the use of the historical-critical method,
despite its modifications by the perspective of faith, leads Küng to an
unacceptable and un-catholic view of Tradition. Has historical criticism
"replaced" Tradition as the authoritative interpreter of Scripture? If so,
does not historical criticism then "stand over" Scripture as well? Is
Tradition a tertiary norm—after Scripture certainly, but after historical
criticism as well?

The second part of the chapter will examine the 'neuralgic point' of
Küng's own methodology—his view of Tradition. Based on the principle that
any methodological question has a theological counterpart, we shall in this
section inquire into the implicit theological notion of Tradition which
informs Küng's methodological position; in this context the question of
catholicity will be asked and answered.

What Is Küng's Final Criterion?

Isolating and identifying theological methodology is difficult enough,
but critiquing it is even more complicated, because it means coming to terms

with an ambiguity which inheres in any methodology. It is the difference between what conveniently may be called <u>theoretical methodology</u> (the stated intentions of a theologian) and <u>applied methodology</u> (what he or she actually does). It is entirely possible for there to be some disparity between the two levels, for a theologian may harbor agenda and biases which are not evident to him or her, but which find their way into the actual doing of theology.[1]

In order to take account of these different levels of methodology, we shall first ask questions about Küng's theoretical methodology (formal considerations), and second, about the applied methodology (material considerations). In a way, we will be "using Küng to critique Küng" by centering on the tension between faith and history. That is, we will want to know whether <u>in principle</u> and/or <u>in practice</u>, history outweighs faith, whether historical criticism leads to the kind of subjectivism which "has the last word over" Scripture and Tradition, and whether Küng's method is fundamentally irreconcilable with catholic or Roman Catholic theology.

Formal Considerations

1. <u>Does historical criticism have the last word over Scripture?</u> Another way of asking this would be, is Scripture in fact <u>norma normans</u>, as Küng avers time and again, or has he, unwittingly perhaps, made historical-critical principles the final judge of Scripture? In terms of theoretical method, this may be answered in the negative in at least four senses.

First of all, Küng's understanding of Scripture, of its course of composition, of the New Testament strata, and so on, is indisputably based on historical-critical principles. But he clearly holds also that historical methods are incapable of verifying scriptural testimonies to God's power and activity; this is for him strictly a matter of confident faith. Chapter I showed how Küng modifies even in his methodological starting point what would otherwise be (according to the knowledge of faith) undiluted historical criticism. From the perspective of faith, Scripture remains for him the Spirit-effected Word of God and as such is beyond the judgment of historical criticism. Concomitant with this is Küng's belief that because the Bible results from the operation of the Holy Spirit in unrestricted human historicity, literary and textual criticism become necessary. When Küng alleges that Scripture must be _investigated_ historically-critically, he is not denying that it still must be _interpreted_ through faith. In this first way, then, historical criticism does not "stand over" Scripture formally speaking; in some sense Scripture is outside the provenance of historical criticism. As Küng stated some time ago, historical studies cannot help believers or the Church in their "truly existential meditation on the word of God in Scripture . . . " At best, such study can only "assist and stimulate us." (TC 20)[2]

Second, Küng modifies historical analysis by his methodological allegiance to the Canon of Scripture; he makes it clear that this kind of loyalty would not be possible from an exclusively historical-critical point of view, but stems from his desire to be a catholic theologian firmly rooted in the faith-tradition of the Church. As Chapter II showed, a strict historical-critical analysis of New Testament early catholicism can lead to the determination of a sub-canon, which would imply a dogmatic rejection of the normativity of Church Tradition. Here Küng clearly affirms the inescapability of what Löhrer had called the hermeneutical circle: that Scripture must be read critically within the horizon of the Church community and its Tradition. (F 460) It is, moreover, only loyalty to Church Tradition which protects the exegete from his or her own subjectivity and places him or her squarely within the _catholic_ Tradition (which is also the ecumenical tradition).

Third, Küng has interpreted the fundamental witness of the New
Testament to be that God revealed himself historically in Israel, became
historical in Jesus Christ, and continues to act historically as the Holy
Spirit in the Church. And so, Küng believes that his historical interpretation is ultimately justified, if not required, by the New Testament
itself. In other words, although obviously the tools and methods of historical study as such are not discussed anywhere in the Bible, still this
method thinks of itself as a faithful version of "letting Scripture
interpret itself," for it claims to take its basic category from the Bible
itself. In this, Küng believes he is simply carrying out what he wrote in
Justification: theological terminology should orient itself to biblical
terminology. Leaving aside for a moment the material questions (whether
this interpretation of the New Testament is true to it, or whether historical categories obtrude on Scripture), we may point out that formally
speaking, in choosing historical categories Küng does not believe he is vio-
lating Scripture by imposing alien material on it.

Fourth, Küng states repeatedly that the final norm of all theology and
church practice is Jesus Christ himself, who is authoritatively attested in
Scripture. Thus even if the Bible is norma normans theologically speaking,
from the standpoint of faith, Jesus Christ is exalted as the ultimate
criterion of all truth. Hence with respect to the Canon we have seen that
Küng did not determine a sub-canon but designated Jesus Christ himself, that
is, a living person, as the 'center' of the Gospel. In so doing Küng
methodologically avoids Käsemann's problematic selection. In addition, the
shift from Scripture being norma normans to Jesus Christ as the norma
normans does not necessarily signal a gross inconsistency on Küng's part,
since he maintains that Jesus Christ is always available first and foremost
in Scripture, hence that no theologian or believer could know this Jesus

Christ except in Scripture. As far as belief is concerned, what matters is
only Jesus Christ as he confronts us here and now. (OBC 160)

2. Does historical criticism have the last word over Tradition? At
the level of theoretical considerations, Küng is clearly anxious to give
Tradition a regulating (albeit secondary) role as a source and norm. First,
catholicity means for him obliging oneself to the various witnesses of
Tradition: to (a) the Canon, to (b) the definitions and confessions of
faith, and to (c) past theological thought. Just as "catholic hermeneutics"
required that Scripture be taken as a whole, so also "catholic hermeneutics"
demands the same with respect to Church Tradition. With respect to (a) the
Canon, Chapter II showed that Küng's allegiance to it comes about as a
result of his loyalty to catholicity more than from a loyalty to historical
criticism. With respect to (b) consulting the testimonies of Church
councils, Küng remarks that he has consistently tried to gain a positive
understanding of the great but lesser known conciliar tradition. (A 178) As
for accepting the authority of councils, he never cast aspersion on the
inner ecumenicity of certain councils (even in face of a denial by non-Roman
Catholics), nor did Küng adjudge Vatican I or II to have erred in their
definitions, nor has he rejected the Chalcedonian "true God, true man"
formulation (which is not to say he has not re-interpreted it), nor has he
proposed that decisions of councils cannot be true or binding, nor that they
lack the assistance of the Holy Spirit. What Küng has challenged is whether
decisions of councils can be a priori infallible due to the Holy Spirit's
assistance, and whether such a priori infallibility need apply to dogmatic
definitions. As far as (c) is concerned, Küng has indeed researched past
theological positions, from the Church Fathers right up to contemporary
times, which all of his books amply exemplify. He is also to be recognized
for his impressive knowledge of Protestant, Orthodox and Jewish theology.

There is a second way Küng accords Tradition a regulating role in the theological schema. In the question of the final criterion of Christian truth, he posits two moments to the Verifikationsprozeß. There is the first moment of community (Gemeinschaft), in which truth is received and in which it lives on today. Second is the factor of tradition (Tradition). The Christian message was not created in our generation, but has been transmitted through a two-thousand year history. This intervening or mediating history can help the individual and the community guard against their own subjectivity and to perceive the truth more deeply and comprehensively. (F 443) The relationship of the theologian to the Tradition of the Church, which should aid him or her in interpreting Scripture, is precisely what Küng means by "catholicity in space and time."

And third, there is the related fact that Küng insists that Scripture be read within the context of the believing Church, which means both within the present faith experience of the Church, and within the Church's past Tradition. He warns against making either the magisterium into a "supercriterion" or the gospel into an uncritical, subjectivistic criterion; the theologian must rather strive to be truly catholic, with the aid of the historical-critical method. (F 444) The "hermeneutical circle" is thus complete; the verification process takes place within and presupposes the Church's faith, yet requires the theologian to assume a critically scientific (historical) posture.

Formally speaking, then, in Küng's theoretical theological methodology there appears to be a lively, if not difficult, tension between faith and history, in which the historical strand conditions but does not determine the strand of faith. Yet this does not obviate the exigence of asking whether the same strand wins out in Küng's applied theological methodology,

that is, whether the ultimate norm for Küng in _practice_ is perhaps otherwise
than he indicates.

Material Considerations

1. In Chapter I it was noted that in Küng's Christological writings he
expressed reservations about whether it is possible to "so easily pass" (as
he thinks W. Kasper does) from functional statements about Jesus of
Nazareth, to the ontological statements about Jesus Christ made by
Chalcedon. The transition is difficult, in Küng's view, because historical
categories do not admit supra-natural causes to explain historical events
(for example, the doctrine of Christ's pre-existence is a-historical or
supra-historical). Küng writes that because the early Church "heard the
gospel with Hellenistic ears" it interpreted the salvific will of God in
Christ in essentialist or Greek metaphysical terms. He recognizes the
fact that the early Church had no other ears with which to listen to and
interpret the gospel, but he adds that "from the modern perspective it must
be said that the Hellenistic concepts were not very apt to express the
original message." (OBC 448; cf. OBC 442) That is to say, because it is a
desideratum for Küng that theology conform itself to biblical language, and
since metaphysical language is not biblical language, _therefore_ speculative
categories are less fitting than historical categories. But the critical
question must be raised, are the nineteenth- and twentieth-centuries doing
anything different in principle by "listening with historical ears," however
unavoidable this may be for the present age, and would not this listening
also be subject to the very same criticism Küng directs to the classical
dogmatic tradition?

Küng would likely answer that historical categories are themselves the
actual biblical categories, and for that reason alone they are appropriate
for theological discourse. He writes,

> Would it not perhaps correspond more to the New Testament evidence
> and to modern man's historical way of thinking if we started out
> like the first disciples from the real human being Jesus, his his-
> torical message and manifestation, his life and fate, his historical
> reality and historical activity, and then ask about the relationship
> of this human being Jesus to God, about his unity with the Father.
> In a word, therefore: can we have less of a Christology in the
> classical manner speculatively or dogmatically 'from above', but--
> without disputing the legitimacy of the older Christology--more of
> a historical Christology 'from below', in the light of the concrete
> Jesus, more suited to modern man? (OBC 133)

But there would arise from Küng's position two further counter-questions.

First, why did the early Church (and the Church of subsequent ages) fail to

see this if it is such an essential characteristic of the Bible? If it were

answered that the Church was bound unavoidably and intractably to its

hellenistic conceptuality, and for this reason did not read revelation in a

predominantly historical way, "from below," then, it might be asked, could

the present-day Church be certain that it is not just as inescapably bound

to its own (historical) conceptuality, and therefore perhaps also blinded

but in another way to the real language of Scripture. How does or how could

the Church of today know whether its historical reading of Scripture

actually corresponds to the Word of God, and that exegesis is not misled by

the prevailing historical intellectus into thinking as if history is indeed

the proper category for understanding revelation? There is a vicious circle

here; one could ask whether, twenty centuries later, we can have a 'pure'

gospel (if this would even be desirable), one not molded to or tainted by a

particular era's conceptuality, a gospel that does not need to be mediated

by the whole of Church Tradition.[3]

And second, in what sense is classical Christology inadequate? Küng

writes that "the importance of this teaching should not be belittled. It

has made history. It gives expression to a genuine continuity of Christian

faith and provides important guidelines for the whole discussion and for

any future interpretation." (OBC 131) But, he goes on to say, because the two-natures doctrine of Chalcedon uses terms and ideas which are hellenistic and no longer understood today, it is inadequate.

We might agree with Küng in this first respect, that a highly metaphysical formulation, if left uninterpreted, is insufficient for today's way of thinking. But he adds what is, at best, an unfortunate expression: that the two-natures doctrine did not solve the difficulties even at that time, and that the same doctrine is in the opinion of many exegetes not simply identical with the original New Testament message about Jesus. "Some regard it as displacing or--up to a point--even corrupting the original message . . ." (OBC 131f.; cf. MG 565f.) In other words, Küng seems to be saying that the Greek metaphysical terminology is inadequate not only for moderns who think historically, but also for those in the early Church who thought metaphysically. The not-so-subtle yet questionable assumption here is that modern historical categories not only make more sense to modern people, but they better correspond to the New Testament, hence they better solve Christological difficulties than their metaphysical counterparts. The salient and difficult question then emerges: on what grounds does the user of historical criticism know that biblical categories are historical categories, if not by his or her own historical interpretation of the Bible?

To say that Scripture must be interpreted historically-critically may be, as mentioned above under formal considerations, simply a result of Küng's maintaining that because the Word of God is expressed in finite, human, historical concepts and terms, it is therefore subject to a critical reading. At the same time, to say that Scripture must be interpreted historically-critically may be also a way of replacing or bypassing Church Tradition, which up until the present age had been the indispensable mediator of Scripture to the Church. Historical criticism (as used by Küng) believes itself capable of going directly to the scriptural texts

themselves, and of extracting the original message without being colored by
interpretations of a text in Tradition. In Küng's method Tradition defi-
nitely recedes into the background in terms of its normativity. Indeed, we
may observe that Tradition assumes a tertiary position as a theological
norm, though it retains secondary position as a theological source.

In contradistinction to these indications in Küng's methodology that
history dominates Scripture, we would say that historical criticism must be
understood to be subject to all limitations which accrue to other methods.
That is to say, even to admit the tremendous wealth of insight and information which historical criticism has yielded, does not--and cannot--mean
that it is any more than a means, not necessarily the best nor even necessarily a better means of interpreting Scripture. For twentieth-century
people it is virtually impossible even to envision another method which
would satisfy so bountifully many of the criteria our age esteems:
objectivity; determination of facts; process and changeability; recognition
of relativity; historical knowledge. But if we can prescind for a moment
from our own very powerful and cohesive intellectual framework, the question
at least may be entertained whether historical criticism is not vaunted
above Scripture if it becomes 'indispensable' or 'necessary' for scriptural
interpretation. If, as the Church proclaims, Scripture is really its ultimate source and norm, then any particular exegetical method--historical
criticism notwithstanding--must be dispensable in principle, regardless of
whether the Church of the present or future might continue to find its
results helpful and might decide to continue to rely on its procedures. If
it is not dispensable in principle (regardless of its status in practice),
then in effect the future Church--which might operate with a conceptuality
other than the historical--would be prevented from developing an exegetical
method appropriate for its time. Historical method may be the most fitting

type for our age, but it cannot be thought of as a final or exclusive tool.
To say this exegetical method is "better" than another presupposes that a
so-called "unhistorical" understanding of Scripture is less true than an
historical one, which is something that simply cannot be established. But
what makes this critique so elusive is that it seems nearly self-evident to
the twentieth-century mind that the present-day historical approach can
better identify the conditions under which Scripture was written (including
the intent of the author), and that therefore it draws closer to the truth.
But again, however helpful and appropriate historical criticism may be to
our age, it must guard against giving the impression of being required by
the New Testament itself.

2. When the Bible is understood foremost in historical terms, and the
central events in it (especially miracles and resurrection) are interpreted
according to the canons of historical knowledge, then indeed the transition
from "below" to "above" becomes exceedingly difficult to make. Historical
thinking, as we have seen Küng employ it, positively imposes certain limitations on the kinds of conclusions that may be drawn about any event:
Scripture cannot be word-for-word inerrant; dogmas cannot be infallible a
priori, God cannot break the laws he himself creates. Yet, there is a means
of making a transition through what Küng calls the "analogy of historicity,"
according to which he discusses the "historicity" of God, Christ and the
Church. Küng avers that the New Testament order--and hence the proper theological order--is from economy to theology, or from "below" to "above". In
his view, theology must begin with the concrete historical manifestations of
God, Christ and the Church, and only then proceed to make statements about
the 'essence' of the same realities. But again, once this critical historical procedure is incorporated as an irrefragable methodological
principle, according to which one judges even past theological formulations,

the same line of questioning presents itself: can historical criticism
systematically establish why the economy-to-theology approach is a better or
more correct one, apart from repeating its claim that its (historical)
interpretation of Scripture shows this to be so?

With respect to the analogy of historicity, by virtue of which Küng
asserts there to be history in God in se, is the extension of the analogy
theologically justified by him? That is to say, the analogy of history may
be as ingenious and cogent for us today as Augustine's psychological analogy
was for the fifth-century Church, yet, an analogy is always only an analogy,
and it cannot be claimed apodictically to describe God as God actually is in
se. Certainly there is contained in Küng's position the perspective of
faith which believes that in Jesus Christ God truly reveals himself, which
means that God appears in revelation as he is in himself. The fact that the
transition from below to above (function to essence) is so difficult for
Küng to make vis-à-vis the Christological tradition, yet is more freely made
with regard to the nature of God, seems to indicate more his fundamental
reservation about dogma, than a confusion about the analogy. Yet, the
question may still be raised: what is the justification for the confidence
(of faith?) that the intra-mundane analogy can be applied to divine reality?
This seems to be a problem in systematic theology which Küng is neither
prepared nor inclined to answer.

Hans Küng says that the trinitarian question hinges on the Christological question: how God was in Christ. The Christological question is to
be investigated historically first, and then dogmatic definitions presumably
are to be formulated on this historical basis. And, he says, trinitarian
theology must come at the end of theology.[4] It is interesting that in his
most recent book, Does God Exist? we find the rudiments of a trinitarian
formulation conceived along historical lines; there Küng speaks of God as

the origin, power and goal of all history, and these are terms which may be interpreted as being symbolic of Father, Spirit and Son respectively. Since he has spent several years exploring ecclesiology and Christology, and if in Does God Exist? he is beginning to move cautiously towards a more fully explicit trinitarian interretation, then it will be necessary for him in future writings to discuss the theological relationship between the economic (historical) trinity and the immanent (historical) trinity, especially in terms of the analogy he has set up. It may be that the historical analogy will yield great insights for the future Church as well; this we cannot yet know. But it is doubtful that the analogy will prove very compelling unless the connection between God as he is in (our) history and God as he is in himself (in his inner history) is made clear from the standpoint of systematic theology. It cannot go unnoticed in this regard that in a book of eight hundred pages on the existence of God, a scant three are on "God in the Spirit," and the final three are on the "Triune God." Apparently thorough-going historical thinking leads Küng to near silence on a triune God.

And so, it should not be considered excessive if one says in all honesty that what one misses most in Küng's theology is a systematic doctrine of the Holy Spirit. For even though, as Küng himself emphasizes, the Church is assisted by the Spirit, how--concretely speaking--can its members know what is or is not of Christ? Despite the answer given to this question by Küng in Fehlbar? (cf. Chapter IV above), most theologians and believers are probably not content with his reply. Ecclesiology would seem to warrant a consideration of the ad extra (or, in his scheme, economic-historical) trinitarian work of God the Holy Spirit; in addition, in terms of methodology, the nature and function of the Holy Spirit is crucial in explaining how we can know that God is in himself as he reveals himself to us in history.

3. Historical criticism as employed by Küng serves to emphasize the mutability, temporality and limitedness of every aspect of the Church's life, even or especially its dogmas. The distinction between the form and the content of a dogma, a distinction which even the Vatican uses[5] in order to admit the relativity of certain time-conditioned embodiments but the permanent truth of the core affirmation, is challenged by Küng, because such a theory does not go far enough to state why, if the form is subject to historical limitations, including error (and so is not a priori inerrant), the content is also not likewise subject.[6] His historical analysis serves concomitantly to play up the role of the Holy Spirit as the one who grants to individuals and to the Church that trusting faith which alone could survive the vicissitudes of historical change. The questions we wish to raise relate to whether this is an essentially correct view, whether it does justice to the faith of the Church, whether concrete and fallible humans in the Church can live in doctrinal unsurety despite their confident faith in the future eschatological triumph of God's will and truth. Another way of asking this would be, is the tension between faith in God's Spirit and Küng's description of historical changeability one with which the Church must live?

There are raised in this two questions, only the second of which is germane to our discussion. The first would be, what is God's will for the Church, and the second, how is the Church to know this will? Küng certainly maintains that God as Holy Spirit has pledged to be present in word and sacrament,[7] hence that these are reliable pointers to God's activity in the Church, apart from the various forms they have assumed in the course of history. These signs may not posses some inherent characteristic which obligated God to choose them as concrete manifestations of his will, yet the incontrovertible fact remains that word and sacrament have always been means in the Church by which Christians came to know God's will, truth and presence. It seems that at least in these two instances God in his infinite wisdom has desired that Christians have the kind of trusting faith Küng describes, yet willed also that the Church have definite, immutable, insuperable, albeit still historical (and therefore to some degree limited) signs of its faith. The question is why dogmatic definitions are excluded in principle from exercising a similar function in the Church. Clearly Küng does not deny altogether the value or binding character of definitions hitherto made, but he does question whether such definitions are reliable or a priori certain manifestations of God's will for the Church.

It is ironic in this connection to note that Küng's historical analysis of divine activity in history highlights the becoming-historical of God to the extent that even divine truth is considered to be historically con-ditioned, and God himself (though without ceasing to be God) becomes also historically conditioned, as it were, when He enters history in Jesus Christ. At the same time, by accentuating the incompleteness and fragmentariness of any historical embodiment, historical criticism renders somewhat unreliable and tendentious the historical forms we do have, and robs something of their ability to concretely, definitively and perduringly express meanings and values.[8] In the realm of dogma and doctrine, the Roman Catholic Church is willing now to recognize a degree of historical con-ditioning and conceptual imperfection in formulas of faith, but it will not go with historical criticism so far down the line to admit dogmatic error as a potential result of historicity. This Church in its teaching office may not entirely satisfy all theologians by the reasons it now adduces for this stance,[9] but what becomes clear is that because it holds a different

theological opinion about the role of the Holy Spirit in "bringing
the Church into all truth," it holds also a different methodological
position regarding Church Tradition. That is, this Church believes God's
will is known not only in word and sacrament, but authoritatively and on
occasion even infallibly in dogmatic definitions. To Küng's charge that the
Roman theory of infallibility is simply a colossal lack of faith in the Holy
Spirit's promises to preserve the Church, there can be raised a counter-
charge: is it also a lack of faith to deny that the Holy Spirit, if it
wills, can bind itself not only to word and sacrament but also to certain
perduring, concrete, structured expressions of truth?[10]

4. When historical thinking is appropriated by theology, one result is
to make a very clear separation between divine and human agency in the
world. What previous theology deemed miraculous deeds, performable only by
a divine person, historical criticism (as employed by Küng) defines as
post-resurrection interpretations of Jesus by the primitive communities.
The positive theological significance of such a separation between God and
man/woman may be seen in this way: it preserves the transcendence and total
otherness of God by confining men and women to very relative and finite
historical modes of existence, yet it also affords a mode through which God
nevertheless can become present to his people in Israel, Christ and Church.
Considered from the positive point of view, the historical analysis impedes
the kind of idolatry which confuses the temporal with the eternal, the human
with the divine, or which tends to restrict and foreshorten God's activity
to any particular event, dogma, word, practice, and so on. Accordingly, in
Küng's analysis, faith is made somewhat independent of historical events
inasmuch as faith must be a free choice; since it is impossible to determine
beyond any historical doubt that there was a factual, historical event such
as the resurrection (or any other miracle), presumably faith is left free;

as Küng explains it, if the resurrection were historically verifiable, faith would not be free but coerced by the evidence and hence no longer faith. At the same time, of course, faith in Christ is unthinkable apart from the event of the resurrection, whether that means apart from an historical event or not.

However, the very same historical analysis that from one perspective may help keep the Church from a certain type of idolatry may encourage another: the elevation of historical categories and historical criteria above that to which they are applied. Certainly there are historians who do not deny a priori the possibility of miracles, but even their disavowal of history's ability to determine such a matter still makes it more difficult to postulate that God could, if God so willed, 'break' or 'suspend' or 'transform' the causal chain and enter history in ways that contravene historical cause and effect.[11] Küng seems quite reluctant to consider seriously this possibility, principally for apologetic reasons.

5. Since historical criticism is so decisive a factor in the formation of the ecumenical hermeneutic, and since the historical-critical method so well serves Küng's apologetic and dogmatic ecumenical principles, in questioning historical criticism in Küngian methodology one is also questioning the ecumenical hermeneutic, or ecumenical theology as such. And, inasmuch as faith also contributes to the formation of the ecumenical hermeneutic, one is questioning also the relationship between faith and history as it applies to ecumenism.

To the earlier questions concerning whether an ecumenical reading of Scripture is ultimately the result of a historical-critical reading of Scripture, Küng could answer that present ecumenical interest is, rather, something that flows from the present faith-consciousness of the Church, which presumably is Spirit-led. But here we encounter a rather difficult

matter in Küngian methodology. Because the ecumenical hermeneutic results
from _faith_ _and_ history, the question of Tradition is raised in a new light:
how important and how reliable is the present-day lived faith-experience
(which Küng and others understand as the desire for reunion) vis-à-vis the
Church's _past_ Tradition? If the present faith is made judge over an
admittedly un-ecumenical past, or if a present awareness is seen as sur-
passing or superseding the past, then the question arises how the present
faith could be so discontinuous with--or at least at variance with--the
past, all within the same Spirit-guided Church. If, further (though this
seems unlikely), the present faith were shown to be ultimately and
exclusively a product of the present _intellectus_ which is then identified
with the present faith, then one age's intellectual framework would again
have come to function normatively in the Church.

Yet precisely here a greater ambiguity is felt. One would hesitate to
say outright that Küng is doing what has just been described, but it is not
wholly clear which comes first for him, historical criticism or ecumenical
faith. In _Justification_ Küng was aware of possibilities for ecumenical
rapprochement in various doctrinal and practical areas besides justification, but at that time he apparently conceived it as a doctrine-
by-doctrine process in which individual controversies would be researched
and areas of possible agreement brought out into the open. But with the
advent of Küng's study of historical criticism, the one-doctrine-at-a-time
approach was evidently superseded by the establishment of overarching
hermeneutical-ecumenical principles which were, after all, made possible by
tenets of historical criticism. And even though historical criticism
relativizes everything, the emphasis on ecumenical unity, and its preoccupation with the "one Christ," is a way to overcome 'absolute relativity' and restore to faith its need for certainty about this Jesus. The

relativization extends to all historically conditioned understandings of Jesus in dogma, art and practice, but Jesus Christ himself stays constant and hence becomes the one non-relative factor in faith. Ecumenical theology capitalizes on this single common bond, and holds moreover that only Scripture (which is the theological source common to all Christians) reliably and authoritatively announces and attests this Jesus Christ. This position on Scripture, of course, is defended on grounds of (ecumenical) faith and (critical) history. Consequently, even though perhaps in chronological terms Küng's interest in ecumenism came first, in overall methodological terms one may at least wonder whether it continues to come first, or whether the current _intellectus_, as shaped by historical thinking, somehow precedes and informs his ecumenical theology.

It is very difficult to evaluate ecumenical theology from within the current age. The modern emergence of ecumenical efforts may indeed be the work of the unifying Spirit in the Church; this seems to be the thinking of Vatican II. And it would be quite odd to say that because of certain problems which attach to a particular theological method, ecumenical inquiry should be placed in abeyance until such methodological problems are solved. It is difficult to imagine that any other theological method could so ably further ecumenical exchange; this means only that questions at least can and should be raised about the relationship between historical criticism and ecumenism. Would ecumenical theology be possible apart from an historical interpretation of Scripture? If the answer is no (which is again unlikely), then ecumenical theology—and the whole idea of ecumenical reunion—would seem to be made contingent on a prevailing _intellectus_, one not necessarily compulsory on the basis of Scripture. This is obviously untenable in a theology and methodology which believes its _norma normans_ to be Scripture.[12]

6. In the section on "Errors in Tradition" in Chapter III, the point
was made that any ascription of error to the past comes about only when a
present standard and a future hope are read back into history, and past
events are judged alongside this standard. The present criterion for Küng
is ecumenicity: whatever in the past promoted division or continues in the
present to impede reunion is deemed to be in error. The ecumenical
hermeneutic was shown in Chapter I to be one consequence of the historical-
critical method, and although it was explained that faith, too, plays a
crucial role in the formation of the hermeneutic, it is evidently predominantly historical criticism by which Küng finds passage to the possibilities
of ecumenical reunion. Related to this is his intimation in Infallible?
that the oldest, common, ecumenical tradition is more normative than the
practices and teachings of the (unecumenical or un-catholic) "Roman" Church
of the middle ages onward. This, too, follows from the ecumenical hermeneutic, and therefore reflects the influence of historical criticism in
the assessment of Tradition. According to Küng's own definition of catholicity, however, Tradition cannot be circumscribed to mean that Church
history prior to the schism with the east is more correct or more normative
than subsequent (Roman Catholic) history, even though the original catholic
Tradition is distinct from the Roman or Orthodox or Protestant tradition. (cf. TC 261ff.)

In the same matter of the present determining the interpretation of the
past, we must note that Küng has openly and frequently detached himself from
the Enlightenment idealist view of history (A 173) which, he maintains,
partially accounts for the promulgation of the last two Marian and two papal
dogmas under the development of dogma framework. At the same time, we may
wonder whether Küng himself has subscribed to an incipient philosophy of
history, one not itself based in the New Testament. Readers are given the

impression that all his views are derived from Scripture itself; even Küng does not believe he is evaluating the past in light of a present norm, but would see his enterprise as letting the original gospel arbitrate the present. But the question raised above emerges here also, are Scripture and Tradition accessible only through a medium alien to both? The area of the philosophy of history is indeed complex, and one cannot demand that Küng enter into an investigation of it. Yet it is nonetheless true that a theology of history is operative in Küng's ecumenical hermeneutic and therefore it stands in need of additional clarification. From the standpoint of systematic theology, Küng's method could only be strengthened if he were to engage in reflection on these areas which require an admittedly more "metaphysical" discussion.

7. The entire enterprise of conciliar exegesis proceeds under the direction of historical criticism. No one would dispute the valuable contributions to our knowledge of the history of dogma. But it cannot be overlooked that the same critical questions which arise concerning the foundations of historical criticism in relation to Scripture have bearing also in the matter of councils. Conciliar definitions were expressions of the Church's faith at a given time; historical method seeks out the greater unity among such definitions because of its conviction that despite relative and diverse formulations, the faith expressed remains faith in the one same Lord.

It is apparently as painful a process for the Church to extend historical criticism to Tradition as it was to Scripture. The difficulty the Church has experienced in this regard stems from its apprehension about the eroding effects of historical methods on Church Tradition and ecclesiastical authority. The Roman Catholic Church does not believe its councils to be unqualifiedly historically conditioned, but Spirit-assisted, even infallible guides to Christian truth. This is a view not easy to reconcile with Küng's critical-historical view which relativizes conciliar definitions to a much greater degree. And no matter how much an analysis such as Küng's tries to preserve the element of faith in Jesus Christ as the constant factor amidst all relativity, the troubling implication remains that the definitions of the dogmatic tradition, which formerly presented this Christ to the Church, are no longer very reliable. The Church is therefore involved in a precarious dilemma between admitting a degree of relativity in its definitions, yet insisting that it may make error-free definitions as well. The last point is a problem for it to work out; the issue has been acutely raised by Küng, though in a way obviously not acceptable to the Roman Catholic teaching office. Still, the Church must justify theologically and historically why, once it attributes partial historicity to its dogmas, some still are exempt a priori from error. On one point at least the Church is correct: as much caution is necessary in conciliar exegesis as in scriptural exegesis, and care must be taken that the method does not come to dominate the material.

8. The shift in what Küng considers the final norm for theology and for "being a Christian" (from "Scripture which is the Word of God" to "Jesus Christ who is attested in Scripture") (cf. Chap. II above) raises an interesting question about the ultimate criterion of truth. Christian truth is not the same as a set of propositions which require assent. Christians believe not in the Bible, nor in Tradition, nor in the Church, nor in dogma, but in Jesus Christ himself. (OBC 163) Consequently both the criterion for Christian truth and truth itself are one and the same, according to Küng. But is the Jesus Christ of the gospel--the "real Christ"--accessible except through an historical-critical analysis?

We may ask in all honesty what Küng actually means by saying, "Jesus
Christ himself, as he is attested in the original witnesses of the New
Testament is the norma normans." (Cf. W&W 162) The appeal to "original New
Testament witnesses" means simply that to the eyes of faith, Scripture
"becomes the Word of God," it testifies in a unique and authoritative way to
Jesus Christ, and thus it is this apostolic witness which is decisive for
the Church of all later centuries. There is surely no doubt that, as he
says, Scripture has its authority by virtue of the one it announces. Yet it
is not clear why it could not be said that Tradition--even, granting Küng's
distinction, the catholic Tradition--likewise has its authority by virtue of
the one it announces. In no way would Jesus Christ cease to be the ultimate
norm if it were admitted that the "Jesus Christ attested in Scripture" must
be mediated by (though not supplanted by) the "Jesus Christ in the dogmatic
tradition." But when the only thing said is "Jesus Christ is the ultimate
norm," and this apart from any mention of a mediation by Tradition, one may
wonder to what degree Jesus Christ is even mediated by Scripture, since
Scripture is itself mediated by historical criticism. The secondary status
of Tradition does not obviate its authority; its task is still to expound
and mediate Scripture to the present.

A Question of Tradition

It is not our intent in these final remarks to furnish Hans Küng with a
list of areas he "should" consider further. However, we have looked at the
salient areas of Küng's methodology which present themselves for critical
questioning, and by taking note of the disparity between the formal and
applied levels of methodology, we were able to ponder to what degree Küng's
theoretical methodology does not preclude his holding some problematic
positions. We would like to advance this critique by inquiring about the
most controverted outcome of his theological method: his view of Tradition.

It was in this context that the question of Küng's catholicity first arose, thus it should also be the context within which we venture an answer.

Apostolicity and Catholicity

One might well say that the question of Tradition is not only methodological but theological as well, for the Church has always believed that Tradition is one of the media by which revelation is preserved and handed on in the Church. The methodological issue concerns how the Church (or theology) is to view, measure, adjudge and employ the heterogeneous manifestations of its faith, including the various witnesses of Scripture, up through the panoply of traditions and Tradition. Hans Küng's answer to the methodological question is quite clear: Tradition is the norma normata, which means that as a source and norm, the Church (or theology) is to view and employ it in an entirely secondary way; Tradition is always for Küng radically subordinated to Scripture.

The theological counterpart to this methodological issue pertains to different theological definitions of Tradition. Here we begin to see the problems with Küng's view of Tradition. First of all, as noted in Chapter III above, with the exception of the 1957 book on justification (which was written before his historical-critical studies), Küng does not define what he means by the term, except to call it the norma normata. Not infrequently he mentions certain elements that belong to Tradition--the Canon; definitions of councils; past theological thought--but this is quite different from explicitly and positively explaining what it is that is norma normata. If indeed he means by the term only the three elements mentioned, then serious problems remain, for he would have construed a rather limited definition of Tradition without ever explaining on what basis these three elements had been singled out. Moreover, Küng would have explained Tradition only as a source, not as a theological norm.

To further this discussion, we may be permitted to extrapolate Küng's theological view of Tradition from what we have seen to be his methodological view of Tradition. Based on the fact that his methodological stance regarding Tradition is predominantly historical-critical in origin, it follows that his theological view likewise would be historical-critical. And so, if we were to apply to Scripture and Tradition the historical-critical principle which runs, "the original text is always normative for any translation of it," then, in the analogy, Tradition would consist of numerous 'translations' or re-interpretations of Scripture, with Scripture being analogous to an original text.[13] In this case, Tradition would appear to consist of everything in the Church's whole history not committed to writing in Scripture; this would include all practices and professions of faith in the Church's rather extensive past which have in one way or another reflected or comprised opinions and practices based on Scripture (evolutio secundum evangelium) as well as those (in Küng's opinion) not necessarily grounded in Scripture (evolutio praeter or contra evangelium). Since he does not say otherwise, there is nothing to prevent the reader from concluding that this is what he might mean theologically by Tradition.

There is a closely related second problem. Since he does not exactly define the term, he is free to use it in dissimilar ways, depending on the context. In some instances he appears to use it to refer to the theological source which may be apposed to Scripture, and the impression is given that there is universal agreement as to what "Tradition" per se means.[14] At other times, too numerous to mention, Tradition seems to mean vaguely the whole of Church history without deference to any particular segment of that history. In other cases the term is qualified, as in "the earliest common ecumenical tradition of the first millenium," or "the apostolic tradition." At still other times, within one passage there may be an equivocation of usages. (Cf. Inf 111f.; TC 357, 424) But in no one of these cases can the reader be certain that he or she understands how Küng intends Tradition to be understood as a norm.

And yet, such an uncritical idea of Tradition would seem unwieldy for theological method, because equal weight would have to be distributed among all elements in Tradition. And so, even though one would search in vain for a theological definition of Tradition, one may, on the basis of our methodological approach, discern an operative though admittedly hidden theological definition of Tradition. Küng certainly does not make use of an explicit differentiation between the one binding Tradition and the numerous traditions, or between 'active' and 'passive' Tradition in Vatican II's sense. And certainly he is not obliged to make use of such distinctions. However, what the methodological analysis has shown is that Küng apparently regards the one binding Tradition to be the catholic (or ecumenical) Tradition, or those aspects (especially the Canon, definitions of faith and past theological positions) which are deemed in accord with "the origins," or with the gospel. All else (evolutio secundum or contra evangelium) belong to traditions, important perhaps at a particular point in the Church's history, but not decisive nor necessarily even of great consequence for the present Church. Above all, these traditions are not necessarily catholic, hence it is on this basis Küng can consider certain Roman Catholic practices or professions of faith (which Roman Catholics regard as belonging to Tradition) as belonging to tradition.[15]

Influencing Küng's criterion in this is a distinction which came to the foreground most decidedly in the infallibility issue. As we found above, his argument in Infallible? An Inquiry and in Fehlbar? hinged on his view that Vatican I's definition of papal infallibility was more "Roman" than "catholic," that the two are not necessarily identical with each other,

that "Roman-Catholic" is a contradictio in adiecto. In light of what he
calls "catholicity in space and time," the theologian's obligation to
tradition becomes the conditio sine qua non of catholicity in theology;
hence the exigence of giving an explicit definition of Tradition becomes all
the more urgent. But in the absence of such precision, one is left to fall
back on the extrapolated definition given above, despite the ambiguity it
entails.

Third, Küng's indefinite idea of Tradition works to his disadvantage in
terms of his basically correct view of catholicity. The historical case he
makes for the distinction between catholicism and Roman Catholicism, or
between catholic Tradition and Roman Catholic traditions, could be
strengthened greatly if he were to speak of Tradition--especially the
catholic Tradition--as being one and the same as the apostolic Tradition.
For the catholic faith is also the apostolic faith. If Küng were to make
explicit that theology is catholic if it is apostolic, then in effect he
would be saying that theology is catholic if it is bound to apostolic faith
or apostolic tradition. In this way, a definite content would be given to
the source called Tradition, and at the same time the rule of faith--
apostolic teaching--would establish the place of Tradition and traditions as
theological norms.

Moreover, Küng's claim that catholicity in exegesis consists in loyalty
to the whole of Scripture also could be made even more compelling, if the
catholic faith were explicitly connected with the apostolic faith.
Scripture itself contains many levels of apostolic traditions about Jesus;
indeed, in one sense, the New Testament is nothing other than the original
apostolic tradition committed to writing, and so only in the sense of its
form (not its content) does it differ from other apostolic traditions.[16] As
mentioned above, when Küng speaks of Tradition, it is not clear whether he

has in mind the apostolic tradition or not, hence the impression is often (if unwittingly) given that Tradition begins after Scripture, since Tradition always has such a derivative or secondary connotation for Küng. This, of course, overlooks the fact that apostolic tradition existed before any Scripture was even recorded, much less made canonical. (TC 424ff.)

In this connection, we may return for a moment to the Canon. It was on the basis of practice, not theological hermeneutics, that the Canon of Scripture was decided, which Küng of course also maintains.[17] The norm for deciding was the apostolic faith preserved already in the Church's earliest tradition. Küng does not demur from saying it was the Church which decided the Canon, but what is perhaps not explicit enough is that it was the catholic church, on the basis of its apostolic faith, which fixed the canonical limits. In this connection, an additional factor seems to be missing, as W. Kasper points out: apostolic succession in the office of bishop.[18] When the apostolic succession is made independent of the office of bishop, Kasper continues, it is untied from the concrete community. In the first centuries, he writes, the Church had three bulwarks against heresy: the Canon of Scripture, the apostolic tradition, and apostolic succession in the office of bishop; these formed as indissoluble a unity, Kasper asserts, as do Scripture and Tradition. And he rightly points out that we have access to the "origins" of the Church only through this three-fold concrete work of the Church.[19]

Küng, on the other hand, seems to collapse the distinctions Kasper so carefully makes. It is not possible to go into a detailed examination of Küng's theory of apostolic succession;[20] suffice it to say here that according to his developed position, the whole Church (not just the bishops) succeeds the apostles in history through the Spirit. This is made concrete in two ways: first, agreement with the apostolic witness in Scripture is

guaranteed by adherence to the Canon, and second, continuity in the
apostolic ministry takes place through service, including service in office.
with every member of the Church serving according to his or her charism. In
connection with the first of these, Küng affirms the existence of the
apostolic tradition, its preservation in Scripture and its ultimate delimitation in the Canon. (TC 356f.) Yet, the de-emphasis on apostolic office
raises the question of Tradition from another angle: how is the original
form of the Church's faith (the apostolic faith attested in Scripture) to be
transmitted or mediated by the post-apostolic Church?

In the methodological arena one speaks of carrying on apostolic faith
by appealing to the criteria on which the Church can rely; theologically,
one speaks of what "Tradition" is, and how through it the Holy Spirit
"brings the Church into all truth." For example, methodologically speaking,
the Roman Catholic Church adheres to the teachings of its magisterium
(teaching office of the bishopric) in order to decide what does or does not
belong to the apostolic faith; theologically speaking, the same Church
believes its teaching office to be vested by the Spirit with a special
charism to transmit, interpret and on occasion infallibly teach divine revelation. Or, methodologically speaking, the Orthodox Church stresses ecumenical councils; theologically speaking, it believes these councils to be
specially assisted by the Holy Spirit. Or, methodologically speaking, the
Protestant sola scriptura (though no longer understood as anti-Tradition) is
informed by the theological reluctance to identify the Spirit with a particular agency outside the Bible. And so, methodologically speaking, Küng
asserts that the ultimate and non-relative criterion the Church must follow
in order to discern and maintain its apostolic faith is Jesus Christ
attested in Scripture; theologically speaking, Küng believes the Holy Spirit

cannot be identified with or restricted to a structure like the office of
bishop or the dogmatic tradition promulgated by that office.

Again, then, once apostolic succession is separated from the office of
bishop, what would Küng be willing to accept as authentic means for the
transmission of the apostolic and catholic faith, if not the magisterium?
Once apostolic succession is disengaged from the office of bishop, the seat
of authority in the Church shifts accordingly. Bishops no longer are the
sole custodians of Tradition; rather, authority is distributed among all
apostolic offices and ministries. For Küng, the office of teacher is distinct from that of bishop, thus theological authority stands alongside, not
beneath episcopal authority. At this point the further question arises: on
what grounds, according to what criteria, and by virtue of what authority,
would the somewhat disenfranchised bishops rule that a theology is no longer
catholic or apostolic? Is the magisterium competent to adjudicate the finer
points of theological argumentation? Clearly, a theology is catholic only
if it is methodologically and theologically bound to the apostolic tradition; but what obligation on the part of the theologian towards the magisterium is implied therewith?

Seen in this light, to ask, Is Küng still Catholic? is to put in
theological form the methodological question about his position vis-à-vis
Tradition. His distinction between catholicism and Roman Catholicism is
historically valid, and his firm intent to consider himself a catholic
theologian in that sense must be taken seriously. One might venture to say
that Küng is evidently no longer Roman Catholic--nor would he wish to be--if
a pre-condition for this is accepting without qualification Vatican I's
definition of papal infallibility or Chalcedon's Christological formulation.
However, this does not mean Küng is still not a catholic theologian, if
catholicity is identified with ecumenicity. As he has defined the term, it

would be quite correct to say, "the catholic theologian is also an ecumenical theologian," because, "the catholic Tradition is also the ecumenical Tradition."

And yet the weakness remains that Küng's definition of catholicity and hence of catholic Tradition does not make adequately clear its relationship to apostolicity and thus to apostolic tradition. Ecumenical theology, too, must reckon with the significance of the one binding Tradition and its relationship to the various (confessional) traditions; above all it must take a stand on what it is willing to accept as authentic means for the transmission of apostolic faith. In the course of his or her reflections, the ecumenically-minded theologian would do well to ponder Küng's own words: "There is no route to the Lord which bypasses the apostles." (TC 356)

Summary

One is led finally to ask about the suitability of Küng's theological methodology, since it is accompanied by the difficulties explored throughout this chapter. The critical questions raised in the foregoing are certainly not unanswerable, and Küng's method is doubtless defensible, despite various problems which it leaves untended. The principal area of controversy is, as we have seen, the normativity of Tradition.

We have seen from various standpoints that Küng is indeed very involved with the Tradition of the Church, through his extensive conciliar research and through wider historical investigation. The matter of the Canon also underscores that, theoretically speaking, he chooses to bind himself to the Church even though materially speaking the impression is left that he gives preferential treatment to certain testimonies (biblical and dogmatic) over others. In addition, we saw at a few critical junctures that historical knowledge in some ways dominates faith. And so, despite Küng's insistence to the contrary, one could say that perhaps he has not done enough in his

theology and methodology to guard against the impression that his is an
overly subjective interpretation of Scripture, or that he has, despite
theoretical assurances to the contrary, in effect foreshortened Tradition by
letting it stand under the judgment of historical criticism. In the matter
of catholicity, Küng ardently believes himself to be theologically and
methodologically bound to the catholic Tradition, as he so defines it. But
his historical-critical view of Tradition, with its attendant dangers of
overlooking the Church's living Tradition as its context and presupposition,
brings him into a clear and inevitable collision with the Roman Catholic
Church.

Nevertheless, it would be inequitable to dismiss Küng's entire
theological endeavor simply because of difficulties which inhere in the
method. One can not deny that critical evaluation must continue, especially
regarding the matter of catholicity and Tradition. Further reflection on
theological methodology--whether that of Küng or of other theologians--is
certainly warranted by many of these considerations, and one might learn
from all this that in any theology there is bound to be much that is true,
much that is of value, regardless of accompanying methodological problems.
Our own view is that Küng often has been misunderstood and misread (or not
read at all), due perhaps as much to the fact that he not infrequently
expresses himself in a way that lends itself to misinterpretation, as to the
equally unfortunate fact that a great many theologians and Church officials
have not endeavored to comprehend his theology in the context of his
methodology, and on that basis to make their evaluation. The first factor
is certainly beyond anyone's control but Hans Küng's; for the second, it may
be hoped that the present investigation has been something of a counterbalance, and that it may prompt further study of this undeniably gifted
theologian.

FOOTNOTES

Introduction

[1]Joseph F. Costanzo, The Historical Credibility of Hans Kung (sic)
(North Quincy, Mass.: The Christopher Publishing House, 1979). This is the
first volume to appear (as of this writing). In preparation by Costanzo are
Catholic Ecclesiology and Kung's (sic) Ecclesial Paradeigma, and The Theological Gnoseology of Hans Kung (sic). The first volume is thoroughly
negative, and tries to identify Kung's 'aporiae'. Costanzo, it may be
noted, is not a trained theologian.

Chapter I

[1]Some consequences of this approach will be reviewed below in Chapter
V.

[2]See the work done by theologian Thomas F. Torrance on science and
religious epistemology, in Theological Science (Oxford University Press,
1969), and The Ground and Grammar of Theology (University of Virginia,
1980).

[3]An example is that black holes are at this point mere mathematical
constructions; there may or may not be a 'real' black hole in space which
conforms to the theoretical construct.

[4]For theology, the Enlightenment philosophical heritage poses an
immense epistemological problem vis-à-vis faith, but not one that cannot be
solved. Although it cannot be argued here in detail--it would require a
rather lengthy investigation--it seems that to escape the agnostic and
relativistic consequences of Kantian metaphysics, one needs to show either
(1) that there is some standard which can measure both the method and
results, a standard not drawn from either, that is, a standard not itself
entirely contingent on the historical, the relative, the human. Or (2),
that the standard used to measure history is itself the origin and ground of
history; Küng opts for a variation on the latter of these.

[5]Thus methodology always has to do with content (data to be analyzed or
the actual conclusions reached), though methodology is distinguishable from
content for purposes of analysis.
An illustration from the physical sciences is apposite. A fifth-
century B.C. physician, looking at diseased tissue with an unaided eye,
might conclude that the disease is a punishment from the gods for evil-
doing. A twentieth-century physician, looking at diseased tissue through an
electron microscope, might conclude something about its viral causes. In
our schema, the point of origin is scientific knowledge at a given point in
time (one which may not exclude theonomous explana-tions); the conduit is
the means of observing the data (human eye or electron microscope); the end
point is the conclusion based on the two distinguishable moments.

[6]The question could arise, from what sources is the way of knowing
drawn, and does this not place the sources as the first moment in
methodology? If this were really the case, one would still have to explain

how it is that different individuals, even different disciplines, may begin
with identical sources but view them quite differently. This indicates that
one's way of knowing is logically antecedent to what is known.

[7]This is by no means an exhaustive account of types of methods.

[8]Clearly, history claims to be a rigorously scientific discipline, and
equally clearly, science involves a great deal of interpretation beyond its
sheer calculations.

[9]For example, the event does not have to be something extraordinary
like virginal conception, which a scientist obviously cannot accept, but
could be the more common yet not for that reason less mysterious event of
God's calling women and men to have life with Him in Jesus' name. When
those so called by God do respond, the scientist (and here also the social-
scientist) might remark that the response is the result of genetic inclina-
tion, neurotic need or socialization. In principle, for the scientist there
is not necessarily any warrant for believing the cause to be God Himself.

[10]This is Van A. Harvey's term, in The Historian and the Believer (New
York: Macmillan & Co., 1966).

[11]"Theologian" here means primarily dogmatic or systematic theologians.
There are undoubtedly biblical and historical scholars who are also
Christian believers, and even non-believers who consider themselves yet
theologians. But it is hard to know exactly what the latter of these would
mean by their appellation.

[12]Of course "faith" means different things to different theologians,
which partly accounts for the view that faith is an unreasonable prejudice.
As we shall see, Küng comes to terms with this by giving a definition of
faith purged of both anti-rationalistic or excessively rationalistic elements, and describes it more as a free decision made through God's grace.

[13]'Heretical' is the religious judgment equivalent to the logical
judgment of 'untrue'. Throughout its history, the faith of the Church seems
to have been remarkably able, no matter how many decades it may have taken,
to ferret out the un-true from the true, heretical (heterodox) from
orthodox.

[14]Theologians are quite amenable to the insights of psychology, but when
it becomes a matter of choosing a psychological explanation or a biblical
one, in some cases the theologian would have to choose scripture. (For
example, "Religion serves to repress people's drives, desires and needs" vs.
"The truth shall set you free.")

[15]Faith and history are not the only alternatives in theological method.
Other methods center around faith and dogma, others around dogma only, and
so on. It is the precise weighting of each element that is decisive in the
method.

[16]This indicates that already in the epistemology there is content: the
commitment to the transcendent God who reveals himself to us in history.
Although the source for Küng's faith is the Bible, this simply supports our
claim that method is conditioned by sources and vice versa.

[17]Chapter V will examine whether faith is pre-eminent in Küng's applied methodology as well.

[18]See below under "The Küngian Hermeneutic," as well as Does God Exist?, Part A., on the scientific standards which Küng thinks theology should emulate (logic; clarity; precision; et. al.), and those which he renounces (exclusion of any higher authority).

[19]Küng's M.A. thesis was also on Barth's doctrine of justification. (W&W 14)

[20]See also "Justification and Sanctification in the New Testament," reprinted in Hans Küng. Theologians Today, ed. Martin Redfern (New York: Sheed & Ward, 1972): 9-48. See also OBC 402-410.

[21]Cf. Chapter IV below; this is the reasoning behind Küng's position in Infallible? An Inquiry, that the insistence on a priori propositional infallibility (in the face of God's promises to the Church) is ultimately a lack of faith in God's Spirit.

[22]See OBC 356-381; see also "Zur Entstehung des Auferstehungsglaubens," Theologische Quartalschrift 154 (1974): 103-117.

[23]See also H. Küng, Was in der Kirche bleiben muss, (Theologische Meditationen 30), Benziger, 1973.

[24]H. Küng, "Being A Christian," The Tablet (19 October 1974), pp. 1021f. See also Signposts For the Future (New York: Doubleday, 1978), p. 41; W&W 131f.

[25]See for example, Van A. Harvey, The Historian and the Believer (New York: The Macmillan Co., 1966); Maurice Mandelbaum, The Problem of Historical Knowledge (New York: Harper & Row, Harper Torchbooks, 1967); Edgar Krentz, The Historical-Critical Method (Philadelphia: Fortress Press, 1975); Henri-Irénée Marrou, The Meaning of History (Baltimore: Helicon, 1966); James D. Smart, The Strange Silence of the Bible in the Church (Philadelphia: The Westminister Press, 1970); Patrick Gardiner, Theories of History (New York: Free Press, 1959); Karl Löwith, Meaning in History. The Theological Implications of the Philosophy of History (Chicago: University Press, 1941).

[26]"What is the Criterion for a Critical Theology? Reply to Gregory Baum," Commonweal 94 (1971), p. 328.

[27]See TC 20f., OBC 129ff. See also Edgar Krentz's confident claim, "Historical criticism is self-correcting. Arbitrary reconstructions and wild theories are doomed to rejection by scholars who measure them against the texts. Texts are uncompromising masters who drive out bad criticism by calling forth better evaluation. The history of criticism shows how the process of correction goes on." In The Historical-Critical Method (Philadelphia: Fortress Press, 1975), p. 66.

[28]At the end of Küng's book on Barth (written prior to historical-critical studies), he wrote an excursus entitled, "The Redeemer in God's Eternity." Therein he argues for the eternal pre-existence of God's Word, saying that his explanation is entirely in line with the New Testament

witness (J 293), with patristic theology (J 295), and grounds the "predominant place of Mary in God's plan of salvation" (J 299). This Christology "from above" is obviously the counterview of Küng's developed Christology. See the discussion in W&W 164f., and the lively debate at the 1977 Stuttgart Colloquium, in W. Jens, hrsg., Um nichts als die Wahrheit. Deutsche Bischofskonferenz contra Hans Küng (Piper, 1978), pp. 321f., 243, 260ff.

[29]Küng points out that his is not a decision in favor of exegetical rather than dogmatic Christology, nor progressive over conservative. Rather, he says, there is a growing consensus today in exegetical and dogmatic theologians from different schools for a starting point 'from below'. (MG 593f.)

[30]OBC 448-449; MG 592; see also W. Kasper, "Christologie von unten?", in Leo Scheffczyk, Grundfragen der Christologie heute (Freiburg: Herder, 1975), p. 153.

[31]In MG 599. He takes the term over from his student, J. Nolte, Cf. W. Kasper's remarks in "Christsein ohne Tradition?" in Diskussion über Hans Küngs "Christ sein" (Mainz, 1976), p. 21.

[32]In "Reponse to Avery Dulles," Union Seminary Quarterly Review 27 (1972), p. 146. Cf. OBC 472ff.

[33]One of the clearest illustrations of this is Küng's position on the historicity of miracles. In "Die Gretchenfrage des christlichen Glaubens? Systematische Überlegungen zum neutestamentlichen Wunder," (Theologische Quartalschrift 152 (1972): 124-233), he argues that the starting point for interpreting miracle stories must be the fact that they are not eyewitness accounts, not scientifically proved documents, not historical, medical or psychological records, but popular narratives which stand fully in the service of proclaiming Christ. (p. 216) Still, miracles cannot be dismissed unilaterally as unhistorical. Küng proceeds to distinguish among strata in the earliest tradition (216ff.), and emphasizes that the gospels were written in light of the risen and exalted Lord, for the community. (p. 219) Historical investigation yields nothing more than this, even if it starts out free from an a priori exclusion of the possibility of miracles. But, Küng continues, whoever maintains miracles in the strict sense of God's breaking natural law, has the burden of proof. It is better to speak of 'signs' (Zeichen) than to use the ambiguous term "Wunder". (p. 220)

[34]Küng writes, "Faith presupposes my personal decision. If it could be proved it would no longer be faith. It should however be a well-founded, responsible decision, made after reflection. But faith should not try to establish historical facts from its own resources. Certainties of faith may not be presented as scientific conclusions . . . ." (OBC 191)

[35]The gamut of positions runs from "innate ideas of God" to "God breaking through time and space realities." The former is easily refutable, the latter obviously more problematic, given our present scientific-historicist legacy.

[36]Cf. Joseph Fitzer, "Hegel and the Incarnation. A Response to Hans Küng," Journal of Religion 52 (1972): 240-267.

[37]OBC 309; cf. n. 18. The criterion here is biblical; the matter of sources and criteria will be taken up in Chapter II below.

[38]Küng writes also that Christian theology should be aware that when it criticizes Hegel's presentation of the becoming of God and the suffering of God, it permits itself also to be criticized since it appears to presuppose the possibility and reality of both. (MG 524)

[39]MG 543. See also MG Exkurs II, "Kann Gott Leiden?" and Gott und das Leid (Theologisches Meditationen 18), (Benziger, 1967).

[40]EG 186; see also MG Chap. VIII.2, and MG Exkurs III, "Die Dialektik der Eigenschaften Gottes." See also OBC 82f.

[41]"Reply to Gregory Baum: What is the Criterion For a Critical Theology?" Commonweal 94 (1971), p. 328; see also OBC 309, and OBC 377 where he writes, "The history of man is taken up in the history of God and . . . the history of God is worked out in the history of man . . . ."

[42]Ibid., p. 320, emphasis mine.

[43]Cf. the debate between Küng and the German Bishops' Conference at the 1977 Stuttgart Colloquium, in W. Jens, hrsg., Um nichts als die Wahrheit (Piper, 1978), especially pp. 260ff. See also KD 113 and W&W 154f.

[44]It may be remarked parenthetically that Küng criticizes Kasper for not following through far enough with historical-critical principles. He writes, "Würde Kasper die von ihm bejahte historisch-kritische Methode auch in den lehramtlich belasteten ("unfehlbaren") Lehrpunkten wie Naherwartung und Jungfrauengeburt ohne hermeneutischen Kompromiss konsequent durchhalten, so käme er auch dort zu ähnlichen Schlüssen wie ich." (Ibid., pp. 173-174) It is instructive that Küng asks Kasper whether he (Kasper) can so readily equate the New Testament Jesus Christ with the Jesus Christ of the dogmatic tradition. There is, as Küng says, a different dogmatic preunderstanding attested by such an equivalence. See below, Chapter III.

[45]Küng's reinterpretation has generated a great deal of controversy; though we are unable to discuss the Christological debate, the reader may refer to the documentation of the German Bishops' Conference, including their triple Declarations against Küng's Christology, in Jens, Um nichts als die Wahrheit, pp. 146-373 and in KD. See also W. Kasper, "Christologie von unten? Kritik und Neuansatz gegenwärtiger Christologie," in L. Scheffczyk, hrsg., Grundfragen der Christologie heute (Herder, 1975), pp. 152-164.

[46]Cf. Medard Kehl, Kirche als Institution (Joseph Knecht, 1976), pp. 123-171.

[47]See below under "Errors in Tradition" in Chapter III.

[48]The English translation (TC 5) reads, "while there are permanent factors, there are no absolutely irreformable areas." The original German reads slightly differently: "Es gibt bleibende Konstanten, aber keine von vornherein irreformablen Bezirke." (Die Kirche, p. 15).

[49]Again, our intent here is only the delineation of the formal ontological aspects, hence this is not intended as a presentation of Küng's views on ecumenism.

[50]Obviously one enters here into the very complex theological and methodological problem of sources and their ordering (for example, whether Tradition is just as normative as Scripture for authorizing later developments). This is the substance of the following two chapters.

[51]See, for example, Colm O'Grady, "Hans Küng's Ecumenical Programme. An Enquiry," Clergy Review 56 (1971): 922-932, and Joseph Costanzo, The Historical Credibility of Hans Kung (sic) (North Quincy, Massachusetts: The Christopher Publishing House, 1979).

Chapter II

[1]It is hardly necessary to give a citation for this, else one would need to refer to virtually every page and argument in Küng's writings.

[2]See Edgar Krentz, The Historical-Critical Method (Philadelphia: Fortress Press, 1975), and Van A. Harvey, The Historian and the Believer, (New York: Macmillan, 1966), Chapter I.

[3]We will return to this in Chapter III below.

[4]"Karl Barths Lehre vom Wort Gottes als Frage an die katholische Theologie," in Einsicht und Glaube, hrsg. J. Ratzinger u. Heinrich Fries (Freiburg: Herder, 1962): 75-97. The essay was included in a Festschrift for Gottlieb Söhngen's seventieth birthday in 1962 so it was likely prepared in 1961. What is essential to remember is during 1960-1962 Küng was involved in an extensive exchange with Ernst Käsemann at Tübingen which affected immeasurably Küng's own position on Scripture. (See W&W 16, also pp. 157ff.). This 1962 essay indicated Küng's growing dissatisfaction with traditional Catholic teaching on the Word of God, in light of the historical-critical studies which opened up a whole new world for him.

[5]It has been objected that Küng's method consists in allowing Catholic doctrine to be questioned by the Protestant principle of the sovereignty of God; in other words, Küng has let Barth dictate in what areas Catholic theology fails in his view to honor God's transcendence. See Colm O'Grady, "Hans Küng's Ecumenical Programme, An Enquiry," Clergy Review 56 (1971), pp. 923ff. In fact it is much more complex; Küng's questioning by no means ends with Catholic theology; he also persistently questions just as stringently Barth's theology from a Catholic point of view, and then questions both from an historical point of view.
     In the present considerations regarding the Word of God, Chapter I showed that Küng rejects the extreme forms of both natural theology and dialectical theology, in favor of an historical theology. For Küng's opinion of the essential differences between him and Barth, see W&W 140ff. In defense of O'Grady it may be pointed out that his particular article was written in 1971; Küng's other major works such as Menschwerdung Gottes, On Being A Christian and Does God Exist? were not yet available.

[6]"Karl Barths Lehre. . .", pp. 79f. In other words, the descriptions of the Word of God which Küng himself had given as representative of Catholic teaching up to 1957 (in Justification), he now found unsatisfactory. Apparently Küng thought that even if one investigated the formal pronouncements of the Roman Catholic theological tradition (whose representatives he cites as support in Justification), one would be hard-pressed to find an adequate basis for countering the objections of someone like Barth. See n. 5 above.

[7]See "Karl Barths Lehre. . .", pp. 80-94 for Küng's summary of Barth's position.

[8]See also SC 315ff. There Küng tries to answer Barth's criticisms of Roman Catholicism on various ecclesiological points of controversy.

[9]"Karl Barths Lehre. . .", pp. 94f. Küng's counter-question to Barth belongs of course to a much wider debate over natural theology. See Justification, pp. 278ff. Küng does not consider Barth's answer the most satisfactory one. See, for example, EC 276, n. 3.

[10]"Karl Barths Lehre. . .", pp. 95-96.* This kind of argumentation is reminiscent of the line Küng directs against Barth in Justification, pp. 32; 92-96; 260-261. In each case Küng's criticism is that Barth does not take seriously enough the human side of grace and justification or, in the present instance, of the human word in the Bible. Barth's fear of usurping God's sovereignty takes the form of (over-) emphasis on the divine; for Küng, the lack of correct emphasis on the human turns out to be the real usurpation of God's sovereignty since it does not take seriously God's real accomplishment in the human subject. Another way of saying this is that Barth's methodology is not historical enough.

[11]See W&W 157f. Küng certainly learned more from Käsemann than is reflected in this article. In fact, he says that his studies with Käsemann opened his eyes to the charismatic dimension of the Church and the consequences of that for Church office. However, this article best reflects the growing hermeneutical principles of Küng based on historical criticism. This is central for our present purposes.

[12]This is exactly the dilemma Heinrich Schleier found himself facing. After his own investigation into early Catholicism and the New Testament concept of office, Schleier became Roman Catholic after having been Protestant. In Structures of the Church Küng uses Schleier's case to advance his own position.

[13]The majority of the following references are to "Early Catholicism" since it is generally a better translation than that in Structures. Also, the discussion in EC follows a slightly different line, one more suited to our purposes. See also SC 135-151; TC 40-46; Th&Ch 24.

[14]Küng adds, "This can often seem less consistent and less impressive than the powerful onesidedness of expounding one line alone; Paul alone can, in certain circumstances, produce a more consistent and impressive effect than the great complexity of the whole New Testament, and the Paul of Paulinism (purged of his 'sacramentalism' and 'mysticism') a still more consistent and impressive effect than the whole Paul. But the real Paul is

the whole Paul, and the real New Testament is the whole New Testament." (EC 269)

[15]Küng actually prefers Karl H. Schelkle's Catholic exposition of the early community order over Käsemann's. See EC 276, n. 2.

[16]This requires, Küng adds, the cooperation of Rome which has often been less than friendly to exegetes and their findings. See EC 286. As he has said elsewhere, "If in many fields, such as exegesis, history of dogma, comparative religion, etc., the Catholic Church still lags far behind Protestant theology, this lamentable fact is not due to a lack of intelligence or unreadiness to work on the part of Catholic theologians, but to lack of freedom." (FT 59)

[17]SC 148. In The Church Küng says, "It is certainly possible to look impartially for a 'centre' in Scripture, by working exegetically from the New Testament texts rather than dogmatically from established preconceptions. It is of course easier to establish such a centre in negative terms rather than in positive terms, to establish that certain things at any rate are not the heart of Scripture, are peripheral rather than central; but this in itself can be a gain. To establish a positive centre is more difficult because of the basic diversity of the individual New Testament writings. Yet, despite the differences, a discriminating and sensitive interpretation will be able to make out the decisive common links and a fundamental inner coherence . . . ." (TC 19f.) As for what Küng thinks that center is, in his address to the Concilium Congress on September 14, 1970, he said, "The Christian message can be expressed in a word: Jesus as the Christ . . . . The Christian message is this: 'In the light and power of Jesus we are able, in the world of today, to live, to act, to suffer, and to die in a truly human way, because totally dependent on God and totally committed to our fellow human beings'." In Catholic Mind 68 (December, 1970): 28-34. The same text is in OBC 602.

[18]J 113. See also p. 116, Scripture ". . . is the unmediated and manifest Word of God in every sentence . . . ."

[19]Even when we place this statement in its context in Justification the bare impact is not attenuated. The context is a discussion on whether Trent intended "with the same sense of reverence" (Denz. 783) to mean that tradition is a divinely inspired source alongside and equal to Scripture. Küng answers that it is only scripture that is inspired and thus it has a priority which no other source can claim. This will be taken up below in Chapter III.

[20]In "Christsein ohne Tradition?" in Diskussion über Hans Küngs "Christ sein" (Mainz, 1976), pp. 26, 29-30.

[21]It is beyond our scope to discuss individual scriptural interpretations which Küng elaborates. However, we may point out that Küng's use of the critical-historical principle which distinguishes among strata in the New Testament accounts for some of the opposition he encountered from the hierarchy, especially concerning The Church and On Being A Christian. With respect to The Church, which Yves Congar called "a sensational re-entry of Paulinism into Catholic thought," (in "L'Église de Hans Küng," Révue des sciences philosophiques et théologiques 53 (1969), p. 697) the Vatican felt Küng de-emphasized the structured aspect of the Church as set down in the

pastoral epistles. In Küng's scheme, to be sure, these epistles would assume secondary status inasmuch as they are "later" writings. The reader may refer to "Das Römische Veto" in H. Häring u. J. Nolte, hrsg., Diskussion um Hans Küng "Die Kirche" (Freiburg, 1971): 25-31 for a short chronicle of Roman proceedings against Küng, as well as to other contributions to this volume (especially those of Carlos Colombo, Yves Congar, Georges Dejaifve, Hermann Diem, P. Grelot, Rudolf Pesch, Otto Semmelroth, George Tavard). Also, W. Jens' documentation, Um nichts als die Wahrheit, contains some information on this.

Second, with respect to Christology, Küng's de-emphasis of Johannine testimony to a pre-existent Logos (since the fourth gospel is less "histori-cal" than the synoptics), led to the sharpest dissent by the German Bishops' Conference. Cf. "The Stuttgart Colloquium," in W. Jens, op. cit., pp. 225-313 and the three Declarations against Christ sein made by this body, also in Jens. See also Raymond E. Brown, "'On Being a Christian' and Scripture," America 129 (1976): 344f.

[22]Küng cites Denz. 3202-3294; 3411; 3652-3654; 3887.

[23]Article 11 reads: "Therefore, since everything asserted by the inspired authors or sacred writers must be held to be asserted by the Holy Spirit, it follows that the book of Scripture must be acknowledged as teaching firmly, faithfully, and without error that truth which God wanted put into the sacred writings for the sake of our salvation."

[24]Cf. W. Kasper, "Christsein ohne Tradition?," pp. 29-30.

[25]In saying that propositions in the Bible cannot a priori be regarded as infallible, close attention must be paid to Küng's exact choice of words, "a priori regarded." Küng is not saying that infallible propositions in the Bible do not exist; rather, he is saying that there is no a priori certainty that there are infallible propositions, or which ones they might be; the truth of biblical propositions is determined a posteriori, by the Church. We will return to this in subsequent chapters.

[26]W. Kasper also observes this shift in "Christsein ohne Tradition?", p. 27. See also n. 41 below.

[27]For example, "According to Mark 2:26 . . . David had entered the house of God under the high priest Abiathar and eaten the loaves of offering; in fact, however, according to Samuel 21:1ff., it was not under Abiathar, but under his father Ahimelech. In Mt. 27:9, the fulfillment of a prophecy of "Jeremiah" is reported, which is in fact a prophecy of Zechariah (11:12ff.), and so on." (Inf 192)

[28]Küng has not followed Käsemann in setting up a center in the New Testament. If one pays careful attention, he has not chosen any doctrinal center for his hermeneutic; rather, Küng has placed a living person at the center, this Jesus Christ himself. From this center all of Scripture must be interpreted, all Church life must proceed, all doctrine must be formulated.

[29]The Church is also, for Küng, the proper confessional context for theology. See especially Chapter IV below. See also Th&Ch.

[30]It may be noted that Küng's nature/un-nature distinction concerning the reality of the Church is not biblical language. Cf. TC section A.II.

[31]The preference for "resurrection" over "incarnation" reflects more than a choice of individual words. "Resurrection," in Küng's view, expresses an event; "incarnation" expresses a hellenistic manner of explaining God's presence in Jesus.

[32]The exact status of conciliar statements will be clarified under "Tradition," Chapter III below. Here only the normativity of Scripture over councils needs to be mentioned.

[33]Humanae Vitae is not directly the product of a council, but Küng faults it likewise for what he views as its non-foundation in Scripture. See Inf. 31-57.

[34]Küng later remarked that the almost total absence of Catholic exegetical scholars at Vatican II had serious consequences for its theology. "Almost everywhere, particularly in the doctrinal decrees . . . there is lacking a solid exegetical, and often too a solid historical basis." (T 110) See also MG, Chapter VII and Exkurs I, "Der Weg zur klassischen Christologie."

[35]It is not exactly clear what Küng means by saying Scripture should guide the selection of speakers, order of discussions, manner of debates.

[36]See Medard Kehl, Kirche als Institution (Knecht, 1976): 123-171 and H. Häring u. J. Nolte, hrsg., Diskussion um Hans Küng "Die Kirche" (Freiburg, 1971) for discussions of Küng's ecclesiology.

[37]See Chapter III below, "Errors in Tradition."

[38]It is firmly not our intention to enter into the extremely complex problems surrounding the New Testament Canon itself, but only to elucidate Küng's position as that has bearing on his theological method. The two polar statements that need nuancing are (a) the Church decided rightly regarding the New Testament Canon; and (b) Scripture is the norma normans.

[39]There are indications that prior to the formal delineation of the New Testament Canon against Marcion, the Church already had a "roughly defined collection . . . which it was beginning to treat as Scripture." (J. N. D. Kelly, Early Christian Doctrines, pp. 57-58.) Marcion's (heretical) list simply spurred the Church to publicly and formally delimit what already was the case in practice. Still, the final figure of twenty-seven books took over two centuries to reach. (Kelly, pp. 56-60)

[40]It was Marcion's own selective reading of the New Testament testimonies which led him to reject all Jewish elements in the New Testament, along with the entire Old Testament.

[41]W. Kasper points out that the significance of the Canon is not only that the Church stands under Scripture, but it stands over subjective scriptural interpretations of individual theologians. Cf. "Christsein ohne Tradition?" in Diskussion über Hans Küngs "Christ sein" (Mainz, 1976), p. 25.

Chapter III

[1]See, for example, Vatican II's "Dogmatic Constitution on Divine Revelation," in W. Abbott, ed., The Documents of Vatican II (The American Press, 1966).

[2]In the later debate on infallibility with Rahner, Küng insists that he first learned how to look at dogma historically from Rahner, and thus could not at all understand Rahner's denunciation of Küng with respect to his historical interpretation of dogma. Küng shrewdly writes, "he (Rahner) can in fact understand my method, without dialectical artistry, as the legitimate consequence of his own; my historical interpretation of the historicity of dogma as the consequence of his speculative interpretation of the historicity of dogma." "To Get to the Heart of the Matter," Homiletic and Pastoral Review 71 (July, 1971), p. 25.

[3]See also Denz. 1787; 1800. Cp. SC 54; 316ff.

[4]Küng does not indicate what exactly would remain once one removed all human elements from tradition. Apparently the same distinction made with respect to Scripture between the divine Word of God and its expression in human words, is operative also here. Küng cites Franzelin who writes, ". . . only divine traditions are in the strict sense and per se the revealed Word of God and therefore capable of being the object of divine faith." (Franzelin cited in Küng, J 114). But once the 'human account of divine revelation' is stripped of its human elements, only the original revelation would remain, that is, the same revelation attested originally in Scripture. See also CRR 115f.

[5]A comment on Küng's parenthetical remark "(since they are not subject to discussion)" is in order. In the German the same sentence reads, "Die amtlichen kirchlichen Lehrdokumente im besonderen sind dem katholischen Theologen eine äusserst wertvolle und unabdingbare Hilfe für das Sichten der kirchlichen Tradition." (Rechtfertigung. Die Lehre Karl Barths und eine katholische Besinnung. Mit einem Geleitbrief von Karl Barth. (Johannes Verlag, 1957), p. 121.) The word "unabdingbare" does not mean "not subject to discussion" but "irrevocable" or "unalterable." The latter, more nuanced translation safeguards the possibility of discussion and interpretation, despite the finality of a statement may have in terms of its being binding. Cp. CRR 115.

[6]An abbreviated version of much of the material of this section may be found in, "Why Are Dogmatic Pronouncements So Difficult To Make Today?" in The Living Church. Reflections on the Second Vatican Council, trans. Cecily Hastings and N. D. Smith (London: Sheed & Ward, 1963): 295-313.

[7]Several other instances can be found in Christological doctrines especially, as Chapter I acknowledged. See also MG Exkurs I, "Der Weg zur klassischen Christologie."

[8]Barth had objected that at Trent, the Church had "taken over" Christ by identifying itself with Christ, by adding to Scripture its own ecclesiastical tradition, and then extending tradition to cover the whole life of the Church. "At Trent tradition ousted Scripture, at Vatican I real

historical tradition was in turn ousted by the present magisterium of the Church." (TC 240) Küng answers these objections here and in SC 305-351.

[9]Note that Küng uses the conjunction and, not the disjunction, or. See Chapter IV under "Methodological Areas of Dissent."

[10]See also H. Küng, "To Get to the Heart of the Matter," Part II, Homiletic & Pastoral Review (July, 1971), p. 21.

[11]For example, see Pius IX "Syllabus of Errors," in 1864 (Denz. 2905); Vatican I's "Dogmatic Constitution on the Catholic Faith" of 1870 (Denz. 3020, 3028); Pius X "Oath Against Modernism" of 1910 (Denz. 354); Pius XII "Humani Generis" of 1950 (Denz. 3881-3882).

[12]Küng gives as an example the 1934 Barmen Declaration against Nazi socialism. (Inf 132) The choice seems somewhat peculiar, since (1) this Declaration was not made by the Roman Catholic Church, and presumably Küng is wrestling with the problems of Catholic magisterium, and (2) it is not the development of a dogma per se.

[13]From Küng's point of view this is the condition awaiting fulfillment in his own case.

[14]Küng gives the history of the term which may be briefly summarized as follows. The history of this axiom began as early as Ignatius of Antioch, and was based on a literal application of Mk 16:16. Several other Church Fathers followed Ignatius, up through Augustine; scholasticism simply carried on the tradition. Boniface VIII in Unam Sanctum (1302) gave very explicit formulation to the idea that the Roman Catholic Church was necessary for salvation. (Denz. 468-469) But the discovery of the New World challenged the axiom since the majority of the world's population existed outside the Roman Catholic Church; in 1854 Pius IX attenuated the meaning of "outside" to make room for the "invincibly ignorant'. Mystici Corporis in 1943 restated the axiom in an unmitigated form, following which the Jesuit Father Feeney tried to maintain the damnation of all outside the Roman Catholic Church. The Vatican Holy Office declared excommunicate all who held such a position. And Vatican II stated that salvation exists outside the Catholic Church. See TC 403-411, and Christenheit als Minderheit. Die Kirche unter den Weltreligionen. (Einsiedeln, Benziger, 1965).

[15]Küng argues in this connection that although Father Feeney was censured, he operated clearly within the logic of a positivistic approach to doctrine. (T 144)

[16]Küng wrote elsewhere that such an extension of the concept of Church is unjustified because (1) it is not based on the New Testament; (2) it is an unnecessary way to show the possibility of salvation for other Christians; (3) it makes it difficult for missionaries to preach to non-Christians both the value of membership and that all persons of good will already belong to the Church; (4) it is a theological construction and disguised arrogance to impute membership entirely apart from free consent. (TC 317)

[17]Küng's interpretation in brief is that salvation is given through Christ alone, whether one is inside or outside the Church per se (T 148f.; TC 318; Christenheit als Minderheit; OBC.

[18]This is identical to the way Küng views past Christological teachings, especially that of Chalcedon. It is to be respected as giving "expression to a genuine continuity of Christian faith" though its apologetic value is greatly reduced because the terms it uses are no longer intelligible. (OBC 131) See also W. Kasper, "Christsein ohne Tradition?" in Diskussion über Hans Küngs "Christ sein" (Mainz, 1976), p. 20.

[19]The import of this position will be seen in Chapters IV and V below.

[20]Much of this material was later translated in the Op Ed page of The New York Times (Jan. 28, 1980) A17, and recently has been reprinted in CIT 159–165, and MIT 75–87.

[21]Cf. W&W 162f.; also "Ein Appell zur Verständigung," in W. Jens, Um nichts als die Wahrheit, pp. 374–389, and OBC 503.

[22]Hans Küng, interview with Robert Murray, The Month 4/4 (1971), p. 121.

[23]See A178; cf. F 337, n. 6. Kasper acknowledges this in "Christsein ohne Tradition?" in Diskussion über Hans Küngs "Christ sein" (Mainz, 1976), p. 19.

[24]The careful distinction must be made between papal infallibility (doctrine) and papal primacy (authority). The exercise of the infallible teaching office had been precisely delimited at Vatican I, but the same is not true of papal primacy.

[25]Küng adds, "The principle of subsidiarity as a formulated legal principle is of recent date. The requirement formulated along with it, however, has behind it not only Catholic tradition, especially of the first millennium, but especially the still-binding model of the apostolic Church. The model clearly excludes—what is possible even when the episcopate is maintained in principle—a factual voiding of the apostolic office of the bishops and the position of the faithful. A monarchic-absolutist or even a dictatorial-totalitarian Church hierarchy is impossible according to the New Testament." (SC 216)

[26]Again the principle of subsidiarity is operative. As the old adage goes, "As much freedom as possible, as much restraint as necessary!"

[27]"It is this principle that must be interpreted on the basis of the Petrine office in Scripture, and not the position of the Petrine office in Scripture on the basis of this legal principle, which moreover is understood in a purely abstract and formal way." (SC 237–238)

[28]Elsewhere Küng writes, "According to the canonistic presentation of the problem, no resolution of this conflict may be expected from the pope's understanding of the matter. Naturally an extraordinary intervention of Divine Providence must not be excluded at the outset in a momentous crisis of this kind. Still less, however, must such divine intervention be postulated at the outset—as a juridical solution, so to speak. It can nevertheless, be precisely the intention of the Lord of the Church that the Church, with the assistance of the Holy Spirit that has been promised to her, herself master this situation by her own decision, as she often has had to do, and has done, in Church history." (SC 238)

[29]Küng's last consideration is the convocation of councils. (SC 285-304) This falls outside our present scope.

[30]The methodology Küng used to arrive at his conclusions is not under discussion at this point, but only the results of his investigations as they pertain to the topic of Church Councils.

[31]". . . for example, the Council of Constantinople in 754 condemned the veneration of images, the Council of Nicaea in 787 confirmed it." (SC 311)

[32]This position obviously opens the door to ecumenical agreement. See SC 336ff.; Inf 193ff. It is also significant for our study to note that such an 'infallibility' can be proved from Scripture whereas, in Küng's opinion, the infallibility of the ecclesiastical teaching office does not have an irrefragable biblical basis.

[33]See below under "Errors in Tradition."

[34]Earlier Küng had written, "Therefore, even when a council errs in a question of faith, even when--were there to be one--a pope errs in questions of faith, the Church--through God's abundant grace in the Holy Spirit-- nevertheless continues to exist permanently in Christ; she remains within His truth, and it is precisely then that the gates of hell will not prevail against her. It is indeed the spirit of Jesus Christ that guides the Church, which makes her strong and preserves her, despite--and against--all human weakness." (SC 339)

[35]Küng writes elsewhere, "Who can tell, perhaps the day will come when it will be fully realized that although the term 'infallibility' does indeed express the binding force of the formulations of the faith, it does not indicate their fragmentary character. With this in mind perhaps a concept will then be found which, better than the term 'infallibility', will present in an encompassing and balanced manner the strict binding force of decrees and at the same time their profoundly incomplete character--retaining the respectively true and permanent content of both elements." In "The Historic Contingency of Conciliar Decrees," Journal of Ecumenical Studies I/1 (1964), p. 111.

[36]Inf. 112; T 24, 93ff.; Th&Ch 10; TC 238f.; "To Get to the Heart of the Matter," Homiletic and Pastoral Review 71 (Aug.-Sept., 1971), p. 29.

[37]Küng's insistence that the Church will persist despite all individual errors in detail, emerges as the final and necessary consequence of the non-idealistic view of history, and its attendant position on the Holy Spirit's activity in Church and Tradition.

Chapter IV

[1]The sources of the infallibility debate bear introduction, since much of the pertinent literature is unavailable to non-German readers.
    (a) Besides various articles and book reviews which followed publication of Infallible? An Inquiry (cf. the bibliography of this dissertation), there are
    (b) The following collected volumes: (1) J. J. Kirvan, ed., The Infallibility Debate (New York, 1971), with contributors G. Baum, G.

Lindbeck, R. McBrien, H. J. McSorley; (2) Concilium Vol. 9 (1973); (3) K.
Rahner, hrsg., Zum Problem Unfehlbarkeit. Antworten auf die Anfrage von
Hans Küng (Herder, 1971). This includes essays by Rahner, L. Sartori, J.
Ratzinger, W. Brandmüller, L. Scheffczyk, Y. Congar, O. Semmelroth, H.
Fries, and was intended as a refutation of Küng. (4) H. Küng, hrsg.
Fehlbar? Eine Bilanz (Benziger, 1973) was published as a counter-volume to
Rahner's. It includes articles by Küng, W. Kasper, M. Löhrer, W. von
Löwenich, and many others, some documentation concerning the debate, as well
as an extensive bibliography.

(c) The famous Rahner-Küng debate in Stimmen der Zeit is available in
English in Homiletic and Pastoral Review 71 (1971): (May, 1971: 10-25;
June, 1971: 9-32; July, 1971: 17-32; Aug.-Sept., 1971: 11-27, 28-31).

(d) Various statements by Vatican officials and Bishops' Conferences,
including correspondence exchanged by them with Küng, are collected in W.
Jens, hrsg., Um nichts als die Wahrheit. Deutsche Bischofskonferenz contra
Hans Küng. Eine Dokumentation (Piper, 1978). The United States Catholic
Conference published in 1980 its own version of correspondence in The Küng
Dialogue.

(e) H. Häring and K.-J. Kuschel compiled Hans Küng. Weg und Werk
(Piper, 1978) which contains a recent interview with Küng, a chronology of
his life, and a complete bibliography through 1978 collected by Margret
Gentner. This is now available in English as Hans Küng. His Work and His
Way (Image Books, 1980).

(f) Finally, though these were not investigated for this study, there
are in the Archives at the Institute For Ecumenical Research at Tübingen
eighteen dossiers on the infallibility debate.

[2]Naturally, not everything may be said in one chapter that might be
said. The reader will have to judge whether our analysis is balanced and
fair.

[3]It is not necessarily polemical to take note of some inaccuracies and
generalities which found their way into the debate. For example, A. Dulles
wrote, "Neither of (the two Vatican) Councils gave very full attention to
the notion of infallibility . . ." (in "Hans Küng's Infallible? An Inquiry,
A Symposium. The Theological Issues," America 124 (1971), pp. 427-428). G.
Baum made several careless (or what Küng called "highly imprecise") remarks
including the infelicitous statement, "(the church) is not committed, as are
the churches that do not claim infallibility, to the biblical language that
nobody understands today and to a Jesus who is a stranger in our culture."
And, "While he makes dogma relative in regard to the abiding scriptural
norm, I think it is theologically sounder and historically more correct to
make dogma relative in regard to the church's ongoing, authoritative self-
definition." (In "Infallibility Beyond Polemics," Commonweal 94 (1971),
pp. 103-105). Küng's stinging response to Baum is in "Hans Küng Replies to
Gregory Baum: What Is the Criterion For a Critical Theology?" Commonweal
94 (1971), pp. 326-330.

C. O'Grady wrote, "The Church, (Küng) writes, is not infallible." (In
"Hans Küng's Ecumenical Programme, An Enquiry," Clergy Review 56 (1971), p.
924). Many theologians also took Küng's statements about the truth and
falsity of propositions out of context, as we shall see below. Even (or
especially) K. Rahner was not entirely accurate in his summary of Küng, as
we shall see below.

[4]See F 312-325, and "A Short Balance-Sheet of the Debate on
Infallibility," in Concilium, Vol. 3, No. 9 (1973), pp. 129-136.

[5]Küng claims that because Rahner was editor of the series "Questiones Disputatae" (of which **Strukturen der Kirche** is Vol. 17), he therefore agreed to the positions expressed therein. See F 319.

[6]See also "The Historic Contingency of Conciliar Decrees," **Journal of Ecumenical Studies** 1 (1964): 109-111.

[7]It is interesting that the excursus occurs in the section entitled "The Church is Holy." Cp. SC 334-335, Inf 124f.

[8]"Short Balance-Sheet," p. 130. See also F 325, and W&W 172-174.

[9]F 325. See Ibid., n. 32, where Küng notes that H. J. McSorley falsely constructs a disjunction between **Structures** and **Infallible?**, in **The Infallibility Debate**, pp. 77ff.

[10]All page numbers in this part of this chapter, unless otherwise indicated, refer to the cloth edition of **Infallible? An Inquiry**. This reference is Inf 14.

[11]The wide debate on Küng's catholicity will be discussed below, although our own answer to the question is placed in Chapter V.

[12]See above, Chapter III, under "Errors in Tradition."

[13]Küng notes that the encyclical's conception of natural law is unhistorical, naive, static and narrow, slightly Manichaean, too abstract, and so on. (35f.)

[14]Cf. **Herder Correspondence** 5/11 (1968), p. 336.

[15]Vatican II **did** have a working definition of the relationship between Scripture and Tradition, though one certainly not akin to Küng's. See "Dogmatic Constitution on Divine Revelation," especially articles 9-10.

[16]Cf. TC Section D.IV.2; and "What is the Essence of Apostolic Succession?" in **Concilium** Vol. 4 (New York: Paulist Press, 1968): 28-35.

[17]Küng relies for his analysis mostly on R. Aubert and V. Conzemius, both certainly impeccable references.

[18]Küng later says not that Vatican I or II erred, but both were "blind to the basic problematic." (Inf 136)

[19]It is hard to tell whether Küng's comments on Hegel's triadic theory of knowledge and propositions are merely parenthetical, or whether they form a basis for Küng's own view. Cf. Inf 149-154.

[20]See for example, M. Fahey, "Europe's Theologians Join the Debate," **America** 124 (1971), p. 430; H. McSorley, **The Infallibility Debate**, pp. 68-73; G. Lindbeck, **The Infallibility Debate**, p. 114; J. J. Carey, "Infallibility Revisited," **Theology Today** 28 (1972), p. 436: ("Anyone who works with the literature of the infallibility debate quickly detects that underlying much of the controversy are some radically different assumptions about theological method."); J. J. Carey, "Hans Küng and Karl Barth: One

Flesh or One Spirit?" Journal of Ecumenical Studies 10 (1973), p. 2;
W. Kasper, "Zur Diskussion um das Problem der Unfehlbarkeit," in F 75f.
The question of different methods touches also on the more complex
question of what constitutes catholicity in methodology; this will be taken
up below, under No. 5, and in Chapter V.

[21]K. Rahner, "A Critique of Hans Küng," Homiletic and Pastoral Review 71
(May, 1971), p. 13.

[22]H. Küng, "To Get to the Heart of the Matter," Part I, Homiletic and
Pastoral Review 71 (June, 1971), p. 10, n. 1.

[23]H. Küng, "To Get to the Heart of the Matter," Part II, Homiletic and
Pastoral Review 71 (July, 1971), pp. 24f., and "To Get to the Heart of the
Matter," Part I, p. 28.

[24]H. Küng, "To Get to the Heart of the Matter," Part II, p. 26.

[25]K. Rahner, "Reply to Hans Küng," Homiletic and Pastoral Review 71
(Aug.-Sept., 1971), pp. 14f.

[26]Ibid., p. 17. We will return to this in Chapter V.

[27]H. Küng, "Postscript," Homiletic and Pastoral Review 71 (Aug.-Sept.,
1971), pp. 28-31. In an interview Küng said of his debate with Rahner,
". . . what is involved is a formal question that precisely as such has a
decisive influence upon theological method and that in practice affects all
the Catholic Church's doctrinal statements on matters of faith and morals."
(W&W 174)

[28]Küng cites three areas: the admission of factual errors of the
teaching office; skepticism about the idea and practice of infallibility;
affirmation of the Church's indefectibility despite errors. (F 367-373)

[29]Critical remarks were registered against the polemical style of Küng's
book. We saw above (under "Pre-history") some of the reasons he gives for
changing his style. K. Rahner found it arrogant and certain to appeal to
those "allergic to Rome, bishops and traditional theology." (In "A Critique
of Hans Küng," p. 11.) G. Baum found Küng's "vehement though brilliant"
polemics "offensive." (In "Infallibility Beyond Polemics," Commonweal 94
(1971), p. 102.) M. Löhrer gently chided, "One might certainly have wished
that Küng had exercised a bit more restraint in his criticism." He adds,
"Küng's criticism of the magisterium strikes me as being severe and . . .
not free from onesidedness. But as far as I can judge, it is never unfair."
(In "Towards a Discussion of Infallibility," Worship 45 (1971), pp. 278f.)
Regarding these objections, Küng refers the reader of Fehlbar? (F 325ff.)
to his Candid Preface in Infallible? where he had written, "Let no one
assume . . . a lack of faith or charity on our part, when . . . courageous
and hopeful speech (parrhesia) is required . . . . If perhaps occasionally
the tone is sharp and the style harsh, this is a reflection, not of the
author's aggressiveness, but of the way in which the matter affects him."
(Inf 12) Another of Löhrer's comments expresses probably the wisest
judgment: "(Küng's) answer can and should be criticized and refined in
individual points. But in no case should it simply be rejected out of
hand." (Löhrer, ibid., p. 279.)

[30]Only those methodological areas which have bearing on other areas of Küng's works will be discussed. Remaining areas are indicated in footnotes.

[31]Cf. J. J. Carey, "Infallibility Revisited," Theology Today 28 (1972), pp. 433-444; G. Lindbeck, "A Protestant Perspective," America 124 (1971), p. 431; A. Dulles, "The Theological Issues," America 124 (1971), p. 428; R. McBrien, The Infallibility Debate, p. 39; H. J. McSorley, The Infallibility Debate, pp. 78-82.

We may point out that starting or not starting with the encyclical is not, strictly speaking, a methodological but a procedural matter. The fact that Küng begins with Humanae Vitae neither comprises nor affects his theological methodology per se. Küng later insisted in Fehlbar? that no one was able to demonstrate convincingly that his analysis of the encyclical was in fact incorrect or even unjustified. Küng also pointed out to Rahner that he could equally well have examined other errors of the ordinary magisterium: the condemnation of Honorius, of religious freedom, and others. (See "To Get to the Heart of the Matter," Part I, pp. 16f.) M. Löhrer wrote, "In my opinion Küng goes too far when he connects the specific problem of infallibility with this encyclical . . . . In view of the uncertain criteriological situation with respect to arguments based on the magisterium ordinarium et universale his reasoning is not persuasive." But he generously added that even if one objects to Küng's starting point, it certainly does not invalidate the remainder of his Inquiry. (See "Towards a Discussion of Infallibility," Worship 45 (1971), pp. 282, 283, 274.) Küng gratefully acknowledged Löhrer's view, in "Response to Magnus Löhrer," Worship 45 (1971), pp. 287-289.

[32]K. Rahner, "A Critique of Hans Küng," pp. 12-16.

[33]Ibid., p. 15.

[34]Ibid.

[35]H. Fries, "Das mißverständliche Wort," in Antworten, pp. 220f.; O. Semmelroth, "A priori unfehlbare Sätze?" in Antworten, p. 199; H. Mühlen, "Der Unfehlbarkeits-Test. Warum H. Küng auf harten Widerspruch stoßen muß," in Antworten, p. 237; K. Lehmann, "Von der Beweislast für 'unfehlbare Sätze'," in Antworten, p. 345.

[36]Congar cited in F 363*. Cf. Y. Congar, "Infallibilität und Indefektibilität. Zum Begriff der Unfehlbarkeit," in Antworten, p. 194.

[37]H. Küng, "To Get to the Heart of the Matter," Part I, p. 16.

[38]Ibid., pp. 17ff.

[39]Ibid., p. 23. See also F 363f. It is not the case, as A. Dulles inaccurately puts it, that "in Küng's estimation, the teaching of Humanae Vitae and the doctrine of infallibility stand or fall together." (In "The Theological Issues," America 124 (1971), p. 428.) As M. Löhrer points out, Küng is interested only in the formal, not the material aspects of Humanae Vitae. (Cf. "Towards a Discussion of Infallibility," pp. 274, 282f).

[40]Inf 105. See also SC 333f. One may recall that the context of Küng's statement is his consideration of the possibility of conflict between pope

and church. Specifically there is the final phrase of Vatican I's definitions: ". . . such definitions of the Roman Pontiff are irreformable of themselves, and not from the consent of the Church (non autem ex consensu Ecclesiae)." Cited in Inf 102.

[41]Cf. M. Löhrer, "Zur Diskussion um das Problem der Unfehlbarkeit," in F 92; H. Fries, "Das mißverständliche Wort," in Antworten, p. 220.

[42]In "The Theological Issues," America 124 (1971), p. 427.

[43]The Infallibility Debate, pp. 84f.

[44]See W. Kasper, "Zur Diskussion um das Problem der Unfehlbarkeit," in F 79; K. Lehmann, "Von der Beweislast für 'unfehlbare Sätze'," Antworten, p. 349; R. McBrien, in The Infallibility Debate, p. 40.

[45]It may be recalled that Küng clearly demurs to the work of a student of his, J. Nolte, and says that his own purpose is not to develop a philosophical foundation because (a) it would disturb the tempo of his book, and (b) it would distort the proportions of the book. (Inf 157)

[46]Y. Congar, "Infaillibilité et indefectibilité," Révue des sciences philosophiques et théologiques 54 (1970), p. 614. C. Davis echoed this complaint in "Küng on Infallibility," Commonweal 91 (1971), pp. 445f.

[47]K. Rahner, "A Critique of Hans Küng," p. 11.

[48]Ibid., p. 17.

[49]Ibid., p. 22. Küng resented Rahner's enjoinders about what he "should" do. See "To Get to the Heart of the Matter," Part I, p. 23.

[50]Ibid., p. 14.

[51]Ibid., pp. 24f.

[52]H. Küng, "To Get to the Heart of the Matter," Part II, p. 21. See also F 389f.

[53]"To Get to the Heart of the Matter," Part II, p. 22.

[54]"Towards a Discussion of Infallibility," p. 281.

[55]H. Fries, "Das mißverständliche Wort," in Antworten, p. 221*. See also J. Ratzinger, "Widerspruche im Buch von Hans Küng," in Antworten, p. 110; K. Lehmann, in Antworten, pp. 361-364.

[56]In "A Protestant Perspective," America 124 (1971), p. 432.

[57]W. Kasper, "Zur Diskussion um das Problem der Unfehlbarkeit," in F 78f*.

[58]L. Scheffczyk, "Satz--Wahrheit und 'Bleiben in der Wahrheit'," in Antworten, p. 161.

[59]K. Rahner, "Reply to Hans Küng," p. 17.

[60]W. Kasper, "Zur Diskussion um das Problem der Unfehlbarkeit," in F 82.

[61]W. Kasper points out that because of the sharpness of Küng's question, it is not surprising that critics seize on the point but do not necessarily answer it. In "Zur Diskussion um das Problem der Unfehlbarkeit," in F 79.

[62]K. Lehmann, in Antworten, p. 363; H. Stirnimann, "'Bleiben in der Wahrheit' im Bereich der Sprache," Freiburger Zeitschrift für Philosophie und Theologie 18 (1971), p. 477.

[63]Cf. K. Lehmann, in Antworten, pp. 351-354; J. Ratzinger, in Antworten, pp. 113-115; W. Kasper, in F 82.

[64]M. Löhrer, "Zur Diskussion um das Problem der Unfehlbarkeit," in F 101*. Cf. W&W 160f.

[65]The dispute was not confined to infallibility; Küng's Christology has elicited further controversy and three separate declarations by the German Bishops' Conference against the book: Feb. 17, 1975 (in Jens, 146-151; KD 94-98); March 3, 1977 (Jens, 329-330; KD 121) and Nov. 17, 1977 (Jens, 349-361; KD 133-140). The Bishops stated in their third declaration, "Consistently applied, the theological method used by Professor Küng, the shortcomings of which have already been mentioned in the Declaration of February 17, 1975, brings about by way of consequence a breach with traditional faith and doctrine in matters of importance. The dissociation of theological method from the previous tradition of the Church and a prejudiced and selective use of Scriptural texts lead to a diminishing (Verkürzung) of the faith." (KD 134)

[66]Formal proceedings against Unfehlbar? Eine Anfrage began in 1971. (Cf. the list of points of disagreement in "Brief der Sacra Congregatio Pro Doctrina Fidei, den 12 Juli 1971," in F 497-500.) On July 5, 1973 the Congregation issued Mysterium Ecclesiae (available in English in The Tablet (14 July 1973), pp. 667-670). Although no author was named, it was clearly directed against Hans Küng. Finally, on February 15, 1975, proceedings against these two books were ended in another Declaration of the Congregation. No condemnation was issued, nor was Küng's teaching license revoked, but he was warned not to teach in public certain of his views (L'Osservatore Romano (English), March 6, 1975).
Mysterium Ecclesiae does not really take up the methodological issues raised by Küng. However, it does make some important "concessions." For example, it admits that dogmas are conditioned by historical factors and that some formulas ought to be replaced by others, depending on new historical circumstances. But it plainly contradicts Küng when it asserts that the content of dogma is not relative, and that the faithful are not permitted to hold for the Church merely a "fundamental permanence in the truth." (See The Tablet (14 July 1973), p. 668. See also K. Rahner's comments on Mysterium Ecclesiae, in The Tablet 227 (Oct. 6, 1973): 956-958; (Oct. 13, 1973): 981-983; (Oct. 20, 1973): 1005-1007).

[67]"A Critique of Hans Küng," pp. 13-14, and "Reply to Hans Küng," p. 14. Cf. Hans Küng in Publik (January 29, 1971), and H. Küng, "Postscript," p. 28.

[68]In "Widerspruche im Buch von Hans Küng," Antworten, pp. 102ff.

[69]The Infallibility Debate, pp. 70-71.

[70]"Hans Küng's Ecumenical Programme," Clergy Review 56 (1971), pp. 928f.

[71]See The Infallibility Debate, compare pp. 41, 57ff.

[72]Baum wrote that "Küng stands wholly within the Catholic theological tradition despite the apparent novelty of his view" and called 'conservative' Küng's position that "post-biblical developments in the church may be valid, but they are purely human and never divinely established events." "Infallibility Beyond Polemics," Commonweal 94 (1971), pp. 104-105.

Lindbeck wrote, "Almost all of what Küng says about revelation, scripture, tradition and the authority and infallibility of the Church is consonant with the Reformation and also, I believe, with the Catholic tradition when this is viewed as a whole." "A Protestant Perspective," America 124 (1971), pp. 431-432; cp. The Infallibility Debate, p. 111.

Marcus Barth wrote, "While Hans Küng can hardly be called a devoted Roman Catholic, he certainly deserves to be regarded as a good Catholic Christian," in "Papal Fallibility," Saturday Review (April 10, 1971), p. 19.

Brown wrote, "Küng must be seen as a Catholic theologian, and his position must be viewed as an attempt to articulate Catholic theology. Indeed, the real question about 'catholicity' in the present dispute is not to be directed against Küng . . . but at his adversaries within Roman Catholicism—not only his fellow theologians, or even various national bishops' conferences, but particularly those in Rome who are challenging him." In Journal of Ecumenical Studies 8 (1971), p. 866.

[73]Originally in F 15-18; in English in W&W 90-95.

[74]In particular the Bishops declared that according to Roman Catholic and Orthodox teaching, the power to make binding true dogmatic statements belongs above all to ecumenical councils. The Catholic Church in addition, they wrote, recognizes that the exercise of this power belongs also to the bishop of Rome, according to conditions established by Vatican I and II. The bindingness and truth of dogma results not from theological discussion or from a consensus of the Church, "but from the charism given to the Church to adhere to and unerringly to interpret the once-given word on the strength of its truth." The Bishops continue, "The acceptance of such a dogmatic declaration in the Church can be significant as a sign of its harmony with the authoritative source, but it does not establish either its truth or its authority." Cf. KD 40f.

[75]Originally in Jens, Um Nichts als die Wahrheit, p. 147. In KD 95.

[76]Originally in W. Jens, Um nichts als die Wahrheit, p. 148. Also in KD 96.

[77]Ibid.

[78]Ibid., p. 97.

[79]F 335; "Short Balance-Sheet," Concilium (1973), p. 131; "To Get to the Heart of the Matter," Part I, p. 23; Part II, p. 26; "Postscript," p. 29; see also F 422, 343; cp. F 347; TC 305ff.

[80]Cf. Küng's differentiation between 'catholic' and 'pseudo-catholic' in "Ein Appell zur Verständigung," in Jens, Um nichts als die Wahrheit, p. 381.

[81]Hans Küng, interview with Robert Murray, in The Month 4/4 (1971), p. 121.

[82]Cf. "To Get to the Heart of the Matter," Part II, p. 26.

Chapter V

[1]W. Kasper tries to work around the same kind of ambiguity, in "Christsein ohne Tradition?" in Diskussion über Hans Küng's "Christ sein" (Mainz, 1976), especially pp. 26-34.

[2]Cf. W. Kasper, ibid., p. 28.

[3]This is precisely what the German Bishops' Conference had in mind when they wrote that Tradition is necessary to mediate Scripture to the present-day Church. See their Declaration of Feb. 17, 1975 (in Jens, pp. 147f.; in KD 94f.).

[4]In "Response to Avery Dulles," Union Seminary Quarterly Review 27 (1972), p. 146.

[5]See Mysterium Ecclesiae, in The Tablet (14 July 1973), pp. 667-670.

[6]See "The Case is Open," for Küng's response to Mysterium Ecclesiae, in The Tablet (14 July 1973), pp. 670-671, and F 439ff. See also Chapter IV above, under "Methodological Areas of Dissent." A good example of application is Küng's view of Mary, in OBC 450-462.

[7]Cf. TC 178. Perhaps this will be explained further in his promised forthcoming book on sacraments (cf. Hans Küng, "To Get to the Heart of the Matter," Part I, Homiletic and Pastoral Review 71 (June, 1971), p. 28, n. 5, and W&W 251.)

[8]For example, there must be some grounds for the Church's belief that bread and wine are reliable and perduring signs of God's presence in his Church, and that bread and wine also are not thoroughly arbitrary signs but really express something about the same God who chose these elements in the first place. The basis for the Church's belief clearly is not a theory of history, which relativizes concrete embodiments.

[9]Even K. Rahner wondered about this, in "Mysterium Ecclesiae," The Tablet (6 Oct. 1973): 956-958; (13 Oct. 1973): 981-983; (20 Oct. 1973): 1005-1007.

[10]One might appeal on this point to the believer's faith and ask if such a view requires not only at least as strong a faith as Küng recommends, but perhaps even stronger, since it would emphasize the very radical difference between the Christian understanding of the world as containing some absolute and non-relative signs and truths, and the world's understanding of truth and symbol as thoroughly historically relative.

[11]Cf. J. Ratzinger, "Wer verantwortet die Aussagen der Theologie?" in Diskussion über Hans Küngs "Christ sein" (Mainz, 1976), pp. 7-18.

[12]None of the comments about ecumenism are meant to suggest that ecumenical agreement is not both desirable and warranted. In terms of theological method, however, and Küng's in particular, a very great precision is required so that ecumenism is not left to stand or fall with a particular theological method, in this case, historical criticism as used by Küng.

[13]The analogy is, of course, limited because Scripture actually contains several interpretations of an original event.

[14]One may also note that in Structures of the Church, where Küng presents Barth's hypercritical question as to whether, for the Catholic Church, there are three sources of revelation (Scripture; Tradition; the Church of the present time), Küng adroitly circumvents the issue by not giving what would seem to have been warranted by Barth's charge: a definition of the Catholic understanding of Tradition. Instead, Küng inserts the question into the context of infallibility, and makes note only of the limitations on an infallible pope in determining Tradition, not of the limitations on Tradition itself. See pp. 315ff.

[15]Küng never said explicitly that the two Marian dogmas, for example, contravene the gospel, but since they are peculiar to Roman Catholicism they do not necessarily belong to catholicism, hence they do not necessarily belong to catholic Tradition.

[16]Joseph F. Mitros, "The Norm of Faith in the Patristic Age," Theological Studies 29 (1968), p. 471, and J.N.D. Kelly, Early Christian Doctrines (New York, 1960), p. 39.

[17]In accepting the Canon as is, Küng is in effect partaking theologically and methodologically in Church Tradition. We may note that this does not take place as a purely formal requirement imposed from without (if one wants to be a Catholic theologian, one must adhere to Church Tradition, including its delimitation of the Canon), but as an antecedent choice for Scripture as it is (because one adheres to the Canon of Scripture as delimited by Tradition, one is therefore catholic). Küng's relationship to Tradition, then, comes about as a consequence of his relationship to Scripture, not vice versa.

[18]In "Christsein ohne Tradition?" in Diskussion über Hans Küngs "Christ sein" (Mainz, 1976), pp. 24f.

[19]Ibid., p. 25.

[20]Cf. SC 154ff.; TC 354ff.; "What is the Essence of Apostolic Succession?" Concilium (1968), pp. 28-35.

BIBLIOGRAPHY

Primary Sources

Books (arranged chronologically)

Küng, Hans. Rechtfertigung. Die Lehre Karl Barths und eine katholische
Besinnung. Mit einem Geleitbrief von Karl Barth. Johannes Verlag,
1957. English translation: Justification. The Doctrine of Karl Barth
and a Catholic Reflection. Foreword by Karl Barth. New York: Thomas
Nelson & Sons, 1964.

_____. Konzil und Widervereinigung. Erneuerung als Ruf in die
Einheit. Herder, 1960. English translation: The Council, Reform and
Reunion. Translated by Cecily Hastings. New York: Sheed & Ward,
1961.

_____. That the World May Believe. London: Sheed & Ward, 1963.

_____. Strukturen der Kirche (Quaestiones Disputatae 17). Herder,
1962. English translation: Structures of the Church. Translated by
Salvator Attanasio. Notre Dame, Indiana: University Press, 1968.

_____. Kirche im Konzil. Herder, 1963. English translation: The
Living Church. Reflections on the Second Vatican Council. London:
Sheed & Ward, 1963.

_____. Congar, Y. and O'Hanlon, D., editors. Council Speeches of
Vatican II. Glen Rock, New Jersey: Paulist Press, 1964.

_____. Freiheit in der Welt. Benziger, 1964. English translation:
Freedom in the World. St. Thomas More. Translated by Cecily Hastings.
Theological Meditations 3. London: Sheed & Ward, 1965.

_____. Theologe und Kirche. Theologische Meditationen 3. Benziger,
1964. English translation: The Theologian and the Church.
Theological Meditations 1. London: Sheed & Ward, 1965.

_____. The Church and Freedom. Theological Meditations 6. Sheed &
Ward, 1965.

_____. Christenheit als Minderheit. Die Kirche unter den
Weltreligionen. Theologische Meditationen 12. Benziger, 1965.
English translation: "Christianity as Minority," pp. 110-161. In
Freedom Today. Sheed & Ward, 1966.

_____. Gott und das Leid. Theologische Meditationen 18. Benziger,
1967.

_____. Die Kirche (Ökumenische Forschungen I, 1). Herder, 1967.
English translation: The Church. New York: Sheed & Ward, 1967.

_____. Truthfulness: The Future of the Church. New York: Sheed &
Ward, 1968.

_____. Menschwerdung Gottes. Eine Einführung in Hegels theologisches Denken als Prologomena zu einer künftigen Christologie (Ökumenische Forschungen II, 1). Herder, 1970.

_____. Unfehlbar? Eine Anfrage. Benziger, 1970. English translation: Infallible? An Inquiry. Translated by Edward Quinn. New York: Doubleday, 1971.

_____. Was ist Kirche? Herderbücherei 376, 1970.

_____. Why Priests? A Proposal for a New Church Ministry. Translated by Robert C. Collins. Garden City, New York: Doubleday & Co., Inc., 1972.

_____. Freedom Today. Translated by Cecily Hastings. New York: Sheed & Ward, 1966.

_____. Was in der Kirche bleiben muß. Theologische Meditationen 30. Benziger, 1973.

_____, hrsg. Fehlbar? Eine Bilanz. Benziger, 1973.

_____. Christ sein. Piper, 1974. English translation: On Being a Christian. Translated by Edward Quinn. Garden City, New York: Doubleday & Co., 1976.

_____. Was ist Firmung? Theologische Meditation 40. Benziger, 1976. English translation: "What is Confirmation?" In Signposts For the Future, pp. 178-203. Garden City: Doubleday, 1978.

_____. Jesus im Widerstreit. Ein jüdisch-christlicher Dialog (mit Pinchas Lapide). Calwer-Kösel, Stuttgart/München, 1976. English translation: "Jesus in Conflict: A Jewish-Christian Dialogue." In Signposts For the Future, pp. 64-87. Garden City: Doubleday & Co., 1978.

_____. Gottesdienst--warum? Theologische Meditationen 43. Benziger, 1976. English translation: "Worship Today - Why?" In Signposts For the Future, pp. 160-177. Garden City: Doubleday & Co., 1978.

_____. Existiert Gott? Antwort auf die Gottesfrage der Neuzeit. Piper, 1978. English translation: Does God Exist? An Answer for Today. New York: Doubleday, 1980.

_____. Signposts For the Future. New York: Doubleday & Co., 1978.

_____. The Church Maintained in Truth. Seabury Press, 1980.

Articles (arranged chronologically)

Küng, Hans. "Ist in der Rechtfertigungslehre eine Einigung möglich?" Una Sancta 12 (1957): 116-121.

_____. "Christozentrik." Lexikon für Theologie und Kirche. Bd. II. (Freiburg i. Br., 1958): 1169-1174.

_____. "Konzil und Episkopat. Zur Theologie das ökumenischen Konzils." Anima 15 (1960): 294-300.

_____. "Theologische Neu-orienterungen in der Weltmission." Priester und Mission (1960): 111-130.

_____. "Das Theologische Verständnis des ökumenischen Konzils." Theologische Quartalschrift 141 (1961): 50-77.

_____. "Venerating Mary. Difficulties in the Way of Reunion." Pax Romana Journal 6 (1961): 13-14.

_____. "Can the Council Fail?" Cross Currents 12 (1962): 269-276.

_____. "The Ecumenical Council in Theological Perspective." Dialog 1 (1962): 40-49.

_____. "Der Frühkatholizismus im neuen Testament als kontroverstheologisches Problem." Theologische Quartalschrift 142 (1962): 385-424. English translation: "'Early Catholicism' in the New Testament as a Problem in Controversial Theology." In the Living Church. Reflections on the Second Vatican Council. Translated by Cecily Hastings and N. D. Smith, pp. 233-293. London: Sheed & Ward, 1963.

_____. "Karl Barths Lehre vom Wort Gottes als Frage an die katholische Theologie." In Einsicht und Glaube. Hrsg. von Joseph Ratzinger und Heinrich Fries, pp. 75-97. Herder, 1962.

_____. "Does a Catholic Have to Defend Everything? The Sign (February, 1963): 11-13.

_____. "Liturgical Reform and Christian Unity." In Hans Küng. Theologians Today. Edited by Martin Redfern, pp. 49-74. New York: Sheed & Ward, 1972.

_____. "Das Eucharistiegebet." Wort und Wahrheit 18/2 (1963): 102-107.

_____. "Veröffentlichungen zum Konzil. Ein Überblick." Theologische Quartalschrift 143 (1963): 56-82.

_____. "Why Are Dogmatic Pronouncements So Difficult to Make Today." In the Living Church. Reflections on the Second Vatican Council, pp. 294-313. Translated by Cecily Hastings and N. D. Smith. London: Sheed & Ward, 1963.

_____. "Zur Diskussion um die Rechtfertigung." Theologische Quartalschrift 143 (1963): 129-135.

_____. "The Historic Contingency of Conciliar Decrees." Journal of Ecumenical Studies I/1 (1964): 109-111.

_____. "The Charismatic Structure of the Church." Concilium (April, 1965): 23-33.

_____. "And After the Council?" Commonweal 82 (1965): 619-623.

_____. "The Council--End or Beginning?" Commonweal 81 (1965): 631-637.

_____. "God's Free Spirit in the Church." In Freedom and Man, pp. 17-30. Edited by J. C. Murray. New York, 1965.

_____. "Was hat das Konzil erreicht?" Universitas, Stuttgart 2 (1966): 461-468.

_____. "A Question to the Church," (Concerning Charles Davis). The Month 38 (1967): 259-261.

_____. "Katholische Besinnung auf Luthers Rechfertigungslehre heute." In Theologie im Wandel. Festschrift zum 150jährigen Bestehen der Katholisch-Theologischen Fakultät an der Universität Tübingen 1817-1967, pp. 449-468. Hrsg. von der Katholische-Theologischen Fakultät der Universität Tübingen. München-Freiburg i. Br., 1967.

_____. "The World Religions in God's Plan of Salvation." In Christian Revelation and World Religions, pp. 25-66. Edited by Joseph Neuner. London: Burns & Oates, 1967.

_____. "Intercommunion." Journal of Ecumenical Studies 5 (1968): 576-578.

_____. "What is the Essence of Apostolic Succession? Concilium (April, 1968): 16-19.

_____. "Mitentscheidung der Laien in der Kirchenleitung und bei kirchlichen Wahlen." Theologische Quartalschrift 149 (1969): 147-165. English translation: "Participation of the Laity in Church Leadership and in Church Elections." Journal of Ecumenical Studies 6 (1969): 511-533.

_____. "Tribute to Karl Barth." Journal of Ecumenical Studies 6 (1969): 233-236.

_____. "Mixed Marriages: What is to be Done?" The Tablet 224 (1970): 518-520.

_____. "What is the Christian Message?" Address to the Concilium Congress of September 14, 1970. Catholic Mind 68 (1970): 28-34.

_____. "Interkommunion und Ökumene (Zur Pariser Pfingsteucharistie)." In Diskussion um Hans Küng "Die Kirche", pp. 293-297. Hrsg. von H. Häring u. J. Nolte. Freiburg, 1971.

_____. "Die Kirche des Evangeliums." In Diskussion um Hans Küng "Die Kirche", pp. 175-222. Hrsg. von H. Häring u. J. Nolte. Freiburg, 1971.

_____. "Schlusswort." In Diskussion um Hans Küng "Die Kirche", pp. 307-310. Hrsg. von H. Häring u. J. Nolte. Freiburg, 1971.

_____. "Unfehlbare Sätze--wer hat die Beweislast? (Antwort an K. Lehmann)." Publik (29.1.1971).

_____. "L'Église selon L'évangile: Response à Yves Congar." Révue des sciences philosophiques et théologiques 55 (1971): 193-230.

_____. "Im Interesse der Sache. Antwort an Karl Rahner (Unfehlbarkeitsdebatte). Stimmen der Zeit 96 (1971): 43-64, 105-122. English translation: "To Get to the Heart of the Matter." Homiletic and Pastoral Review 71 (June, 1971): 9-21; (Aug.-Sept., 1971): 17-32.

_____. "Postscript." Homiletic and Pastoral Review 71 (Aug.-Sept., 1971): 28-31.

_____. "Response to Magnus Löhrer." Worship 45 (1971): 287-289.

_____. "Why I Am Staying in the Church." America 124 (1971): 281-283.

_____. "What is the Criterion for a Critical Theology? Reply to Gregory Baum." Commonweal 94 (1971): 326-330.

_____. "Die Gretchenfrage des christliche Glaubens? Systematische Überlegungen zum neutestamentlichen Wunder." Theologische Quartalschrift 152 (1972): 214-223.

_____. "Response to Avery Dulles." Union Seminary Quarterly Review 27 (1972): 143-147.

_____. "Justification and Sanctification According to the New Testament." In Hans Küng. Theologians Today, pp. 9-48. Edited by Martin Redfern. London: Sheed & Ward, 1972.

_____. "A 'Working Agreement' to Disagree." America 129 (1973): 9-11.

_____. "A Short Balance-Sheet of the Debate on Infallibility." Concilium (March, 1973): 129-136.

_____. "The Case is Open. Reply to Mysterium Ecclesiae." The Tablet 227 (1973): 670-671.

_____. "Ein Kommentar: Karl Rahner noch katholisch?" In Fehlbar? Eine Bilanz, pp. 521-514. Hrsg. von Hans Küng. Benziger, 1973.

_____. "Ein Bilanz der Unfehlbarkeitsdebatte." In Fehlbar? Eine Bilanz, pp. 305-461. Hrsg. von Hans Küng. Benziger, 1973.

_____. "Incapable of Learning?" America 129 (1973): 58-60.

_____. "Papal Infallibility: O Felix Error!" Journal of Ecumenical Studies 10 (1973): 361-362.

_____. "Parties in the Church? A Summary of the Discussion." Concilium (August, 1973): 133-146.

_____. "La prehistoire de 'Infaillible? une interpellation'." In Église infaillible ou intemporalle?, pp. 13-31. Paris, Desclée de Brouwer, 1973.

_____. "Die Religionen als Frage an die Theologie des Kreuzes." Evangelische Theologie 33 (1973): 401-423.

234

_____. "Unfehlbarkeit kann tödlich sein (Die Seite der Herausgeber)."
Theologische Quartalschrift 153 (1973): 72-74.

_____. "Zur Entstehung des Auferstehungsglaubens. Versuch einer
systematischen Klärung." Theologische Quartalschrift 154 (1974):
103-117.

_____. "Anmerkungen zu Walter Kasper, 'Christologie von unten?'." In
Grundfragen der Christologie heute (Quaestiones Disputatae 72),
pp. 170-178. Hrsg. von L. Scheffczyk. Herder, 1975.

_____. "Anonyme Christen--wozu? Antwort an Heinz Robert Schlette."
Orienterung (1975): 214-216.

_____. "Jesus und sein Gott." Theologie der Gegenwart 18 (1975):
1-10.

_____. "Statement on Women Priests. Theology No Barrier." National
Catholic Reporter (December 12, 1975).

_____. "Antwort an meine Kritiker. Theologie für den Menschen?" in
Frankfurt Allgemeine Zeitung (22. Mai 1976). Reprinted in W. Jens,
hrsg., Um nichts als die Wahrheit. Deutsche Bischofskonferenz contra
Hans Küng. Piper, 1978. Pp. 191-207.

_____. "Thesen zur Stellung der Frau in Kirche und Gesellschaft."
Theologische Quartalschrift 156 (1976): 129-132.

_____. u. Lohfink, G. "Keine Ordination der Frau? (Die Seite der
Herausgeber)." Theologische Quartalschrift 157 (1977): 144-146.

_____. "An Ecumenical Inventory." In Signposts For the Future,
pp. 88-94. Garden City: Doubleday & Co., 1978.

_____. "The Christian in Society." In Signposts For the Future,
pp. 46-63. Garden City: Doubleday & Co., 1978.

_____. "Ein Appell zur Verständigung." In Um nichts als die Wahrheit.
Deutsche Bischofskonferenz contra Hans Küng, pp. 374-389. Hrsg. von W.
Jens. Piper, 1978.

_____. "On Being a Christian: Twenty Theses." In Signposts For the
Future, pp. 2-40. Garden City: Doubleday & Co., 1978.

_____. "Vatican III: Problems and Opportunities for the Future."
In Toward Vatican III. The Work That Needs to be Done, pp. 67-90.
Edited by D. Tracy, H. Küng, and J. B. Metz. New York: Seabury, 1978.

_____. "Women in Church and Society." In Signposts For the Future,
pp. 155-159. Garden City: Doubleday & Co., 1978.

_____. "Toward a New Consensus in Catholic (and Ecumenical) Theology."
In Consensus in Theology. A Dialogue With Hans Küng and Edward
Schillebeeckx. Ed. by L. Swidler. Philadelphia: Westminister Press,
1980.

Interviews (arranged chronologically)

Küng, Hans. "Conversation at the Council, with J. C. Murray, G. Weigel, G. Diekman, V. Z. Yzermans, and H. Küng." The American Benedictine Review 15 (1964): 341-351.

_____. In the Tablet (15 February 1969): 168.

_____. With Claude François Jullien, "Christianity With a Human Face." Commonweal 94 (1971): 106-107.

_____. With Robert Murray. The Month 232 (1971): 117-121.

_____. "Die Meinung von Hans Küng. Fragen der Redaktion an den Tübinger Theologen. Irrtümer über die Kirche?" Herder Korrespondenz 227 (1973): 422-427.

_____. "Mysterium Ecclesiae. Interview With Hans Küng." The Tablet 227 (1973): 835-839.

_____. With John Wilkens. The Tablet 229 (1975): 381-382.

_____. "Disput zwischen Hans Küng und Heinz Zahrnt." Herder Korrespondenz 29 (1975): 362-363.

_____. "An Interview with Hans Küng," by H. Häring and K.-J. Kuschel. In Hans Küng. His Work and His Way. Ed. by H. Häring and K.-J. Kuschel. Doubleday, 1980. Pp. 127-183.

Secondary Sources (arranged alphabetically)

Antweiler, Anton. "Fragen zur 'Erklärung der Deutschen Bischofskonferenz zum Buch von Prof. Dr. Hans Küng "Unfehlbar? - Eine Anfrage"'." Freiburger Zeitschrift für Philosophie und Theologie 18 (1971): 499-511.

Aubert, Roger. Le concile et les conciles. Paris, 1960.

von Balthasar, Hans Urs. "Erbe als Auftrag." In Diskussion um Hans Küng "Die Kirche", pp. 257-267. Hrsg. von H. Häring u. J. Nolte. Freiburg, 1971.

_____. "Gekreuzigt für uns." In Diskussion über Hans Küngs "Christ sein", pp. 83-94. Mainz, 1976.

Barth, Marcus. "Papal Infallibility." Saturday Review (April 10, 1971): 17-19.

Baum, Gregory. "Infallibility Beyond Polemics." Commonweal 94 (1971): 103-105.

_____. "Truth in the Church--Küng, Rahner, and Beyond." The Ecumenist 9/3 (1971): 33-48.

Beeson, Trevor. "Hans Küng and the Search for Truth." Christian Century 92 (1975): 498-499.

236

Berkhof, Hendrikus. "Ökumenische Strukturen." In Diskussion um Hans Küng "Die Kirche", pp. 246-248. Hrsg. von H. Häring und J. Nolte. Freiburg, 1971.

Bourke, Myles M. "Kirchenverfassung und Eucharistiefeier." In Diskussion um Hans Küng "Die Kirche", pp. 127-133. Hrsg. von H. Häring und J. Nolte. Freiburg, 1971.

_____. "Reflections on Church Order in the New Testament." Catholic Biblical Quarterly 30 (1968): 493-511.

Bouyer, Louis. "Enttäuschte Sympathie." In Diskussion um Hans Küng "Die Kirche", pp. 43-57. Hrsg. von H. Häring und J. Nolte. Freiburg, 1971.

Brandmüller, Walter. "Hans Küng und die Kirchengeschichte: Kritische Anmerkungen zu seinem Buch Unfehlbar?." In Zum Problem Unfehlbarkeit. Antworten auf die Anfrage von Hans Küng, pp. 117-133. Hrsg. von Karl Rahner. Herder, 1971.

Brown, Raymond E. Review of Infallible? An Inquiry, by Hans Küng. Liturgical Arts (1972): 72-73.

_____. "'On Being a Christian' and Scripture." America 129 (1976): 343-345.

Brown, Robert McAfee. "The Coming of Küng." Commonweal 78 (1963): 133-135.

_____. "The Setting of the Infallibility Dispute: A Protestant Appraisal." Journal of Ecumenical Studies 8 (1971): 865-867.

Butler, B. C. The Church and Infallibility. New York: Sheed & Ward, 1954.

Carey, John J. "Infallibility Revisited." Theology Today 28 (1972): 426-438.

_____. "Hans Küng and Karl Barth: One Flesh or One Spirit?" Journal of Ecumenical Studies 19 (1971): 1-16.

Cochrane, A. C. "The Promise of God and Ecclesiastical Propositions." Journal of Ecumenical Studies 8 (1971): 872-876.

Colombo, Carlo. "Nur das Neue Testament?" In Diskussion um Hans Küng "Die Kirche", pp. 74-78. Hrsg. von H. Häring und J. Nolte. Freiburg, 1971.

Congar, Yves. "Infaillibilité et Indefectibilité." Révue des sciences philosophiques et théologiques 54 (1970): 601-618. Translated as "Infallibilität und Indefectibilität. Zum Begriff der Unfehlbarkeit." In Zum Problem Unfehlbarkeit. Antworten auf die Anfrage von Hans Küng, pp. 174-195. Hrsg. von Karl Rahner. Herder, 1971.

_____. "Après Infallible? de Hans Küng: Bilans et Discussions." Révue des sciences philosophiques et théologiques 58 (1974): 243-252.

_____. "'Die Kirche' von Hans Küng." In Diskussion um Hans Küng "Die Kirche", pp. 155-175. Hrsg. von H. Häring und J. Nolte. Freiburg, 1971.

Cooke, Vincent. "Hans Küng on Propositions and Their Problematic." Thomist 39 (1975): 753-765.

Coppens, J. "L'Église dans l'optique de controverses récentes." Ephemerides Theologicae Louvainienses 47 (1971): 478-488.

Costanzo, Joseph F. The Historical Credibility of Hans Kung. North Quincy, Mass.: The Christopher Publishing House, 1979.

Crowe, M. B. "St Thomas and the Greeks: Reflections on the Argument in Hans Küng's 'Infallible?'." Irish Theological Quarterly 39 (1972): 253-275.

Davis, Charles. "Küng on Infallibility." Commonweal 93 (1971): 445-447.

Deissler, Alfons. "Zum Umgang mit dem alten Testament." In Diskussion über Hans Küngs "Christ sein", pp. 35-43. Mainz, 1976.

Dejaifve, Georges. "Die Frage des Amtes." In Diskussion um Hans Küng "Die Kirche", pp. 98-106. Hrsg. von H. Häring und J. Nolte. Freiburg, 1971.

_____. "Etre chrétien selon Hans Küng." Nouvelle révue théologique 97 (1975): 251-266.

_____. "Un débat sur l'infaillibilité. La discussion entre K. Rahner et H. Küng." Nouvelle révue théologique 103 (1971): 583-601.

Diem, Hermann. "Spannungseinheit im Kirchenbegriff." In Diskussion um Hans Küng "Die Kirche", pp. 223-229. Hrsg. von H. Häring und J. Nolte. Freiburg, 1971.

Donovan, D. "Küng and Kasper on Christ." Ecumenist 15 (1977): 17-23.

Duggan, G. H. Hans Küng and Reunion. Westminister: Newman Press, 1964.

Dulles, Avery. "Widerspruch zu Trient?" In Diskussion um Hans Küng "Die Kirche", pp. 92-94. Hrsg. von H. Häring und J. Nolte. Freiburg, 1971.

_____. "Hans Küng's Infallible? An Inquiry, A Symposium. Part I: The Theological Issues." America 124 (1971): 427-428.

_____. "The Theology of Hans Küng: A Comment." Union Seminary Quarterly Review 27 (1972): 137-142.

_____. "Infallibility Revisited." America 129 (1973): 55-58.

_____. "Dogmatic Theology and Hans Küng's 'On Being A Christian'." America 132 (1976): 341-343.

Ehrlich, Rudolph J. "The Protestant-Roman Catholic Encounter." Scottish Journal of Theology 16 (1976): 341-343.

Eichorst, Calvin J. "Demythologizing the Papacy: A Prophetic Inquiry." Dialog 10 (1971): 272-280.

Eichorst, Clifford J. "From Outside the Church to Inside: Toward a Triumph of Grace in Catholicism." Dialog 12 (1975): 190-196.

238

England, Robert D. "Hans Küng: A Consideration." Churchman 90 (1976): 34-43.

Fahey, Michael A. "Hans Küng's Infallible? An Inquiry, A Symposium. Part II: Europe's Theologians Join the Debate." America 124 (1971): 429-431.

Farrer, Austin M., Murray, Robert, Dickinson, J. C., and Dessain, C. S. Infallibility in the Church: An Anglican-Catholic Dialogue. London: Darton, Longman & Todd, 1966.

Fitzer, Joseph. "Hegel and the Incarnation: A Reponse to Hans Küng." Journal of Religion 52 (1972): 240-267.

Flanagan, Donald. Review of Hans Küng and Reunion, by G. H. Duggan. Irish Ecclesiastical Record 103 (1965): 303-307.

Fleming, W. "The Christological Experiment of Hans Küng." Biblical Theology Bulletin 7 (1977): 77-88.

Ford, John T. "Infallibility--From Vatican I to the Present." Journal of Ecumenical Studies 8 (1971): 768-791.

Forrest, M. "The Theology of Hans Küng." Priest 20 (1964): 300-304, 583-588.

Fransen, Piet. "Hans Küng on Karl Barth." Month 36 (1966): 40-47.

Fries, Henrich. "Das mißverständliche Wort." In Zum Problem Unfehlbarkeit. Antworten auf die Anfrage von Hans Küng, pp. 216-232. Hrsg. von Karl Rahner. Herder, 1971.

Goltzen, Herbert. "Eine ökumenische Ekklesiologie." In Diskussion um Hans Küng "Die Kirche", pp. 239-245. Hrsg. von H. Häring und J. Nolte. Freiburg, 1971.

Grelot, P. "La Structure ministérielle de l'Église d'après saint Paul: A propos de "L'Église" de H. Küng." Istina 15 (1970): 389-424.

Grillmeier, Alois. "Jesus von Nazaret - im Schatten des Gottessohnes?" In Diskussion über Hans Küngs "Christ sein", pp. 60-82. Mainz, 1976.

Häring, Hermann und Kuschel, Karl-Josef, hrsg. Hans Küng. Weg und Werk. Piper, 1978. English translation: Hans Küng. His Work and His Way. Doubleday, 1980.

_____. und Nolte, J. "Das Römische Veto. Kurze Chronik." In Diskussion um Hans Küng "Die Kirche", pp. 25-31. Hrsg. von H. Häring und J. Nolte. Freiburg, 1971.

Heaney, John J. "A Dogmatic Church?" American Ecclesiastical Review 158 (1968): 361-367.

_____. "Catholic Hermeneutics, the Magisterium, and Infallibility." Continuum (1969): 106-119.

Hebblethwaite, Peter. "The Critics of Küng." The Month 4/2 (1971): 81-84.

Hughes, John Jay. "Infallible? An Inquiry Considered." Theological Studies 32 (1971): 183-207.

Jaubert, Annie. "Unfehlbar? Beobachtungen zur Sprache des Neuen Testaments." In Fehlbar? Eine Bilanz, pp. 105-113. Hrsg. von Hans Küng. Benziger, 1973.

Jens, Walter, hrsg. Um nichts als die Wahrheit. Deutsche Bischofskonferenz contra Hans Küng. Eine Dokumentation. Piper, 1978.

Kasper, Walter. "Christologie von unten? Kritik und Neuansatz gegenwärtiger Christologie." In Grundfragen der Christologie heute, pp. 141-170. Hrsg. von Leo Scheffczyk. Herder, 1975.

_____. "Für eine Christologie in geschichtlicher Perspektive. Replik auf die Anmerkungen von Hans Küng." In Grundfragen der Christologie heute, pp. 179-183. Hrsg. von Leo Scheffczyk. Herder, 1975.

_____. "Zur Diskussion um das Problem der Unfehlbarkeit." Stimmen der Zeit 188 (1971): 363-376. Reprinted in Fehlbar? Eine Bilanz, pp. 74-89. Hrsg. von Hans Küng. Benziger, 1973.

_____. "Christsein ohne Tradition?" In Diskussion über Hans Küngs "Christ sein", pp. 19-34. Mainz, 1976.

Kehl, Medard. Kirche als Institution. Zur Theologischen Begründung des institutionellen Charakters der Kirche in der neueren deutschsprachigen katholischen Ekklesiologie. (Frankfurter theologische Studien 22). Frankfurt: Josef Knecht, 1976.

Kelly, J. N. D. Early Christian Doctrines. New York: Harper & Row, 1960.

Kern, Walter. "Das Christsein und die Christologie." Stimmen der Zeit 193 (1973): 516-528.

_____. "Hegel theologisch gesehen und anders." Stimmen der Zeit 189 (1972): 125-133.

Kirvan, J. J., editor. The Infallibility Debate. New York: Paulist Press, 1971.

Koch, Hans Georg. "Neue Weg in der Christologie? Zu einigen christologischen Neuerscheinungen." Herder Korrespondenz 29 (1975): 412-418.

Kremer, Jacob. "Marginalien eines Neutestamentlers." In Diskussion über Hans Küngs "Christ sein", pp. 44-59. Mainz, 1976.

Krentz, Edgar. The Historical-Critical Method. Philadelphia: Fortress Press, 1975.

Lash, N. "Reflections on On Being A Christian." The Month 19 (1977): 88-92.

Lecler, Joseph. "Irritierende Dialektik." In Diskussion um Hans Küng "Die Kirche", pp. 58-62. Hrsg. von H. Häring und J. Nolte. Freiburg, 1971.

Lehmann, Karl. "Von der Beweislast für 'unfehlbare Satze'." In Zum
    Problem Unfehlbarkeit. Antworten auf die Anfrage von Hans Küng,
    pp. 340-371. Hrsg. von Karl Rahner. Herder, 1971.

_____. "Hans Küng auf Kollisionskurs?" Publik (11.9.1970): 21.

_____. "Christsein ökumenisch." In Diskussion über Hans Küngs "Christ
    sein", pp. 112-121. Mainz, 1976.

Lindbeck, George A. "Hans Küng's Infallible? An Inquiry, A Symposium.
    Part III: A Protestant Perspective." America 124 (1971): 431-433.

Löhrer, Magnus. "Towards a Discussion of Infallibility." Worship 45
    (1971): 273-287.

_____. "Zur Diskussion um das Problem der Unfehlbarkeit." In
    Fehlbar? Eine Bilanz, pp. 90-101. Hrsg. von Hans Küng. Benziger,
    1973.

von Löwenich, Walter. "Ist Küng noch katholisch?" In Fehlbar? Eine
    Bilanz, pp. 15-18. Hrsg. von Hans Küng. Benziger, 1973.

Mackey, J. "Küng and Kasper Compared." Living Light 14 (1977): 147-153.

Mascall, Eric L. "Anglokatholische Desiderata." In Diskussion um Hans
    Küng "Die Kirche", pp. 229-233. Hrsg. von H. Häring und J. Nolte.
    Freiburg, 1971.

McGrath, P. J. "The Concept of Infallibility." Concilium 9 (1973).

_____. "Hans Küng on Infallibility." The Tablet 225 (1971): 639-
    642.

_____. "The Statement on Professor Küng's Book." The Furrow 22
    (1971): 764-769.

McKenzie, John L. "Hans Küng on Infallibility. This Tiger Is Not
    Discreet." National Catholic Reporter (March 26, 1971).

McSorely, Harry J. "A Response to Küng's Inquiry on Infallibility."
    Worship 45 (1971): 314-325, 384-404. Reprinted in The Infallibility
    Debate, (without title), pp. 67-106. Edited by J. J. Kirvan. Paulist
    Press, 1971.

Mehok, Charles J. "Hans Küng and George Tyrrell on the Church." Homiletic
    and Pastoral Review 72 (1972): 57-66.

Mitros, Joseph F. "The Norm of Faith in the Patristic Age." Theological
    Studies 29 (1968): 444-471.

Montefiore, Hugh W. "Ein klassisches Werk." In Diskussion um Hans Küng
    "Die Kirche", pp. 267-272. Hrsg. von H. Häring und J. Nolte.
    Freiburg, 1971.

Mühlen, Heribert. "Der Unfehlbarkeits-Test. Warum H. Küng auf harten
    Widerspruch stoßen muß." In Zum Problem Unfehlbarkeit. Antworten auf
    die Anfrage von Hans Küng, pp. 233-257. Hrsg. von Karl Rahner.
    Herder, 1971.

Novak, Michael. "The Küng Case." Christian Century 92 (1975): 300-301.

O'Brien, Elmer. "The Council and Reunion. Reflections on a Recent Book." The Month (1962): 15-49.

O'Grady, Colm. "Hans Küng's Ecumenical Programme: An Enquiry." Clergy Review 56 (1971): 922-932.

Pesch, Otto. "The Küng Decision: An Act of Reconciliation?" The Tablet (March 9, 1975): 238-239.

Pesch, Rudolf. "Amtsstrukturen im Neuen Testament." In Diskussion um Hans Küng "Die Kirche", pp. 133-154. Hrsg. von H. Häring and J. Nolte. Freiburg, 1971.

Picou, Jean. "L'ecclesiologie de Hans Küng: Aperçus Critiques." Nova et Vetera 44 (1969): 241-258.

Quinn, Edward. "Tübingen and Rome." Downside Review 89 (1971): 317-323.

Rahner, Karl. "Questions of Controversial Theology on Justification," Theological Investigations Vol. 4, pp. 189-218. Baltimore: Helicon Press, 1976.

_____. "Kritik an Hans Küng. Zur Frage der Unfehlbarkeit theologischer Sätze." Stimmen der Zeit 186 (1970): 361-377. English translation: "A Critique of Hans Küng Concerning the Infallibility of Theological Propositions." Homiletic and Pastoral Review 71 (May, 1971): 10-21.

_____. "Replik. Bemerkungen zu Hans Küng, 'Im Interesse der Sache'." Stimmen der Zeit 187 (1971): 145-160. English translation: "Reply to Hans Küng In the Form of an Apologia pro theologia sua." Homiletic and Pastoral Review 71 (Aug.-Sept., 1971): 11-27.

_____, hrsg. Zum Problem Unfehlbarkeit. Antworten auf die Anfrage von Hans Küng. Freiburg, Herder, 1971.

_____. "Mysterium Ecclesiae." The Tablet 227 (1973): 956-958, 981-983, 1005-1007.

_____. "Zu Hans Küngs neuestem Buch." Theologie der Gegenwart 18 (1975): 80-87.

_____. "Zur Ekklesiologie." In Diskussion über Hans Küngs "Christ sein", pp. 105-111. Mainz, 1976.

Ratzinger, Joseph. "Widersprüche im Buch von Hans Küng." In Zum Problem Unfehlbarkeit. Antworten auf die Anfrage von Hans Küng, pp. 97-116. Hrsg. von Karl Rahner. Herder, 1971.

_____. "Wer verantwortet die Aussagen der Theologie." In Diskussion über Hans Küngs "Christ sein", pp. 7-18. Mainz, 1976.

Redfern, Martin, editor. Hans Küng. Theologians Today. New York: Sheed & Ward, 1972.

Riedlinger, Helmut. "Maria in der Wahrheit des Glaubens." In Diskussion über Hans Küngs "Christ sein", pp. 122-132. Mainz, 1976.

Scheffczyk, Leo. "Die theologische Diskussion um das Unfehlbarkeitsdogma." Münchener Theologische Zeitschrift 22 (1971): 282-295.

_____. "Satz--Wahrheit und 'Bleiben in der Wahrheit'." In Zum Problem Unfehlbarkeit. Antworten auf die Anfrage von Hans Küng, pp. 174-195. Hrsg. von Karl Rahner. Herder, 1971.

_____, hrsg. Grundfragen der Christologie heute (Quaestiones Diputatae 72). Frieburg i. Br., Herder, 1975.

Schepers, M. B. "Fehlende Mystik." In Diskussion um Hans Küng "Die Kirche", pp. 63-68. Hrsg. von H. Häring und J. Nolte. Freiburg, 1971.

Schnackenburg, Rudolf. "Wahrheit in Glaubenssätzen. Überlegungen nach dem 1. Johannesbrief." In Zum Problem Unfehlbarkeit. Antworten auf die Anfrage von Hans Küng, pp. 134-147. Hrsg. von Karl Rahner. Herder, 1971.

Schneider, Theodor. "Zur Trinitätslehre." In Diskussion über Hans Küngs "Christ sein", pp. 95-104. Mainz, 1976.

Schütte, Heinz. "Richtigstellungen." In Diskussion um Hans Küng "Die Kirche", pp. 107-113. Hrsg. von H. Häring und J. Nolte. Freiburg, 1971.

Schwager, Raymund. "Das Dogma von der Unfehlbarkeit. Zur bisherigen Diskussion um Küngs "Unfehlbar?"." Herder Korrespondenz 27 (1973): 524-529.

Semmelroth, Otto. "A priori unfehlbare Sätze?" In Zum Problem Unfehlbarkeit. Antworten auf die Anfrage von Hans Küng, pp. 196-215. Hrsg. von K. Rahner. Herder, 1971.

_____. "Ernstgenommene Geschichte?" In Diskussion um Hans Küng "Die Kirche", pp. 94-97. Hrsg. von H. Häring und J. Nolte. Freiburg, 1971.

Simons, Francis. Infallibility and the Evidence. Springfield: Templegate Publishers, 1968.

Smyth, K. "Forms of Church Government--A New Essay Examined." Irish Theological Quarterly 39 (1963): 53-66.

Stevens, C. "Infallibility and History." Journal of Ecumenical Studies 10 (1973): 384-387.

Stirnimann, Heinrich. "'Bleiben in der Wahrheit' im Bereich der Sprache." Freiburger Zeitschrift für Philosophie und Theologie 18 (1971): 475-498.

Stoeckle, Bernhard. "Zum Ethos und zur Ethik." In Diskussion über Hans Küngs "Christ sein", pp. 133-143. Mainz, 1976.

Tavard, George H. "Option für das Ursprüngliche?" In Diskussion um Hans Küng "Die Kirche", pp. 84-91. Hrsg. von H. Häring und J. Nolte. Freiburg, 1971.

Thils, Gustave. L'infaillibilité pontificale, sources--conditions--limites. Gembloux: J. Duculot, 1969.

_____. "'Unfehlbar?' de Hans Küng." Révue théologique de Louvain 2 (1971): 88-96.

Tierney, Brian. "Infallibility in Morals: A Response." Theological Studies 35 (1974): 507-517.

_____. "Origins of Papal Infallibility." Journal of Ecumenical Studies 8 (1971): 841-864.

van Voorst, L. Bruce. "Küng and Rahner: Dueling Over Infallibility." Journal of Ecumenical Studies 8 (1971): 841-864.

_____. "Follow-up on the Küng-Rahner Feud." The Christian Century (Aug. 25, 1971): 997-1000.

Weber, J.-J. "A propos du livre de Hans Küng sur l'infaillibilité." La Documentation Catholique 68 (1971): 532-538.

Witte, Johannes L. "Ist Barths Rechtfertigungslehre grundsätzlich katholisch?" Münchener Theologische Zeitschrift 10 (1959): 38-48.

Yarnold, E. J. "Küng Examined." The Month 4/3 (1971): 74-80.

Documentation

"The Future of the Episcopate." Herder Correspondence 5/12 (1968): 355-360.

Declaration of 1360 Catholic Theologians, on the Freedom of the Theologian. Herder Correspondence (English) 6/2 (1969): 46-48.

Letter of Yves Congar to Hans Küng. In Diskussion um Hans Küng "Die Kirche", pp. 298-301. Hrsg. von H. Häring u. J. Nolte. Freiburg, 1971.

Reply of Hans Küng to Yves Congar. In Diskussion um Hans Küng "Die Kirche", pp. 301-305. Hrsg. von H. Häring u. J. Nolte. Freiburg, 1971.

"Déclaration du Bureau d'études doctrinales de l'épiscopat français, le 19 mars 1971." La Documentation Catholique 68 (1971): 336.

"Küng's Statement," of June 25, 1971, in The Month 4/3 (1971): 73.

"Wider die Resignation in der Kirche." Herder Korrespondenz 26 (1971): 230-231. English trans., National Catholic Reporter (March 31, 1972).

The Küng Dialogue. Facts and Documents. United States Catholic Conference, 1980.

Um nichts als die Wahrheit. Deutsche Bischofskonferenz contra Hans Küng. Eine Dokumentation. Hrsg. von W. Jens. Piper, 1978.

Kolping, Adolf. "Hans Küng and die Unfehlbarkeitsdebatte," a letter to Küng. Herder Korrespondenz 27 (1973): 646-649.

244

"Die Stellungnahme der Deutschen Bischofskonferenz." Herder Korrespondenz 29 (1975): 182-185.

"Déclaration des évêques autrichiens." La Documentation Catholique 72 (1975): 262.

"Communique des évêques suisses." La Documentation Catholique 72 (1975): 262.